Normative Change and Security Community Disintegration

Simon Koschut

Normative Change and Security Community Disintegration

Undoing Peace

Simon Koschut
Otto Suhr Institute for Political Science
Freie Universität Berlin
Berlin, Germany

ISBN 978-3-319-80780-5   ISBN 978-3-319-30324-6 (eBook)
DOI 10.1007/978-3-319-30324-6

© The Editor(s) (if applicable) and The Author(s) 2016
Softcover reprint of the hardcover 1st edition 2016
This work is subject to copyright. All rights are solely and exclusively licensed by the Publisher, whether the whole or part of the material is concerned, specifically the rights of translation, reprinting, reuse of illustrations, recitation, broadcasting, reproduction on microfilms or in any other physical way, and transmission or information storage and retrieval, electronic adaptation, computer software, or by similar or dissimilar methodology now known or hereafter developed.
The use of general descriptive names, registered names, trademarks, service marks, etc. in this publication does not imply, even in the absence of a specific statement, that such names are exempt from the relevant protective laws and regulations and therefore free for general use.
The publisher, the authors and the editors are safe to assume that the advice and information in this book are believed to be true and accurate at the date of publication. Neither the publisher nor the authors or the editors give a warranty, express or implied, with respect to the material contained herein or for any errors or omissions that may have been made.

Cover illustration: © EdBookPhoto/Alamy Stock Photo

Printed on acid-free paper

This Palgrave Macmillan imprint is published by Springer Nature
The registered company is Springer International Publishing AG Switzerland

To Nancy
Whose wisdom and warmth has been a continuous source of inspiration

Preface

A community rests on the commitment of its members to intuitively follow and reproduce the social norms that are constitutive to its formation. In this sense, I agree with Heidegger (1969) who claims that the shared understanding that constitutes a community is, more often than not, 'ready-to-hand' (*zuhanden*) instead of simply 'present-at-hand' (*vorhanden*). As Bauman (2001, p. 11) notes, 'we hardly ever notice the air we breathe, unless it is the foul and malodorous air of a stuffy room that we happen to inhale.' As long as this system of tacitly respected 'settled' norms is internalized by all members, the community will probably outlive almost any 'unsettling' changes in its external or domestic environment. Once members begin to question the shared meaning of their social relationship, and its underlying norms, and stop caring for each other's well-being, however, the 'air will turn foul' and the community may subsequently head down the road to disintegration.

The investigation of normative change is becoming increasingly popular in international relations (IR). Most studies, however, focus on its progressive connotation. The possibility of a weakening or even disappearance of an established peaceful normative order, by contrast, tends to be often either neglected or implicitly assumed. This book develops a theoretical and empirical argument about the disintegration of security communities and the subsequent breakdown of stable peace among nations through a process of norm degeneration. A security community is considered to be 'a group which has become integrated, where integration is defined as the attainment of a sense of community, accompanied by formal or informal institutions or practices, sufficiently strong and widespread to assure peaceful change among members of a group with "reasonable" certainty over a "long" period of time' (Deutsch et al. 1957).

The reasons for writing this book are twofold. First, I seek to address a theoretical problem: How can we analytically conceptualize regressive and disintegrative processes in international politics? How do these processes differ from processes of peaceful integration? Coming from a Constructivist background, I—like many of my colleagues—encountered what I have described in this book as a 'progressivist bias' in much of research on the social construction of norms and security communities. The second reason for writing this book concerns an empirical problem. I was intrigued by the upsurge of disintegrative dynamics and tendencies within the North Atlantic Treaty Organization (NATO) during and after the war in Iraq and, more recently, the European Union (EU), following the Euro crisis and the refugee crisis, respectively. These phenomena presented me with the empirical puzzle for this book: Why and how might people and states give up on their prior achievements in terms of peaceful integration? What keeps such security communities together and, more importantly, what drives them apart?

To address these questions, this book draws together two key bodies of contemporary IR literature—norms and security communities—and brings their combined insights to bear on the empirical phenomenon of disintegration. The book advances the contemporary body of research on the important role of norms and ideas by analytically extending recent Constructivist arguments about international norm degeneration to the regional level and by applying them to a particular type of regional order (a security community) in order to explain the latter's demise. In contrast to widespread beliefs in both academia and policy circles that the process of peaceful regional integration is (more or less) linear and irreversible, the empirical observations presented in this book show that the members of a security community can themselves easily undo peace among them.

This book is the result of a long journey, both literally and metaphorically speaking, and I am grateful to a great number of people who offered their guidance, encouragement, and company in developing this project. When I first started thinking about the idea for this book right after completing my PhD, I was fortunate enough to work as a visiting lecturer at the John F. Kennedy Institute at the Freie Universität Berlin. I am pleased to have the opportunity to acknowledge the help and goodwill of a splendid group of scholars whom I was privileged to have worked with there.

A first draft of the theory chapter and the introduction were written while I was a Fritz Thyssen Fellow at the Weatherhead Center for International Affairs (WCFIA) at Harvard University. Beth Simmons, then the director of the Center, and Karl Kaiser, then the director of the Program on Transatlantic Relations, were truly caring academic supporters during my stay at the WCFIA, and so have been many others, including Stephen Walt, Alastair Iain Johnston, Felix Heiduk, Ulrich Krotz, Ronja Kempin, Steven Bloomfield, Michelle Eureka, Megan Margulies, Thomas Murphy, and Ann Townes. Max Büge, with whom I was lucky enough to share an office at the WCFIA, was the best office mate one could imagine, and I trust that he knows how much so. Spending the whole year writing is a great luxury, and I gratefully acknowledge the Fritz Thyssen Stiftung's financial support to enable me to focus on my research in such an inspiring and highly welcoming academic environment.

At the Friedrich Alexander University (FAU) at Erlangen-Nürnberg, I developed my case studies and wrote the conclusion of the book. For four years, the FAU provided me with an academic home (and a stunning view from my office, overlooking the castle and the old town). Here, I was able to work with an equally inspiring and cordial crowd of people. Andreas Falke, then my boss and mentor, provided me with generous free space to develop new ideas and to continue writing. I feel lucky and honored to have been able to work under his chairmanship during these years. Sarah Beringer was my colleague and 'partner in crime' at the chair, and I am grateful for her wisdom and cheerful laughs. Also, I would like to thank my dear colleague and running mate, Gian Luca Gardini, as well as Christina Stolte, who have both been a constant source of support and sympathy. Special thanks go to Sören Brinkmann, Wolfgang Ramsteck, Matthias Fifka, Günther Ammon, Nelia Miguel Müller, Rüdiger Zoller, Walther Bernecker, Dirk Holtbrügge, and Christoph Schumann. Even though they have not read or directly commented on this manuscript, I feel that a series of frequently spirited discussions over the past years has greatly helped to sharpen and strengthen the project. Finally, I have to thank my students at the FAU for their enduring enthusiasm and curiosity.

This book is also my *Habilitationsschrift*. Hence, I would like to extend my sincere gratitude to the University of Potsdam, where I submitted my *Habilitation*, as well as to my board of reviewers, Andrea Liese, Anja Jetschke, and Heinz Kleger. More than anyone else, Kleger, who was also my *Doktorvater*, taught me to think beyond disciplinary boundaries. He is a model of scholarly integrity and open-mindedness and I could not have wished for a better teacher.

Ironically, this book's journey ends where it began. As I am writing these lines, I have returned to the Freie Universität Berlin, this time joining the Otto Suhr Institute for Political Science as a visiting professor. I feel very privileged and honored to be working with such a superb group of scholars here, and I am pleased to thank Tanja Börzel and Thomas Risse for granting me this valuable opportunity.

Beyond those names above, a heterogeneous collection of friends and colleagues, in one way or another, contributed to this book, commenting on parts of the manuscript, offering their own knowledge and expertise, or helping in a variety of other ways. My parents, Wolfgang and Ursula Koschut, as well as my brother David, have been a neverending source of encouragement and so have been my 'American parents', Cathy and David Annas. Sarah Roughley, my editor at Palgrave, deserves praise and respect for her friendly patience and professional support. Lucile Eznack, Regina Heller, Stephan Stetter, Stephen Aris, Andreas Wenger, Simon Hollis, Matthias Dembinski, and Andrea Oelsner as well as the anonymous reviewers have pushed me to think harder and provided valuable comments that helped to prepare the final draft.

My greatest debt is to my family: my children Enja and Elio, and most importantly Nancy. Her continuing generosity and emotional support in challenging times and during my frequent absences from home deserve my unconditional love and gratitude. This book is dedicated to her.

Simon Koschut
Berlin, Germany

References

Heidegger, M. (1969). *On time and being*. Chicago: University of Chicago Press.
Bauman, Z. (2001). *Community: Seeking Safety in an Insecure World*. Cambridge: Polity Press.

Contents

1 Introduction 1

2 Security Community Disintegration:
  An Analytical Framework 41

3 'Successful' Disintegration: The German
  Security Community 93

4 'Unsuccessful' Disintegration: The Transatlantic
  Security Community 165

5 Conclusions 241

References 261

Index 265

List of Abbreviations

AfD	Alternative für Deutschland/Alternative for Germany
ASEAN	Association of Southeast Asian Nations
AWACS	Airborne Early Warning and Control System
CIA	Central Intelligence Agency
CJTF	Combined Joint Task Force
CSCE	Conference on Security and Cooperation in Europe
EC	European Community
ECOWAS	Economic Community of West African States
EPC	European Political Cooperation
ESDI	European Security and Defence Identity
EU	European Union
FPÖ	Freiheitliche Partei Österreichs/Freedom Party of Austria
ICC	International Criminal Court
IFF	Identification Friend or Foe
KFOR	Kosovo Force
KLA	Kosovo Liberation Army
MERCOSUR	Mercado Común del Sur/Southern Common Market
NACC	North Atlantic Cooperation Council
NAFTA	North American Free Trade Agreement
NATO	North Atlantic Treaty Organization
NSA	National Security Agency
OSCE	Organization for Security and Cooperation in Europe
PDD	Presidential Decision Directive
PfP	Partnership for Peace
SACEUR	Supreme Allied Commander Europe
SADC	Southern African Development Community

SEATO	Southeast Asian Treaty Organization
UN	United Nations
UNOSOM	United Nations Operation in Somalia
UNPROFOR	United Nations Protection Force
USA	United States of America
VOPP	Vance–Owen Peace Plan
WEU	Western European Union

List of Figures

Fig. 2.1   The disintegration of security communities   58

List of Tables

Table 2.1   Normative order of a security community   47
Table 5.1   Scope of normative change in security communities   250

CHAPTER 1

Introduction

THE PUZZLE

Why do states that have achieved a state of stable peace re-enter a state of war against each other? What happens when mutual trust and dependable expectations of peaceful behavior between states and societies transform into a state of uncertainty and rivalry? When and under what conditions do mutual trust and the absence of violent conflict in International Relations (IR) deteriorate into mutual suspicion or even war? Why are some cases of security community disintegration 'successful' while others are not? In short, what holds security communities together and, more importantly, what drives them apart?

This book explores and develops theoretical and empirical implications of the disintegration of pluralistic security communities and the subsequent breakdown of stable peace[1] among nations based on a shared normative order. A security community is considered to be 'a group which has become integrated, where *integration* is defined as the attainment of a sense of community, accompanied by formal or informal institutions and practices, sufficiently strong and widespread to assure peaceful change among members of a group with "reasonable" certainty over a "long" period of time' (italics in the original: Deutsch 1954, p. 33). Peaceful change is defined as 'the resolution of social problems, normally by institutionalized procedures, without resort to large-scale physical force' (Deutsch et al. 1957, p. 5). Security communities can be said to exist in the world in various institutional forms and stages of maturity, including the North Atlantic Treaty Organization (NATO), the European Union (EU), the Association of Southeast Asian Nations (ASEAN), Common Market of the South (MERCOSUR), the Economic Community of West African States (ECOWAS), or the countries of the Southern African Development Community (SADC) (Shaw 1998; Selebi 1999; Lund and Roig 1999; Acharya 2001; Hammerstad 2005; Kacowicz 2005).

While most scholars study the conditions under which such peaceful orders among previously antagonistic states and people can be established, I investigate the conditions under which peaceful orders may deteriorate. While many authors seek to explain how security communities develop collective social norms, my primary focus is on what causes these collective norms to erode. While the main branches of literature examine how security communities form and evolve, I wish to explore how these communities disintegrate.

Generally, processes of disintegration of political communities at the international level have rarely been the subject of systematic theoretical and empirical analysis (notable exceptions are: Eppler and Scheller 2013; Stetter et al. 2011; Anderson et al. 2008; Anhut 2005).[2] In particular, there is a significant lack of systematic theoretical and empirical analysis with regard to security community disintegration. Given the fact that virtually all scholars who have studied security communities agree on the possibility of their decline, it seems puzzling that few of them have ever seriously elaborated on or theorized security community disintegration. The inventors of the security community concept, Karl W. Deutsch and his associates, for example, give some background conditions that promote the disintegration of nation-states and empires (what they refer to as amalgamated political communities) but hardly even touch on the conditions that may untie political community between sovereign states (what they define as pluralistic security communities) (Deutsch et al. 1957, pp. 59 and 65). The other major work on the subject, compiled by Emanuel Adler and Michael Barnett (1998, p. 58), simply states that, 'the same forces that "build up" security communities can also "tear them down"'. Likewise, the authors in an edited volume on *Stable Peace Among Nations* (Kacowicz et al. 2000) ask how stable peace can be consolidated in a security community but do not address the interrelated question of how stable peace may unravel. Amitav Acharya (2001) argues that processes of peaceful socialization in world politics may move either way and can thus explain both the establishment and unraveling of a security community.

Yet, Acharya does not expand on his argument further. In short, with only a few exceptions,[3] there is hardly any comprehensive study that deals exclusively with the question of how and why security communities might disintegrate or disappear. It is the purpose of this book to contribute to balancing this conceptual, theoretical, and empirical disparity and thus hopefully narrow an intellectual gap.

While I do not deny the importance of studying the emergence of stable peace and security communities among nations, I argue, as other authors have (Acharya 2001; Müller 2006; Haglund 2006, 2007; Risse 2008), that at least equal attention should be given to the unraveling of these communities. Exploring security community disintegration challenges the often implicit taken-for-grantedness of norms and stable peace in IR, promotes our understanding of how existing security communities can be maintained, and may help to explain social change in the international system more generally.

Disintegration may be broadly defined as the process by which an object or unit breaks down or loses cohesion. In this sense, disintegration functions as the mirror image or counter concept to integration, which involves the process of parts merging into a whole (Spencer 1857). More specifically, disintegration describes 'a multi-level phenomenon, which displays the inability of societal institutions and communities to provide for the existential background conditions of living together, mutual social recognition, and the physical integrity of its members' (my own translation, Imbusch and Heitmeyer 2008, p. 13). On a general level, the key to any disintegrative process is 'the collapse of people's commitment to the community's values' (Merritt 1981, p. 208). Thus, disintegration needs to be conceptually distinguished from both decay, which describes a loss in a unit's capabilities and resources, as well as disaggregation, which implies the mere division of a particular unit into its component parts (Merritt 1973).

This definition implies that security communities are never simply given but involve constant efforts to reproduce their established social order. Such a dynamic understanding of peaceful integration seems plausible when we look at the breakdown of political order, for example, in failed or fragile states, zones of limited statehood, and the dissolution of states such as the former Soviet Union or the former Yugoslavia (Rosenau and Czempiel 1992; Rotberg 2004; Risse and Lehmkuhl 2006). Moreover, in a globalizing world, integration is certainly not limited to the territorial nation-state but has become a regional and global phenomenon as formerly state-bound societies develop transnational identities, networks, and group cohesion as members of a regional society (Giddens 1991; Buzan 2004).

In the following sections, I will present the basic argument of this book and situate it within the existing body of research. Subsequently, I explain my research design and methodology. Finally, I close with a brief summary of the chapters in this book.

THE ARGUMENT

Why do some security communities survive periods of instability and crisis while other security communities disintegrate? The answer, it is argued, lies in the relative scope of normative change within these security communities. To be sure, fundamental changes in IR may occur due to material changes in the distribution of power and capabilities in the international system but more often than not, change at the international and regional level happens when new ideas and norms are introduced into a particular social relationship thereby altering and replacing shared social meanings, and, ultimately, the material conditions within a social group (Milliken 1999; Buzan 2004). I will refer to this phenomenon here as normative change.

Normative change involves both the emergence and establishment of new norms as well as the degeneration and replacement of existing norms (for a similar definition, see Sandholtz 2008). Since I am interested in the disintegration of security communities, this book will focus on the latter process. Examples that deal with norm emergence include the banning of antipersonnel landmines (Coleman 2013), the Chemical Weapons Convention (Price 1997), the anti-torture norm (Liese 2009), or the emergence of an American epistemic community on nuclear arms control (Adler 1992). Empirical examples of normative change involving norm degeneration can be found by looking at the abolition of slavery in the USA, the end of apartheid in South Africa (Klotz 1995), or the recent US weakening of the norm not to torture (Sikkink 2013).

In this book, I suggest that similar norm dynamics may also be found in security communities. In doing so, this book draws together two key bodies of contemporary IR theoretical literature—norms and security communities—and brings their combined insights to bear on the empirical phenomenon of disintegration. Based on the pioneering work of Karl Deutsch, security communities can be understood as normative communities in the sense that they presuppose a normative order 'with some level of compliance and agency for enforcement'. 'Enforcement' refers to institutions and agreements 'freely entered into (...) reliably enforced or peacefully changed'. By 'compliance', Karl Deutsch means 'general agreement about (...) the substance of the matter being complied with (...) the legitimacy of the enforcing agent or (...) the rightfulness of the procedure being used' (Deutsch et al. 1957, p. 8). Emanuel Adler and Michael Barnett display a similar understanding by arguing that, 'normative discourse and actions reflect (...) the norms of the specific community, and refers to how its norms differ from those outside the (security) community' (Adler and Barnett 1998, p. 56) Finally, Amitav Acharya (2014, p. 104) argues that in a pluralistic security community, '(i)nter-state relations are governed by well-defined norms'. If we take these assumptions about the normative character of security communities seriously it may be equally assumed that normative change 'for the worse'—that is, the erosion and replacement of existing peaceful norms about intra-group meanings—should destabilize a security community and could thus serve as a plausible explanation for the disintegration of pluralistic security communities. This is the main argument of this book.

In IR, norms have been defined as 'collective expectations about proper behavior of actors with a given identity' (Jepperson et al. 1996, p. 54; for a similar definition see: Finnemore 1996; Klotz 1995). Ideas are the 'beliefs held by individuals in a particular social environment' (Goldstein and Keohane 1993, p. 3). Norms and ideas are interrelated concepts. Certain ideas can become part of a normative framework, that is, a system of shared institutions and habits among a particular group of actors (Björkdahl 2002, p. 58).[4] In this case, we may speak of 'normative ideas' (Jackson 1993, p. 112; see also: Acharya 2004). From a (conventional) Constructivist perspective, normative ideas frame knowledge-based practices by defining the cognitive boundaries of social reality (Adler 1997b, pp. 325–26).

There is certainly no dearth of scholarly work on norms and ideas in IR. This book advances the contemporary body of research on the important role of norms and ideas by analytically extending recent Constructivist arguments about international norm degeneration to the regional level and by applying them to a particular type of regional order (security community) in order to explain the latter's demise. This should further existing knowledge about norm dynamics within and across regions and hopefully add new insights to the study of security communities.

My basic argument that norm degeneration in a security community can lead to its disintegration rests on five assumptions that will be summarized here and explained in more detail in the following chapter. First, based on Karl W. Deutsch's statements outlined above, it can be claimed with some confidence that norms define intersubjective social meanings and thus constitute a pluralistic security community. It is important to add, however, that the content of such security community norms needs to be further specified in order to be of analytical usage. For example, scholars might detect normative change in an area that may be completely irrelevant to the members of a particular security community. In order to avoid this problem, I argue (based on Karl Deutsch's conception) that a pluralistic security community rests on three fundamental norms ('meta-norms'), which together form its normative order: the norm of common values, the norm of multilateral practice, and the norm of meaningful communication. Norms are deemed fundamental when they acquire a broad moral reach while, at the same time, attain a very low degree of contestation (Wiener 2008, p. 66). The norm of common values includes so-called primary values that are usually written down in foundational documents and treaties, constantly reiterated through symbols and speech acts, and often contrasted against outside values. The norm of multilateral practice prescribes peaceful conflict resolution and the practice of self-restraint on the inside. On the outside, it includes the use of force against outsiders based on collective defense. The norm of meaningful communication calls for genuine and timely consultation and mutual responsiveness among members. Together, these three fundamental norms make up the normative order of a security community.

Second, it is argued that the survival of a pluralistic security community depends on the persuasiveness of and collective allegiance among its members to this normative order. As spelled out above, the basic argument put forward in this book is that security communities cease to exist when its norms are no longer followed and when collective meanings are no longer meaningful. The weakening of the normative order in a security community is thus said to depend on the presence of unpunished norm violations (lack of social control) as well as the absence of constant norm iteration (interruption of socialization processes). Specifically, it is suggested that such normative change involves the persuasiveness of new ideas, the disruption of symbolic interaction, institutional failure, and, crucially, social unlearning. What makes an idea persuasive is its ability to relate to current political and economic problems. Symbolic interaction is understood as meaningful exchange among a group of actors. Institutional failure refers to the inability of regional and domestic political organizations to adapt their norms to changing times, often resulting in subsequent societal disappointment and frustration. Social unlearning involves the rejection and overwriting of previous norms and knowledge.

The third assumption raised here states that the process of security community disintegration follows an outside-in logic similar to its formation process but under opposing signs: Major external change ('shocks') sets off a combination of social and internal changes in a security community (persuasiveness of new ideas, disruption of symbolic interaction, institutional failure, social unlearning) that, in turn, leads to an undermining and erosion of collective norms, identity, and trust (normative change). Major external change includes great events or systemic shocks like revolutions, major wars, or the collapse of large communities or empires. External change of this kind forces members of a security community to critically reflect on their collective norms and identities. Social and internal change typically results from external change and undermines meaningful interactions among the members of a security community themselves involving in-group/out-group differentiation and the attribution of social roles. While major external change provides a window of opportunity for norm contestation within a security community, social and internal changes can be expected to influence the outcome of such contestation. Normative change refers to a close of socialization processes together with a breakdown of social control among its members. Critically, these norm dynamics involve agency (understood as the capacity to affect change).

As a fourth assumption, it is thus suggested that the process of disintegration in a security community can be framed along conflict lines between opposing normative agents. This conflict line broadly runs between norm leaders/regimes, on the one hand, and norm challengers, on the other hand, rivaling each other over implementing their respective normative order within the security community, thereby shaping and altering social meanings. Norm leaders seek to promote and enforce the established normative order of a security community. Norm leaders are bound together as a norm regime, which 'governs' and 'manages' a security community through political socialization and social control including the teaching of community norms and the sanctioning of inappropriate behavior at the level of intergovernmental and transnational institutions, networks, and other forms of social interaction. Needless to say, some norm leaders may also contest existing community norms. Norm challengers, by contrast, are actors who are dissatisfied with the existing normative order of the security community and actively try to change it. It is suggested here that the interplay between norm contestation among powerful norm leaders ('core states') within the norm regime that weakens the normative order from above, on the one hand, and the emergence of transnational social movements that actively challenge the existing normative order from below, on the other hand, provides a potent combination for normative change in a security community.

Finally, it is argued that the process of security community disintegration can be chronologically structured as a sequence of four consecutive stages (dysfunction, decline, denial, and disintegration) each playing a distinct part in the breakup of the normative order. At the dysfunctional stage, new ideas are introduced against the backdrop of an external 'shock' and are actively promoted by norm challengers seeking to change the established normative order. If these ideas gain legitimacy and if norm leaders subsequently fail to incorporate these new ideas or fail to act responsively, norm challengers will further gain in strength and legitimacy. As a result, the normative order may begin to degenerate and the security community enters a stage of decline. To save the security community, norm leaders of the security community may then make significant tactical concessions to norm challengers while, at the same time, refusing to acknowledge that their behavior contradicts their normative beliefs. This puts them in a stage of denial. Finally, if this condition persists the normative order among members of the security community arrives at the stage of disintegration as security community norms disappear and/or are replaced.

To sum up, security community disintegration is presented here as a dynamic process of norm degeneration involving agency. As pointed out above, there have been three other studies that deal with the phenomenon of the disintegration of security communities. It is thus necessary to engage with their alternative explanations in order to lay out explicitly the specific contributions of this study.

Charles Kupchan (2010), for example, explores a number of historical cases of both successes and failures of stable peace. However, his analytical focus is more broadly on 'zones of stable peace', which according to Kupchan, include three types (rapprochement, security community, and union). As a result, his empirical cases represent only two instances of security community failure. Moreover, since Kupchan's definition of 'failure' includes even the 'attempt to form a zone of stable peace', his book effectively deals with only one actual historical case in which a pluralistic security community existed and subsequently disintegrated (Concert of Europe) and even in this case, Kupchan remains skeptical whether a mature security community existed in the first place by stating that 'war among the members of the Concert, though a remote prospect, was not entirely unthinkable' (Kupchan 2010, pp. 8–9 and 34).

Harald Müller (2006) develops a theory of decay of security communities that relies both on material and ideational factors. He develops four core criteria that constitute a mature, tightly coupled security community (values, identity, responsiveness, trust) and argues that their exposure to systemic or domestic change may weaken the security community. Müller's argument shares some commonalities with my own argument in the sense that we both view norms to be essential for understanding why security communities in general, and the transatlantic security community in particular, may be weakened, and focus on the elevated role of core states as the embodiment of its normative structure.

Apart from these commonalities, however, there are a number of important distinctions to be made. One important difference lies in the conceptual relationship between norms and values. Müller treats norms and values interchangeably by arguing that 'norms are values translated into prescriptions and proscriptions of behavior' (Müller 2006, p. 4). He thus condenses the two concepts into a single criterion, which he describes as 'common values and norms'. My own conceptualization, on the contrary, treats norms as a superordinate concept. Common values thus constitute only one part of the general normative order of a security community among others. Accordingly, the analytical model employed in this book specifically concentrates on norm dynamics in a security community. This constitutes another important distinction from Harald Müller's theory of decay. Even though Müller occasionally refers to specific norms like the 'consultation norm' or the 'norm of responsiveness' in his empirical investigations, he does not develop a coherent analytical framework to trace these norm dynamics in a security community at the micro-level. Rather, he subsumes these norms under a category entitled 'ideational normative criteria' along with two other essential categories and 11 additional criteria that all interact with each other. In fact, here lies the strength of his model: Harald Müller develops a 'wide' model of security community disintegration that is able to capture a broad spectrum of possible factors (norms being one among many) and a larger number of cases which permits more generalized answers and predictions. The downside to this macro-approach is that the model becomes too complex to capture norm dynamics at the micro-level. My model of security community disintegration follows a different approach. By specifically focusing on norm dynamics, I develop a 'narrow' model in order to trace the micro-politics of norm degeneration (e.g., the disruption of symbolic interaction or social unlearning) in a security community. In doing so, my model is able to trace normative change in a security community; however, in a limited number of cases and at the expense of making generalized predictions.

Finally, Thomas Risse analyzes the transatlantic crisis over Iraq as a potential case for the breakdown of the transatlantic security community. In summarizing the findings of an edited volume on *The End of the West* (Anderson et al. 2008), he argues that a pluralistic security community is constituted by four elements: common interests, interdependence, shared norms, and collective identity (Risse 2008, p. 268). When the combined strength of these elements weakens, he argues, then the security community will be weakened as well and, ultimately, fall apart. Similar to Harald Müller, Thomas Risse and the authors in the volume thus also use a 'wide' model to explain security community disintegration that relies on a wide array of material and ideational factors. Hence, the same distinctions outlined above separate their model from my own. I certainly do not claim that norms and ideas can be expected to explain the process of security community disintegration completely. Neither do I pretend that material factors do not matter in the process of security community disintegration. My argument, as explained above, is rather that these material conditions follow from rather than precede normative change.

NORMATIVE CHANGE AND SECURITY COMMUNITIES

Having outlined my argument and alternative explanations, the following section will situate this argument within the contemporary state of the art on security communities and tie its assumptions more thoroughly to the research agenda on normative change. This should give the reader a better understanding of the richness and contested nature of the security community concept while also showing how my own argument about the disintegration of security community relates to some important questions in the IR literature on normative change.

Security Communities

There is a rich and growing body of literature dealing with various facets and patterns of the security community concept. Many scholars have made use of the concept and expanded its original scope in order to make it more applicable to the study of contemporary IR, broaden its empirical use, and position it as an alternative concept to other forms of security governance such as regional alliances, regimes, organizations, and imperial orders (for an overview, see Koschut 2014c). Here, Emanuel Adler's and Michael Barnett's (1998) path-breaking book picked up the thread of earlier works that sought to integrate the concept of security community within a Constructivist research framework (see, e.g., Risse-Kappen 1996). Subsequent authors followed suit triggering a whole new generation of scholarly work on the subject. Alexander Wendt (1999), for example, heavily relies on the concept in his exploration of friendship patterns and the Kantian state of anarchy. Bruce Cronin (1999) introduces the concept of transnational identity to the study of security communities. Janice Bially Mattern (2005) looks at the significance of language and discourse in a security community (what she calls 'representational force').

To be sure, not all recent scholarly work on security communities has taken a strictly Constructivist turn. For an instance, Raimo Väyrynen (2000) contrasts the security community concept to the concept of stable peace and criticizes Constructivist research for its allegedly limited attention to the material conditions of security communities. Hans Mouritzen (2001) claims that both state and non-state actors can initiate security communities. Håkan Wiberg (2003) finds that security communities 'evolve from military alliances based on common threats'. Barry Buzan and Ole Wæver (2003) include the concept in their study on so-called regional security complexes. Laurie Nathan (2006) and Andrej Tusicisny (2007) both underline the importance of domestic factors for maintaining a security community. In the wake of EU enlargement and NATO military interventions against nonmembers, some authors have specifically focused on the relationship between security communities and outsiders (Bellamy 2004; Gheciu 2005; Adler 2008). Other empirical works on the subject include Kacowicz et al. (2000); Vucetic (2001); Vesa and Möller (2003); Kværnø and Rasmussen (2005); Möller (2007); Bjola and Kornprobst (2007); Pouliot (2008); Grillot et al. (2007); Kitchen (2009); Kupchan (2010), and Koschut (2014b).

Constructivist input has thus arguably led to a revival of the original Deutschian concept in IR without necessarily limiting the concept to one particular theoretical approach. In fact, Emanuel Adler and Patricia Greve (2009) even suggest to theoretically combine analytically distinct but spatially overlapping regional structures of security orders such as balance of power and security community. Amitav Acharya (2001) and others claim that liberal–democratic interpretations of security communities are overestimated and outdated as certain parts of the Asia-Pacific area are undergoing a significant transformation process toward the formation of a security community (Leifer 1989; Zhang 1995; Bellamy 2004; Acharya 2005; Emmerson 2005; Pugh 2003; Ba 2005; Collins 2007; Burke and McDonald 2007; Tan 2007; Haacke and Morada 2010; Koschut 2012). However, this latter argument has not remained uncontested, with some scholars questioning whether ASEAN and other non-Western institutional frameworks actually qualify as security communities (Nathan 2006; Khoo 2004; Väyrynen 2000).

More recently, some scholars have attempted to align the concept of security community with the practice turn in IR. Perhaps most relevant to the study at hand is Emanuel Adler's notion of 'communities of practice', which he and Vincent Pouliot have adapted from Etienne Wenger (1998). In his book *Communitarian International Relations*, Emanuel Adler (2005, p. 15) advocates a practice theory approach to IR that 'take(s) the international system as a collection of communities of practice: for example, communities of diplomats, of traders, of environmentalists, and of human rights activists'. This approach has featured prominently in research on security communities in recent years (Pouliot 2007, 2008; Bueger and Stockbruegger 2012). Building on organizational theory and insights from philosophy, psychology, and sociology, this latter branch of literature argues that security communities are 'communities of practice as they tacitly practice peaceful change' through background knowledge or habitus (Adler 2005, p. 17; see also: Pouliot 2008; Adler and Greve 2009; Hopf 2010; Adler and Pouliot 2011). These authors view practices[5] as the natural and self-evident way of solving interstate disputes in a security community at the exclusion of violent practices. Introducing yet another perspective, I align the security community concept with the recent emotion turn in IR by arguing that security communities are emotional communities understood as 'groups in which people adhere to the same norms of emotional expression and value—or devalue—the same or related emotions' (Koschut 2014a; on norms and emotions, see also: Eznack 2012; Hutchison 2012).

To sum up, there is a rich and growing body of literature dealing with the concept of security community. However, as pointed out earlier, while the contemporary state of the art on security communities offers a plethora of scholarly writings on their ascent and formation, there is little to nothing on their decline and disintegration. This lack of adequate theoretical and empirical attention to the issue of security community disintegration serves as the starting point for this book. How do norms fit into this picture?

As outlined above, Karl Deutsch and his associates grant a significant role to the normative character of security communities. Most Constructivist accounts of security communities cited above equally suggest that collective normative understandings play a significant role in the development of security communities by providing its members with a sense of 'we-ness' and collective meanings. Conventional (or mainstream) Constructivism,[6] for example, holds that the environment in which actors operate is both social and material. From this perspective, material structures are given meaning by the social context through which they are interpreted. In other words, while material power is an important factor in the development of security community, it acquires meaning only through the cognitive structure of knowledge—the presence or absence of shared meanings and understandings among a group of actors—which constitutes the 'social fabric' of a regional order. This conception understands the conditions for regional security and peace less as a material condition (presence or absence of military capabilities) and instead more as a social construction (presence or absence of shared meanings and norms) (Adler and Barnett 1998). In this sense, a pluralistic security community can be understood as a 'social fact of interstate peace' (Pouliot 2007, p. 375) and a 'cognitive region' (Koschut 2014a, p. 534; Adler 1997a, p. 249) that exists primarily because people collectively believe in its norms and act accordingly.

In terms of scope, the study of security communities as geographically bounded areas of peaceful change requires a regional understanding and framing of norms. In IR, regional norms play an important role not only because they relate to particular geographical spaces but, more importantly, because, in contrast to the universal character of international or global norms, regional norms represent particular common understandings, meanings, and identities (Florini 1996; Katzenstein 2005; Jetschke and Lenz 2013). This is where my argument differs, for example, from some approaches in practice theory, which argue that collective identity is not a necessary condition for the development of security communities (Pouliot 2008). Emphasizing a regional understanding of norms in IR, scholars have pointed to the creation of European norms (Checkel 1999, 2005; Diez 2005), Asian norms (Acharya 2004, 2011; Rüland 2014), Latin American norms (Castle 2000; Kacowicz 2005), Arab norms

(Barnett 1995; Lynch 1999), or African norms (Jackson and Roseberg 1982; Herbst 2007). This book builds on the view that regional norms play an important role in IR not only because they relate to particular geographical spaces but, more importantly, because regional norms shape and represent particular as opposed to universal understandings, meanings, and identities and thus promote a communitarian as opposed to a cosmopolitan understanding of IR (Koschut 2014c). From this perspective, regional norms, expressed through regionally shared terms of discourse, symbols, narratives, language, emotions, habits, and practices gain significance in a security community (Murphy 1991, p. 30; Buzan and Wæver 2003, p. 48; Katzenstein 2005, p. 12). The analytical scope of this book is thus on the fit between competing regional norms rather than the fit between competing international norms or between international and domestic norms.

To sum up, a security community can be understood as a social relationship defined here as the behavior of a plurality of actors whose individual normative discourse and practices (parts) take account of that of the others and is oriented in these terms through collective meaningful content (whole). From such a Constructivist point of view, disintegrative processes can be based on a redefinition of norms and identities within a security community. In this book, I use a motivationally 'internalist' Constructivist interpretation of social action[7] by focusing on the reflexive internalization of 'taken-for-granted norms' as I seek to show how particular regional norms of peaceful change move from being taken-for-granted and internalized by the members of a security community (logic of appropriateness) to instrumental norm compliance or disregard and rational considerations of costs and benefits (logic of consequence) (Checkel 2005, p. 804; Wendt 1999, pp. 310–11). While the explanatory power of norms for processes of security community formation has been firmly established by numerous scholars (see, e.g., Murphy 1991; Adler and Barnett 1998; Legro 1997; Finnemore and Sikkink 1998; Wendt 1999; Tannenwald 1999; Acharya 2001; Buzan and Wæver 2003; Katzenstein 2005), their role in the disintegration of security communities, with a few exceptions noted above, remains largely void.

In the next section, I further elaborate on how normative change may occur in a security community by structuring the Constructivist literature on norms along two strands—norm emergence, on the one hand, and norm degeneration, on the other hand—to show how both are helpful in explaining security community disintegration. To be absolutely clear, this should by no means imply that Constructivist studies on norm emergence ignore the problem of norm degeneration or vice versa. For example, Thomas Risse and Stephen Ropp (2013, p. 15) clearly acknowledge that 'the existence of (...) (counter-)discourses and narratives, together with the associated deterioration in (...) behavior of the countries from which the emanate, obviously undermines our initial assumption regarding "unidirectionality"'. The distinction between these different Constructivist strands is simply meant to structure the contemporary state of the art on normative change, thereby allowing for a clearer analytical differentiation between processes of norm emergence and norm degeneration.

Norm Emergence

While it is well-established that norms and ideas can generally help understand an outcome, the particular modalities, mechanisms, and application of ideational and normative processes are still unclear and deeply contested in the field. The Constructivist literature in particular, at least its mainstream, has provided invaluable insights as to how such processes promote the consolidation of norms in world politics. At the same time, however, the literature has arguably produced a 'progressivist bias' in Constructivist theory that tends to focus on successful norm internalization (Wiener 2009, p. 179; see also: Rosert and Schirmbeck 2007). The possibility of norm degeneration—like the possibility of security community disintegration—remained for long a neglected aspect in mainstream Constructivist research. Alex Wendt (1999), for example, argues that actors, at some point (which he calls the Kantian culture), will regard certain norms as legitimate and will thus internalize and constantly reproduce a given normative order. At the evolutionary stage of a Kantian culture, states move beyond the level of uncertainty in a Hobbesian (enmity) and Lockean culture (rivalry) by developing mutual trust and a collective identity based on a shared normative order to settle their disputes peacefully and form pluralistic security communities. At this stage of norm internalization, Wendt asserts, norms become conventional and taken for granted which makes conformity almost self-evident. Since actors are not forced to do this due to coercion or incentives but because they simply no longer consider alternative forms of behavior, any change to this normative order is inherently difficult if not impossible.

Once norms of peaceful change have become 'frozen' in this way, Wendt sees little chance for an already established pluralistic security community to degenerate into a state of uncertainty or even violent conflict. This is because members of a security community acquire certain normative privileges such as dependable expectations of peaceful change, which they will be hesitant to give up. Wendt thus concludes, 'although there is no guarantee that international time will move forward toward a Kantian culture (...) I do think one can argue that it will not move backward, *unless there is a big exogenous shock*' (emphasis added, Wendt 1999, p. 312 see also Wendt 2003, p. 492). Wendt (1999, p. 312) goes on by elevating this 'progressivist' mind-set to the level of a quasi-law in IR:

> With respect to its endogenous dynamic, the argument suggests that the history of international politics will be *unidirectional*: if there are any structural changes, they will be historically *progressive*. Thus, even if there is no guarantee that the future of the international system will be better than its past, at least there is reason to think it will not be worse (emphasis added).

Other scholars suggest a similar progressive continuum of norm internalization (Finnemore and Sikkink 1998).

A similar pattern has developed with regards to the study of security communities. Practice theory, for example, shares much of Wendt's pessimism about the unraveling of security communities. Since practical knowledge or habits are performed as underlying routines and 'unthinking action' without self-reflection by actors they are naturally hard to change unless interrupted by external 'shocks' (Hopf 2010; see also: Mitzen 2006). Echoing Wendt, Sean Shore (1998) argues that the path-dependent nature of pluralistic security communities sets in motion a self-reinforcing pattern of reciprocal actions that, though by no means inevitable, is increasingly difficult to halt. He illustrates his point by citing the case of the demilitarized US–Canadian border (on this point, see also Haglund 2007).

Still, the literature on norm emergence by no means forecloses the possibility of norm degeneration. Even though Alex Wendt and others appear skeptical regarding norm degeneration and security community disintegration, they do acknowledge the possibility of norm regression through major external change ('a big exogenous shock', see: Wendt 1999, p. 312). Charles Tilly (1995), for example, argues that the decline of political communities causes people to reconsider who they are and with whom they want to associate. This line of argument can also be found in Michael Barnett's (1996) study of the decline of a pan-Arab identity following the Persian Gulf war and subsequent alignment of many Arab states with the former 'Other' (USA). In the same volume, Thomas Berger (1996) suggests that any reinterpretation or redefinition of existing beliefs, norms, and identities must be preceded by 'a major external shock'. This argument is equally prevalent in Emanuel Adler's and Michael Barnett's (1998) seminal study on security communities. The argument that major external change can undermine or loosen affiliation with collective norms and identities is based on a social-constructivist interpretation of Mancur Olson's (Olson (1982) has been changed to Olson (1965) as per the reference list. Please check if okay.1965) argument that systemic 'shocks' increase incentives and capabilities for domestic political groups and individuals who seek change and also provide argumentative ammunition to advocate political change.

In sum, the Constructivist literature on norm emergence suggests that normative change in a security community would most likely result from major changes in the external environment that shift the international system as a whole or at least alter significant parts of it. However (granted that we know 'major change' when we see it), this does not answer the question as to *how* such normative change actually takes place. In other words, which mechanisms, processes, and agents are set in motion by major external change? This book shares the basic assumption that major external change plays a role in the disintegration of security communities. However, it is argued that the story does not end there. As pointed out above, it is assumed here that major external change is only the starting point in the process of security community disintegration initiating a set of social and internal changes that may eventually lead to normative change.

Norm Degeneration

Many authors have recently addressed the possibility of normative change. Still, most have tended to concentrate on its 'progressivist' connotation explained above and hardly touch upon or take for granted the dynamics that may lead to the weakening or disappearance of existing norms. Increasingly, a number of scholars have begun to tackle this problem by conceptualizing normative change 'for the worse'. Predominantly situated within the Constructivist research framework, these scholars have developed innovative approaches and explanations that deal with the puzzle of norm erosion, regress, degeneration, and disappearance in world politics by building on insights generated by growing research on norm contestation during the last decade (Wiener 2004, 2007; Sandholtz 2007, 2008; Sandholtz and Stiles 2009; Wiener and Puetter 2009; Hoffmann 2010; Jetschke and Liese 2013).

Elvira Rosert and Sonja Schirmbeck (2007, p. 258), for example, show how the US norm of the non-first-use/first-strike nuclear option was gradually weakened after the end of the Cold War. They define norm erosion as 'the re-expansion of the scope of action of an actor, previously restricted by the norm, at the expense of the respective norm' and put particular emphasis on the role of agency in this process. A related account is presented by Christopher Daase (2003) who studies the eroding legitimacy of a global nuclear norm of non-proliferation and non-usage. His approach stresses social hierarchies and power struggles between nuclear have and have-nots. Tim Dunne (2007) uses a similar approach in arguing that, in the course of 9/11, human rights norms have been undermined by the most powerful actors at the international level. Thomas Dolan (2013), Daryl Press et al. (2013) as well as Koschut (2014b) have shown how conflict between competing international and domestic norms of appropriate behavior may result in an expansion of the latter at the expense of the former.

Ryder McKeown (2009) and Kathryn Sikkink (2013) investigate the weakening of the torture taboo in USA after 9/11. Mirroring Finnemore and Sikkink's norm life cycle, McKeown (2009, pp. 11–12) presents a 'norm death series' beginning with norm internalization, followed by reverse norm cascades at the domestic and international level, and eventually the expiration of a norm. His account of norm regression centers on the role of norm challengers (which he calls 'norm revisionists') and mechanisms of issue framing, arguing, and persuasion in the US debate on torture. Sikkink (2013, p. 162) uses empirical evidence from US non-compliance with the prohibition of torture during the George W. Bush Administration to test the 'spiral model' of human rights change (Risse et al. 1999, 2013). Her findings suggest the possibility of a norm 'backlash' or 'reversal' occurring within a country where a particular norm has been firmly established and highlight the material invulnerability of a powerful hegemon to internal and external pressures.

Dynamics of normative argumentation play a central role in a study by Regina Heller, Martin Kahl, and Daniele Pisoiu (2012). In their analysis, they demonstrate how governmental actors implemented security and counterterrorism measures at the expense of human and civil rights after

9/11 using discursive and rhetorical tools to legitimize policy choices. Building on the 'life cycle' of norms, they conceptualize norm regression as a process of 'inverse norm development' based on 'triggers, agents of change, and "tipping points" for diffusion' (Heller et al. 2012, p. 282). Lucile Eznack (2012) emphasizes the role of affect and emotions that enable states to rebuild degenerated norms of appropriate behavior through 'relational repair'. Finally, Diana Panke and Ulrich Petersohn (Panke and Petersohn 2012) identify two necessary conditions that may account for the degeneration of a particular international norm (presence of norm challengers/unpunished norm violations). While all of these scholars certainly differ in their conceptual and empirical approaches, this—by no means exhaustive—overview shows that there are a number of shared features regarding the study of the weakening of shared norms at the international level that carry relevance for the study of norm degeneration in a security community.

To begin with, most scholars emphasize the role of agency in the process of deconstructing norms of appropriate behavior. This is an important aspect to note since many Constructivist accounts on norm emergence have tended to underestimate the role of agency at the stage of internalization. While agency certainly plays a critical role in establishing a particular norm, once a norm as been internalized it appears to transform into a structure-like concept that constrains the behavior of actors yet, at the same time, deprives them any access to change the norm. As a result, agency tends to get lost in internalization (Checkel 1998, p. 2, Rosert and Schirmbeck 2007, p. 257). This analytical loss of agency at the stage of internalization appears problematic given that the existence of norms depends precisely on their need for reiteration by relevant actors (Hopf 2010, p. 544, see also: Wiener and Puetter 2009). As Nicholas Onuf (1994, p. 18) reminds us:

> Every time agents choose to follow a rule, they change it—they strengthen it by making it more likely that they and others will follow the rule in the future. Every time agents choose not to follow a rule, they change the rule by weakening it, and in so doing they may well contribute the constitution of some rule.

To sum up, Constructivist scholars studying norm degeneration are 'bringing agency back in' by focusing on the way actors may undermine and transform internalized norms of appropriate behavior. This implies that agency should also take a prominent role in processes of norm degeneration in a security community. More specifically, it draws attention to the critical role of the conflict between norm challengers and norm leaders within a security community outlined above.

Second, concerning process, most scholars who study the weakening of norms use sequential models based on consecutive stages and steps that are able to historically trace the process of norm erosion. In this sense, they mirror and extend Constructivist studies on norm emergence by picking up were others have left. It is important to point out that, while the individual stages and steps of norm degeneration differ, there is a clear rejection of path dependency. This means that processes of norm degeneration need not necessarily lead to norm disappearance. Diana Panke and Ulrich Petersohn (2012, p. 721) as well as Lucile Eznack (2012), for example, show that a weakened norm may also be repaired. On a methodological level, this leads to an unavoidable focus on historical case studies (with all its pitfalls and complications) because the outcome under investigation lies in the past (I will return to this problem below). Thus, whereas Constructivists who study norm emergence are able to point to the future, Constructivists studying norm degeneration have to analytically focus on the past. This suggests that investigating security community disintegration equally needs to focus on the past—a fact that will be highly relevant for selection of suitable cases below.

Finally, regarding mechanisms, scholars who study norm degeneration tend to place emphasis on the discursive weakening of international norms. In a similar way, norm emergence has been empirically evaluated predominantly through speech acts, normative arguments, and issue framing. For example, Thomas Risse and Kathryn Sikkink (1999, p. 13) point out that the process of norm emergence 'emphasizes processes of communication, argumentation, and persuasion. Actors accept the validity and significance of norms in their discursive practices'. Scholars who study the weakening of norms emphasize similar mechanisms, but under opposite signs.

Many Constructivist accounts of norm emergence as well as norm degeneration have arguably tended to focus on language and texts while undervaluing how norms are actually put into practice (Neumann 2002). Because of that, practice theory has criticized these Constructivist accounts for its alleged 'discursive bias' and offered new insights how norms of appropriate behavior are not only (de-)constructed through discourse but also through practice (Pouliot 2008; Hopf 2010; Brunnée and Toope 2010). This criticism is not entirely unjustified but overrated. For example, the spiral model of human rights change developed by Thomas Risse, Stephen Ropp, and Kathryn Sikkink certainly does 'call attention both to what actors do (...) but also what they say (...)' (Sikkink 2013, p. 148). In any case, studying norm degeneration in a security community should take both discursive and practical elements into account. More importantly, the fact that norm degeneration appears to involve similar processes but under opposing signs suggests that similar social processes that are important in the buildup of the normative order of a security community may also be inversely relevant to its breakup. For example, whereas the development of shared regional institutions is conducive to security community formation, the failure of such institutions may lead to security community disintegration.

To sum up, as I hope to have shown here, the Constructivist literature on normative change can be grouped into two strands. One strand focuses on processes of norm emergence and norm internalization. It suggests that security community disintegration would result from a major external 'shock'. A second strand turns attention to processes of norm degeneration and norm replacement. It implies that security community disintegration would mirror the process of security community formation but under opposing signs and turns attention to the critical role of norm challengers in that process. In this sense, the combined Constructivist insights on norm emergence/degeneration tend to support the main argument and assumptions about the disintegration of security community outlined above: Constructivist studies on norm emergence provide valuable insights about how major external change may disrupt the normative order and thus trigger processes of norm degeneration in a security community. Constructivist accounts of norm degeneration are particularly helpful in shedding light on the subsequent social and internal dynamics leading to normative change.

In this section, I have carved out what we know about normative change and security communities in IR and linked these insights to my own argument about when and how security communities may disintegrate. To this end, I have shown the depth and dexterity of the concept of security community by broadening its analytical framework as well as by tying its theoretical assumptions more thoroughly to the research agenda on norm emergence/degeneration. This provides the groundwork for developing an analytical framework for normative change in a security community in the subsequent chapter. In the following section, I explain how I intend to apply this framework in this book.

RESEARCH METHOD AND CASE SELECTION

In the next chapter, I develop an analytical framework for the disintegration of security communities, which elaborates on the assumptions made here. Subsequently, two historical case studies are employed to empirically illustrate the plausibility and applicability of the framework. In this section, I outline the research method used and explain the selection of cases.

Methodology

This book relies on the method of difference by establishing a set of two dissimilar cases. In the former case (the German Confederation), norm degeneration within a security community resulted in its eventual disintegration. In the latter case (NATO), norm degeneration took place yet did not lead to the breakup of that security community. Of course, comparing a single 'successful' case of security community disintegration with a single 'unsuccessful' case of disintegration significantly limits the chances to arrive at definite causal explanations and generalizations, let alone predictions (Ray 1995, p. 132). Indeed, it is not the primary aim of this study to provide any definitive or generalized causal answers. Instead, I wish to create an argument based on a narrative that highlights the nature and dynamics of norm degeneration and agency within a security community using logical inference to judge analysis. And, as Audie Klotz and Cecilia Lynch (2007, p. 21) underline, '(t)hese judgments depend on the researcher's question and analytical goal, not the number of cases'.

The empirical cases are structured along the analytical framework developed in the following chapter. This provides a set of comparable analytical categories and mechanisms as well as actors and the relationships between them. At the beginning of each case, I reconstruct the normative order of the respective security community as a structural base line to empirically capture processes of normative change. I then build a historical narrative to highlight the agency of particular individuals and groups within the security community relying on the analytical categories of norm leaders and norm challengers. In doing so, I develop a story line that seeks to trace processes of normative change within a security community structuring the argument along a temporal sequence of events and consecutive stages. At the end of each case, I revisit the normative order from the beginning to evaluate the scope of normative change. In the concluding chapter of this book, I return to the framework developed in Chap. 2 to evaluate its overall analytical validity in light of the empirical findings from both cases and show some implications of the findings in terms of theory building and make suggestions for further research.

All of this is done using two types of empirical sources and data. First, I look at the subjective opinions and perceptions of political decision-makers as well as other politically relevant groups and individuals. Here, I will rely predominantly on the use of available discourse, symbols, narratives, and language use in historical documents and other text forms. For example, a good way to methodologically detect and evaluate a weakening of existing meanings and shared norms is through discourse analysis and social narratives.[8] As social historians have pointed out, 'social narratives (…) (are) not only a means of representing life, used self-consciously by historians, novelists, and storytellers, but a fundamental cultural constituent of the lives represented (…) and is crucial for understanding the course and the dynamics of historical change' (Sewell 1992, pp. 482–83; see also Klotz and Lynch 2007, p. 45). To illustrate this point, some scholars have used the narratives of industrial workers in Wilhelmian Germany in order to understand and explain the cohesiveness of the German working class. Steinmetz (1992), for example, finds that narratives played an important role as a category of human consciousness and actually aided in the construction of a collective social identity. A similar effect can be attributed to the members of a security community as they identify with each other through mutual communication and interaction. Community narratives can thus be said to both represent and (de-)construct social reality within cognitive regions, normative structures, and shared identities. By looking at the subjective opinions and perceptions of political decision-makers as well as other politically relevant groups and individuals, I pose the following questions: Did the actors appear to genuinely believe that the other members of the community would not use physical force against them? Did the actors identify with and share the norms and meanings of the community?

Second, I complement ideational perceptions and discourse with observable material conditions and practices such as resource allocations and physical interaction to analyze if and how changing norms and ideas actually resulted in changing behavior. Here, I ask the question whether or not the capabilities and practice to physically fight one another actually changed within a particular group of states. For example, did the members of the community build up or reduce their military installations and presence along common borders? Did its members continue to participate in joint decision-making and did they make use of common institutions?

To sum up, I contrast what actors 'say' with what they actually 'do' which reflects the methodological integration of discourses and practices in the study of normative change described above. Hence, transformed ideational perceptions and material conditions are merged into a coherent framework to systematically trace normative change in a security community.

Case Selection

Since security communities, in contrast to alliances or regimes, can be said to involve particular strong bonds among its members this suggests that cases of disintegration naturally tend to be rare (Müller 2006, p. 2; Risse 2008, p. 267). This might lead one to question the practical relevance of the problem at hand. In other words, is the problem of security community disintegration really a 'problem' for IR scholars and practitioners when there are only few empirical cases? A quick look at contemporary cases of security communities, however, vividly confirms the practical relevance of studying security community disintegration. For example, given the recent Euro crisis, could one safely assume that the European security community might not break up one day? Or, following the Iraq war, is the notion of a disintegrated transatlantic security community entirely unfeasible? In both cases, the obvious answer is no. As Karl Deutsch et al. (1957, p. 122) put it: 'if integration *seems* to be achieved at some future time, we should be careful not to assume that it is permanent. Disintegration has, of course, taken place in the past after a long period of apparent integration, and this could also happen to an ostensibly integrated North Atlantic area' (emphasis in the original).

A related challenge may be to provide a convincing explanation why the historical cases employed in this book are instances of the same type: a security community. This relates directly to the question why the cases in this book have been selected. The German Confederation, on the one hand, is the only confirmed case of pluralistic security community disintegration studied by Karl Deutsch et al. (1957, p. 11). Hence, the mere fact that Deutsch and his associates explicitly mention the German Confederation as a case of pluralistic security community disintegration makes it an obvious candidate for a case study in a book that deals with exactly this phenomenon. NATO, on the other hand, is a textbook example of a pluralistic security community (Deutsch et al. 1957; Cox 2005; Pouliot 2006; Bjola and Kornprobst 2007; Anderson et al. 2008; Kitchen 2009; Koschut 2010). In this sense, I selected two 'hard cases' of pluralistic security communities, which should make the findings in this book more resilient against counterarguments and alternative explanations. Of course, to state that Deutsch and others characterize both cases as pluralistic security communities says relatively little about the specific characteristics that both cases have in common as instances of the same type of event. It thus seems necessary to further outline specific indicators that point to the existence of a security community in each case.

Karl W. Deutsch defined a security community as 'one in which there is real assurance that the members of that community will not fight each other physically, but will settle their disputes in some other way' (Deutsch et al. 1957, p. 5). Peaceful resolution of interstate conflicts, according to Deutsch, rests upon two prerequisites that indicate the existence of a pluralistic security community: (a) the attainment of a sense of community (shared meanings, collective identity) and trust and (b) the presence of collective norms of behavior, common institutional procedures of enforcement and shared practices of compliance (Deutsch et al. 1957, p. 5). More specifically, these prerequisites include multilateral decision-making procedures, unfortified borders, changes in military planning, a common definition of a threat, and the discourse and language of community (Adler and Barnett 1998, pp. 55–6).

Evidence of these indicators can be found in both cases under investigation (and will be spelled out in further detail in each case). First, in both cases members can be found to share a particular sense of community, 'we-feeling' and trust rooted in shared beliefs, meanings, and mutual identification as the conservative–aristocratic German states and the transatlantic liberal–democratic West, respectively. Second, both the German as well as the transatlantic security community share particular norms of appropriate behavior and institutional mechanisms to resolve internal conflict peacefully and the historical record shows that the probability of military conflict among its members remains unthinkable over a long period of time. In this sense, the historical cases used in this book can indeed be claimed to represent instances of the same type: a security community.

Having said that, a few caveats remain nevertheless. One is that each case naturally exposes historically different paths and circumstances. However, there are also a striking number of recurring patterns and relationships as well as similar processes and mechanisms that can be traced in both cases.

Still, one might argue that the case selection is diachronic as it spans not only across different historical time periods but also includes a disparate set of actors, for example city-states, kingdoms, and nation-states. There is some truth to that and I am well aware of its limitations. In fact, no two historical events are exactly alike. Yet, as explained above, both cases are analytically consistent and woven together conceptually by the concept of security community. According to Karl W. Deutsch, they are both security communities 'in which keeping the peace among the participating units was (and is) the main political goal overshadowing all others' (Deutsch et al. 1957, p. 31).

In this context, it is important to point out that I do not intend to exclude parametric variations in historical developments nor do I embark on diachronic reductionism by overgeneralizing the empirical findings. In line with this approach, the findings at the end of this book should be understood as probabilities rather than final conclusions. As Karl W. Deutsch points out, '(p)ast examples are suggestive, not conclusive. They point in a general direction, but not toward a specific destination. (...) We are using past experience to find out what arrangements appear possible, which appear probable, and which appear more probable than others. We are dealing not only with possibilities, but with priorities of probabilities' (Deutsch et al. 1957, p. 11). Those who may still doubt the use of historical cases to study security community disintegration yet accept Deutsch's assumptions on security communities (which are entirely derived from historical cases) carry the burden of explaining why different historical contexts and actors seem to matter in the former case but not so in the latter. While this research design is thus well suited for the study at hand certain curtailments must be accepted.

Limitations

No single research can provide answers to every question and this one is no exception. Even though this book contains at least one empirical case of 'successful' security community disintegration, the list of instances where security community disintegration may have occurred in the past is by no means exhaustive. It is also important to emphasize that the particular reading of both cases represents my own interpretations based on the historical evidence and primary sources available. Other researchers may come to different conclusions or they may find conflicting historical material. Having said that, the case studies will not provide for potentially missing variables or error in the empirical data. The study has to rely on the available data at hand and cannot fabricate additional sources, for example, by conducting public opinion polls or interviews with relevant decision-makers. To compensate for this, the case studies employ a broad range of historical data and archival materials allowing for an in-depth empirical analysis of normative structures, actors, and processes that may point to normative change and the subsequent disintegration of the security community.

Moreover, the empirical cases under investigation only consider a particular kind of political community, namely a European/Western-style security community in which the expectation of war as a means of political behavior among its members has become unthinkable. Hence, the findings at the end of this book are not automatically applicable to other types of political communities or non-Western security communities and I do not pretend to present them as the universal standard. My case selection stems from my own familiarity and knowledge of the region and certainly not from a desire to promote a 'Western' or Euro-centric image of security communities. Also, the empirical analysis involves only cases of collective norms and community formation at the regional level that may or may not be relevant for the study of international norms or communities at the global level. Finally, as outlined above, the study will not produce any reliable predictions on whether or when existing pluralistic security communities may unravel in the future. What the study will provide, however, is an analytical framework and an empirical narrative that identifies certain probabilities, conditions, and mechanisms, which hopefully will be able to shed more light on disintegrative processes and normative change in a security community.

Plan of the Book

The aim of this book is to explain the disintegration of pluralistic security communities through processes of normative change. In order to achieve this objective, the book is divided into five chapters.

The introductory chapter should provide the reader with a basic idea of the problem at hand along with the general argument and assumptions as to what factors are thought to be primarily responsible for the disintegration of pluralistic security communities. To this end, I proposed that security community disintegration results from the degeneration of community norms (normative change).

In the second chapter, I further develop this argument about normative change in a security community by building a coherent analytical framework around it. This framework assumes that the path of security community disintegration is similar to its formation but under opposing signs. For this purpose, Chap. 2 is divided into four parts. In the first part, I explain the normative order of a security community including the norm of common values, the norm of multilateral practice, and the norm of communication as a structural baseline for the subsequent case studies. In the second part, I conceptualize the nature of agency in a security community by framing it as a conflict between norm leaders and norm challengers. In the third part, I develop three levels of change (external, social and internal, normative) that constitute security community disintegration. Finally, I integrate normative structure, agency, and process by building a four-stage dynamic model (dysfunction, decline, denial, disintegration) to analytically trace the path of disintegration in a security community, which will then be applied to the empirical cases.

The first case under investigation is concerned with the formation and subsequent disintegration of the German Confederation, which dissolved in 1866. Chapter 3 presents the German Confederation as a pluralistic security community with common institutions and norms to resolve conflict peacefully accompanied by a collective German conservative–aristocratic identity. It builds a historical narrative showing how the established normative order of the German pluralistic security community was gradually replaced by a new normative order among the German states following the external 'shock' of liberal–democratic revolutionary change in Europe. The case of norm erosion in the German security community leading to its eventual disintegration exposes norm conflicts between a group of transnational norm challengers and norm leaders, on the one hand, as well as normative conflict among the norm leaders themselves (in particular, the two core states, Prussia and Austria), on the other hand. It is argued that both conflicts were interrelated and mutually reinforced each other leading to normative change and the eventual disintegration of the German security community.

Chapter 4 deals with the second empirical case involving the NATO. NATO forms the core organizational structure for the transatlantic security community. It will be shown how norm leaders initially struggled to adapt to the major external 'shock' following the end of the Cold war, leading to serious norm conflicts among norm leaders, and culminating in the crisis over the Iraq war which arguably took the transatlantic security community to the brink. However, in contrast to the German security community, despite the serious crisis over Iraq and a partial redefinition of its normative order notwithstanding, the transatlantic security community continues to exist. War among its members is still unthinkable and there is no indication of a member considering the resolution of conflicts by threatening the use of force. At the same time, however, disintegrative tendencies and norm conflicts persist suggesting that, while war remains unthinkable in the North Atlantic area, normative change remains a possibility.

The closing chapter of this book revisits the main argument and assumptions made in the first two chapters and reviews them in light of the empirical findings extracted from Chaps. 3 and 4. In particular, Chap. 5 draws out tentative answers to the empirical puzzle as to why security community disintegration took place in one case (German Confederation) but not (yet) in the other case (NATO). Finally, I offer some theoretical implications as well as suggestions for further research.

Notes

1. Even though the concept of 'stable peace' must be kept analytically separate from the security community concept the two obviously overlap in theoretical and empirical terms. Generally, a security community can be considered the most advanced form of stable peace (Kacowicz and Bar-Siman-Tov 2000, p. 16; see also: Boulding 1978; George 1992; Russett and Starr 1992).
2. Most scholarly work on disintegration has been done by sociologists (see, e.g., Honneth 1994; Heitmeyer 1997; Anhut 2005; Imbusch and Heitmeyer 2008).
3. To my knowledge, the only notable exceptions are Harald Müller (2006), Thomas Risse (2008), and Charles Kupchan (2010). I will engage with their arguments in further detail in the section below.
4. Norms need to be distinguished from institutions (in the sociological sense). Norms are 'single standards of behavior' as opposed to a 'collection of practices and rules' (institutions) (Finnemore and Sikkink 1998, p. 891). For reasons of analytical clarity, I generally use the term 'collective norms' or 'normative order' when referring to the latter definition.
5. Practices are defined as 'socially meaningful patterns of action which, in being performed more or less competently, simultaneously embody, act out, and possibly reify background knowledge and discourse in and on the material world' (Adler and Pouliot 2011, p. 6).

6. In contrast to critical Constructivists who emphasize the flexible quality and essentially contested nature of norms and identities at the international level, conventional Constructivism focuses on the relatively stable quality of norms and state behavior within a community with a given identity (see, e.g., the 2009 Special Issue of the Journal of International Law and International Relations on 'Contested Norms in International Law and International Relations', especially Wiener and Puetter 2009, p. 16; on the distinction between critical and conventional Constructivism, see: Fierke 2007; Klotz and Lynch 2007).
7. The distinction between motivationally externalist and motivationally internalist Constructivist research can be found in Pouliot (2008, pp. 262–64).
8. See, for example, Müller 1994; Zangl and Zürn 1996; Zehfuss 1998; Weldes and Saco 1996; Hansen 2006; Epstein 2008; Herschinger 2012.

References

Acharya, A. (2001). *Constructing a security community in Southeast Asia. ASEAN and the problem of regional order.* London: Routledge.
Acharya, A. (2004). How ideas spread: whose norms matter? Norm localization and institutional change in Asian regionalism'. *International Organization, 8*(2), 239–275.
Acharya, A. (2005). Do norms and identity matter? Community and power in Southeast Asia's regional order. *Pacific Review, 18*(1), 95–118.
Acharya, A. (2011). Norm subsidiarity and regional orders: Sovereignty, regionalism, and rule-making in the third world. *International Studies Quarterly, 55*(1), 95–123.
Acharya, A. (2014). *Rethinking power, institutions and ideas in world politics: Whose IR?* London: Routledge.
Adler, E. (1992). The emergence of cooperation. National epistemic communities and the international evolution of the idea of nuclear arms control. *International Organization, 46*(1), 101–146.
Adler, E. (1997a). Imagined (security) communities: Cognitive regions in international relations. *Millennium, 26*(2), 249–277.
Adler, E. (1997b). Seizing the middle ground. Constructivism in world politics. *European Journal of International Relations, 3*(3), 319–363.
Adler, E. (2005). *Communitarian international relations. The epistemic foundations of international relations.* New York: Routledge.
Adler, E. (2008). The spread of security communities. Communities of practice, self-restraint, and NATO's post-Cold War transformation. *European Journal of International Relations, 14*(2), 195–230.
Adler, E., & Barnett, M. (1998). A framework for the study of security communities. In E. Adler & M. Barnett (Eds.), *Security communities* (pp. 29–66). Cambridge: Cambridge University Press.

Adler, E., & Greve, P. (2009). When security community meets balance of power. Overlapping regional mechanisms of security governance. *Review of International Studies*, 35(1), 59–84.
Adler, E., & Pouliot, V. (Eds.). (2011). *International practices*. Cambridge: Cambridge University Press.
Anderson, J., Ikenberry, G. J., & Risse, T. (2008). *The end of the west? Crises and change in the Atlantic order*. Ithaca: Cornell University Press.
Anhut, R. (2005). Die Konflikttheorie der Desintegrationstheorie'. In T. Bonacker (Ed.), *Sozialwissenschaftliche Konflikttheorien. Eine Einführung* (pp. 381–409). Opladen: Leske and Budrich.
Ba, A. D. (2005). On norms, rule breaking, and security communities: A constructivist response. *International Relations of the Asia-Pacific*, 5(2), 255–266.
Barnett, M. (1995). Nationalism, sovereignty, and regional order in Arab politics. *International Organization*, 49(3), 479–510.
Barnett, M. (1996). Identity and alliances in the Middle East. In P. J. Katzenstein (Ed.), *The culture of national security* (pp. 400–448). New York: Columbia University Press.
Bellamy, A. J. (2004). *Security communities and their neighbours. Regional fortresses or global integrators?* New York: Palgrave Macmillan.
Berger, T. U. (1996). Norms, identity, and national security in Germany and Japan. In P. J. Katzenstein (Ed.), *The culture of national security* (pp. 317–356). New York: Columbia University Press.
Bially Mattern, J. (2005). *Ordering international politics: Identity, crisis and representational force*. New York: Routledge.
Bjola, C., & Kornprobst, M. (2007). Security communities and the habitus of restraint. Germany and the United States on Iraq. *Review of International Studies*, 33(2), 285–305.
Björkdahl, A. (2002). Norms in international relations: Some conceptual and methodological reflections. *Cambridge Review of International Affairs*, 15(1), 9–23.
Boulding, K. E. (1978). *Stable peace*. Austin: University of Texas Press.
Brunnée, J., & Toope, S. J. (2010). *Legitimacy and legality in international law: An interactional account*. Cambridge: Cambridge University Press.
Bueger, C., & Stockbruegger, J. (2012). Security communities, alliances and macro-securitization: The practices of counter-piracy governance. In M. J. Struett, M. T. Nance, & J. D. Carlson (Eds.), *Piracy and maritime governance* (pp. 98–124). London: Routledge.
Burke, A., & McDonald, M. (2007). *Critical security in the Asia-Pacific*. Manchester: Manchester University Press.
Buzan, B. (2004). *From international to world society? English school theory and the social structure of globalization*. Cambridge: Cambridge University Press.
Buzan, B., & Wæver, O. (2003). *Regions and power. The structure of international security*. Cambridge: Cambridge University Press.

Castle, D. B. (2000). Leo Stanton Rowe and the meaning of Pan-Americanism. In D. Sheinin (Ed.), *Beyond the ideal: Pan-Americanism in international affairs*. Westport: Praeger.

Checkel, J. T. (1998). The constructivist turn in international relations theory. *World Politics, 50*(2), 324–348.

Checkel, J. T. (1999). Norms, institutions, and national identity in contemporary Europe. *International Studies Quarterly, 43*(1), 84–114.

Checkel, J. T. (2005). International institutions and socialization in Europe. Introduction and framework. *International Organization, 59*(4), 801–826.

Coleman, K. P. (2013). Locating norm diplomacy: Venue change in international norm negotiations. *European Journal of International Relations, 19*(1), 163–186.

Collins, A. (2007). Forming a security community. Lessons from ASEAN. *International Relations of the Asia-Pacific, 7*(2), 203–225.

Cox, M. (2005). Beyond the West: Terrors in Transatlantia. *European Journal of International Relations, 11*(2), 203–233.

Cronin, B. (1999). *Community under anarchy. Transnational identity and the evolution of cooperation*. New York: Columbia University Press.

Daase, C. (2003). Das Ende vom Anfang des nuklearen Tabus. Zur Legitimitätskrise der Weltnuklearordnung'. *Zeitschrift für Internationale Beziehungen, 10*(1), 7–41.

Deutsch, K. W. (1954). *Political community at the international level. Problems of definition and measurement*. Garden City: Doubleday.

Deutsch, K. W., Burrell, S. A., Kann, R. A., Lee, M., Jr., Lichterman, M., Lindgren, R. E., Loewenheim, F. L., & van Wagenen, R. W. (1957). *Political community and the North Atlantic area. International organization in the light of historical experience*. Princeton: Princeton University Press.

Diez, T. (2005). Constructing the self and changing others: Reconsidering normative power Europe. *Millennium, 33*(3), 613–636.

Dolan, T. M. (2013). Unthinkable and tragic: The psychology of weapons taboos in war. *International Organization, 67*(1), 37–63.

Dunne, T. (2007). "The rules of the game are changing": Fundamental human rights in crisis after 9/11. *International Politics, 44*, 269–286.

Emmerson, D. K. (2005). Security, community, and democracy in Southeast Asia. Analyzing ASEAN. *Japanese Journal of Political Science, 6*(2), 165–185.

Eppler, A., & Scheller, H. (Eds.). (2013). *Zur Konzeptionalisierung europäischer Desintegration. Zug- und Gegenkräfte im europäischen Integrationsprozess*. Baden-Baden: Nomos.

Epstein, C. (2008). *The power of words in international relations: Birth of an anti-whaling discourse*. Cambridge, MA: Massachusetts Institute of Technology Press.

Eznack, L. (2012). *Crises in the Atlantic alliance. Affect and relations among NATO members*. New York: Palgrave Macmillan.

Fierke, K. M. (2007). *Critical approaches to international security.* Cambridge: Polity.
Finnemore, M. (1996). *National interests in international society.* Ithaca: Cornell University Press.
Finnemore, M., & Sikkink, K. (1998). International norm dynamics and political change. *International Organization, 52*(4), 887–917.
Florini, A. (1996). The evolution of international norms. *International Studies Quarterly, 40*(3), 363–389.
George, A. L. (1992). From conflict to peace: Stages along the road. *United States Institute of Peace Journal, 5*(6), 7–9.
Gheciu, A. (2005). *NATO in the new Europe. The politics of international socialization after the Cold War.* Stanford: Stanford University Press.
Giddens, A. (1991). *Modernity and self-identity: Self and society in the late modern age.* Stanford: Stanford University Press.
Goldstein, J., & Keohane, R. O. (1993). Ideas and foreign policy: An analytical framework. In J. Goldstein & R. O. Keohane (Eds.), *Ideas and foreign policy. Beliefs, institutions, and political change* (pp. 3–30). Ithaca: Cornell University Press.
Grillot, S., D'Erman, V., Cruise, R. J. (2007). *Developing security community in the Western Balkans. The role of the EU and NATO.* Paper prepared for the EUSA Tenth Biennial International Conference, Montréal, Canada, May 17–19.
Haacke, J., & Morada, N. M. (2010). The ASEAN Regional Forum and cooperative security: Introduction. In J. Haacke & N. M. Morada (Eds.), *Cooperative security in the Asia-Pacific. The ASEAN Regional Forum* (pp. 1–12). New York: Routledge.
Haglund, D. G. (2006). Québec's "America problem": Differential threat perception in the North American security community. *American Review of Canadian Studies, 36*(4), 552–567.
Haglund, D. G. (2007). A security community – "if you can keep it": Demographic change and the North American zone of peace. *Norteamérica, 2*(1), 77–100.
Hammerstad, A. (2005). Domestic threats, regional solutions? The challenge of security integration in Southern Africa. *Review of International Studies, 31*(1), 69–87.
Hansen, L. (2006). *Security as practice: Discourse analysis and the Bosnian war.* London: Routledge.
Heitmeyer, W. (Ed.). (1997). *Was treibt die Gesellschaft auseinander?* Frankfurt am Main: Suhrkamp.
Heller, R., Kahl, M., & Pisoiu, D. (2012). The "dark" side of normative argumentation. The case of counterterrorism policy. *Global Constitutionalism, 1*(2), 278–312.
Herbst, J. (2007). Crafting regional cooperation in Africa. In A. Acharya & A. I. Johnston (Eds.), *Crafting cooperation regional international institutions in international politics* (pp. 129–144). Cambridge: Cambridge University Press.

Herschinger, E. (2012). "Hell is the other": Conceptualising hegemony and identity through discourse theory. *Millennium, 41*(1), 65–90.
Hoffmann, M. J. (2010). Norms and social constructivism in international relations. In R. A. Denemark (Ed.), *The international studies encyclopedia* (Vol. 8, pp. 5410–5426). Oxford: Wily-Blackwell.
Honneth, A. (1994). *Desintegration*. Frankfurt am Main: Fischer.
Hopf, T. (2010). The logic of habit in international relations. *European Journal of International Relations, 16*(4), 539–561.
Hutchison, E. (2012). Affective communities as security communities. *Critical Studies on Security, 1*(1), 127–129.
Imbusch, P., & Heitmeyer, W. (2008). *Integration – Desintegration*. Wiesbaden: Verlag für Sozialwissenschaften.
Jackson, R. H. (1993). The weight of ideas in decolonization: Normative change in international relations. In J. Goldstein & R. O. Keohane (Eds.), *Ideas and foreign policy. Beliefs, institutions, and political change* (pp. 111–138). Ithaca: Cornell University Press.
Jackson, R. H., & Roseberg, C. G. (1982). Why Africa's weak states persist. The empirical and the juridical in statehood. *World Politics, 35*(1), 259–282.
Jepperson, R., Wendt, A., & Katzenstein, P. J. (1996). Norms, identity, and culture in national security. In P. J. Katzenstein (Ed.), *The culture of national security* (pp. 33–75). New York: Columbia University Press.
Jetschke, A., & Lenz, T. (2013). Does regionalism diffuse? A new research agenda for the study of regional organizations. *Journal of European Public Policy, 20*(4), 626–637.
Jetschke, A., & Liese, A. (2013). The power of human rights a decade after: From euphoria to contestation. In T. Risse, S. C. Ropp, & K. Sikkink (Eds.), *The persistent power of human rights: From commitment to compliance* (pp. 26–42). Cambridge: Cambridge University Press.
Kacowicz, A. M. (2005). *The impact of norms in international society. The Latin American experience, 1881–2001*. South Bend: Notre Dame University Press.
Kacowicz, A. M., & Bar-Siman-Tov, Y. (2000). Stable peace. A conceptual framework. In A. Kacowicz, Y. Bar-Siman-Tov, O. Elgström, & M. Jerneck (Eds.), *Stable peace among nations* (pp. 11–35). Lanham: Rowman and Littlefield.
Kacowicz, A., Bar-Siman-Tov, Y., Elgström, O., & Jerneck, M. (Eds.). (2000). *Stable peace among nations*. Lanham: Rowman and Littlefield.
Katzenstein, P. J. (2005). *A world of regions. Asia and Europe in the American imperium*. Ithaca: Cornell University Press.
Khoo, N. (2004). Deconstructing the ASEAN security community. A review essay. *International Relations of the Asia-Pacific, 4*, 35–46.
Kitchen, V. M. (2009). Argument and identity change in the Atlantic security community. *Security Dialogue, 40*(1), 95–114.

Klotz, A. (1995). *Norms in international relations. The struggle against apartheid.* Ithaca: Cornell University Press.

Klotz, A., & Lynch, C. (2007). *Strategies for research in constructivist international relations.* Armonk: M.E. Sharpe.

Koschut, S. (2010). *Die Grenzen der Zusammenarbeit. Sicherheit und transatlantische Identität nach dem Ende des Ost-West-Konflikts.* Baden-Baden: Nomos.

Koschut, S. (2012). Friedlicher Wandel ohne Demokratie? Theoretische und empirische Überlegungen zur Bildung einer autokratischen Sicherheitsgemeinschaft'. *Zeitschrift für Internationale Beziehungen, 19*(2), 41–69.

Koschut, S. (2014a). Emotional (security) communities: The significance of emotion norms in inter-allied conflict management. *Review of International Studies, 40*(3), 533–558.

Koschut, S. (2014b). Transatlantic conflict management inside-out: The impact of domestic norms on regional security practices. *Cambridge Review of International Affairs, 27*(2), 339–361.

Koschut, S. (2014c). Regional order and peaceful change: Security communities as a via media in international relations theory. *Cooperation and Conflict, 49*(4), 519–535.

Kupchan, C. A. (2010). *How enemies become friends. The sources of stable peace.* Princeton: Princeton University Press.

Kværnø, O., & Rasmussen, M. (2005). EU enlargement and the Baltic region. A greater security community? In A. Kasekamp (Ed.), *The Estonian foreign policy yearbook 2005* (pp. 83–92). Tallinn: Estonian Foreign Policy Institute.

Legro, J. W. (1997). Which norms matter? Revisiting the "failure" of internationalism. *International Organization, 51*(1), 31–63.

Leifer, M. (1989). *ASEAN and the security of South-East Asia.* London: Routledge.

Liese, A. (2009). Exceptional necessity: How liberal democracies contest the prohibition of torture and ill-treatment when countering terrorism. *Journal of International Law and International Relations, 5*(1), 17–47.

Lund, M. S., & Roig, E. (1999). Southern Africa: An emerging security community. In M. Mekenkamp, P. van Tongeren, & H. van de Veen (Eds.), *Searching for peace in Africa: An overview of conflict prevention and management activities* (pp. 391–395). Utrecht: European Centre for Conflict Prevention.

Lynch, M. (1999). *State interests and public spheres. The international politics of Jordan's identity.* New York: Columbia University Press.

McKeown, R. (2009). Norm regress: US revisionism and the slow death of the torture norm. *International Relations, 23*(1), 5–25.

Merritt, R. L. (1973). Decay in social systems. In M. D. Rubin (Ed.), *Systems in society* (pp. 71–103). Washington, DC: Society for General Systems Research.

Merritt, R. L. (1981). Political disintegration in postwar Berlin. In R. L. Merritt & B. Russett (Eds.), *From national development to global community. Essays in honor of Karl W. Deutsch* (pp. 206–232). London: George Allen and Unwin.

Milliken, J. (1999). The study of discourse in international relations: A critique of research and method. *European Journal of International Relations, 5*(2), 225–254.
Mitzen, J. (2006). Ontological security in world politics: State identity and the security dilemma. *European Journal of International Relations, 12*(3), 341–370.
Möller, F. (2007). *Thinking peaceful change. Baltic security policies and security community building*. Syracuse: Syracuse University Press.
Mouritzen, H. (2001). Security communities in the Baltic Sea region: Real and imagined. *Security Dialogue, 32*(3), 297–310.
Müller, H. (1994). Internationale Beziehungen als kommunikatives Handeln. Zur Kritik der utilitaristischen Handlungstheorien. *Zeitschrift für Internationale Beziehungen, 1*(1), 15–44.
Müller, H. (2006). A theory of decay of security communities with an application to the present state of the Atlantic alliance (Working paper). Berkeley: University of California at Berkeley.
Murphy, A. (1991). Regions as social constructs. The gap between theory and practice. *Progress in Human Geography, 15*(1), 22–35.
Nathan, L. (2006). Domestic instability and security communities. *European Journal of International Relations, 12*(2), 275–299.
Neumann, I. B. (2002). Returning practice to the linguistic turn. *Millennium, 31*(3), 627–651.
Olson, M. (1965). *The logic of collective action. Public goods and the theory of groups*. Cambridge, MA: Harvard University Press.
Onuf, N. (1994). The constitution of international society. *European Journal of International Law, 5*(1), 1–19.
Panke, D., & Petersohn, U. (2012). Why international norms disappear sometimes. *European Journal of International Relations, 18*(4), 719–742.
Pouliot, V. (2006). The alive and well transatlantic security community: A theoretical reply to Michael Cox. *European Journal of International Relations, 12*(1), 119–127.
Pouliot, V. (2007). Pacification without collective identification: Russia and the transatlantic security community in the post-Cold War era. *Journal of Peace Research, 44*(5), 605–622.
Pouliot, V. (2008). The logic of practicality. A theory of practice of security communities. *International Organization, 62*(2), 257–288.
Press, D. G., Sagan, S. D., & Valentino, B. A. (2013). Atomic aversion: Experimental evidence on taboos, traditions, and the non-use of nuclear weapons. *American Political Science Review, 107*(1), 188–206.
Price, R. (1997). *The chemical weapons taboo*. Ithaca: Cornell University Press.
Pugh, M. (2003). The world order politics of regionalisation. In M. Pugh & W. P. S. Sidhu (Eds.), *The UN and regional security: Europe and beyond* (pp. 31–46). Boulder: Lynne Rienner.

Ray, J. L. (1995). *Democracy and international conflict. An evaluation of the democratic peace proposition.* Columbia: University of South Carolina Press.
Risse, T. (2008). The end of the west? Conclusions. In J. Anderson, G. J. Ikenberry, & T. Risse (Eds.), *The end of the west? Crises and change in the Atlantic order* (pp. 263–290). Ithaca: Cornell University Press.
Risse, T., & Lehmkuhl, U. (2006). *Governance in areas of limited statehood. New modes of governance? Research program of the research center (SFB) 700* (SFB-governance working paper series 1). Berlin: Research Center SFB 700.
Risse, T., & Ropp, S. C. (2013). Introduction and overview. In T. Risse, S. C. Ropp, & K. Sikkink (Eds.), *The persistent power of human rights* (pp. 3–25). Cambridge: Cambridge University Press.
Risse, T., & Sikkink, K. (1999). The socialization of international human rights norms into domestic practices: Introduction. In T. Risse, S. C. Ropp, & K. Sikkink (Eds.), *The power of human rights: International norms and domestic change* (pp. 1–38). Cambridge: Cambridge University Press.
Risse, T., Ropp, S. C., & Sikkink, K. (1999). *The power of human rights: International norms and domestic change.* Cambridge: Cambridge University Press.
Risse, T., Ropp, S. C., & Sikkink, K. (2013). *The persistent power of human rights.* Cambridge: Cambridge University Press.
Risse-Kappen, T. (1996). Collective identity in a democratic community: The case of NATO. In P. J. Katzenstein (Ed.), *The culture of national security* (pp. 357–399). New York: Columbia University Press.
Rosenau, J. N., & Czempiel, E. O. (1992). *Governance without government: Order and change in world politics.* Cambridge: Cambridge University Press.
Rosert, E., & Schirmbeck, S. (2007). Zur Erosion internationaler Normen: Folterverbot und nukleares Tabu in der Diskussion'. *Zeitschrift für Internationale Beziehungen, 14*(2), 253–288.
Rotberg, R. I. (2004). *When states fail: Causes and consequences.* Princeton: Princeton University Press.
Rüland, J. (2014). The limits of democratizing interest representation: ASEAN's regional corporatism and normative challenges. *European Journal of International Relations, 20*(1), 237–261.
Russett, B. M., & Starr, H. (1992). *World politics. The menu for choice.* New York: W. H. Freeeman.
Sandholtz, W. (2007). *Prohibiting plunder: How norms change.* Oxford: Oxford University Press.
Sandholtz, W. (2008). Dynamics of international norm change: Rules against wartime plunder. *European Journal of International Relations, 14*(1), 101–131.
Sandholtz, W., & Stiles, K. W. (2009). *International norms and cycles of change.* Oxford: Oxford University Press.

Selebi, J. (1999). Building collaborative security in Southern Africa. *African Security Review, 8*(5), 3–12.

Sewell, W. H., Jr. (1992). Introduction: Narratives and social identities. *Social Science History, 16*(3), 479–488.

Shaw, T. M. (1998). African renaissance/African alliance: Towards new regionalisms and new realism in the great lakes at the start of the twenty-first century. *Politeia, 17*(3), 60–74.

Shore, S. M. (1998). No fences make good neighbors: The development of the US-Canadian security community. 1871–1940. In E. Adler & M. Barnett (Eds.), *Security communities* (pp. 333–367). Cambridge: Cambridge University Press.

Sikkink, K. (2013). The United States and torture: Does the spiral model work? In T. Risse, S. C. Ropp, & K. Sikkink (Eds.), *The persistent power of human rights* (pp. 145–163). Cambridge: Cambridge University Press.

Spencer, H. (1857). Progress: Its law and causes. *Westminster Review, 67*, 445–465.

Steinmetz, G. (1992). Reflections on the role of social narratives in working-class formation: Narrative theory in the social sciences. *Social Science History, 16*(3), 489–516.

Stetter, S., Masala, C., & Karbowski, M. (Eds.). (2011). *Was die EU im Innersten zusammenhält. Debatten zur Legitimität und Effektivität supranationalen Regierens.* Baden-Baden: Nomos.

Tan, S. S. (2007). *The role of knowledge communities in constructing Asia-Pacific security: How thought and talk make war and peace.* Lewiston: Edwin Mellen.

Tannenwald, N. (1999). The nuclear taboo: The United States and the normative basis of nuclear non-use. *International Organization, 53*(3), 433–468.

Tilly, C. (1995). *Popular contention in Great Britain, 1758–1834.* Cambridge, MA: Harvard University Press.

Tusicisny, A. (2007). Security communities and their values: Taking masses seriously. *International Political Science Review, 28*(4), 425–449.

Väyrynen, R. (2000). Stable peace through security communities: Steps towards theory-building. In A. Kacowicz, Y. Bar-Siman-Tov, O. Elgström, & M. Jerneck (Eds.), *Stable peace among nations* (pp. 108–129). Lanham: Rowman and Littlefield.

Vesa, U., & Möller, F. (2003). *Security community in the Baltic Sea region? Recent debate and recent trends* (Occasional paper 88). Tampere: Peace Research Institute.

Vucetic, S. (2001). The stability pact for South Eastern Europe as a security community-building institution. *Southeast European Politics, 2*(2), 109–134.

Weldes, J., & Saco, D. (1996). Making state action possible: The United States and the discursive construction of "the Cuban problem", 1960–1994. *Millennium, 25*(2), 361–398.

Wendt, A. (1999). *Social theory of international politics.* Cambridge: Cambridge University Press.
Wendt, A. (2003). Why a world state is inevitable. *European Journal of International Relations,* 9(4), 491–542.
Wenger, E. (1998). *Communities of practice. Learning, meaning and identity.* Cambridge: Cambridge University Press.
Wiberg, H. (2003). *A Baltic security community?* Paper presented at the international conference deepening the process of integration in the Baltic Sea region: Roles of actors, competition between institutions and the issue of identity, Szczecin, 11–14 December.
Wiener, A. (2004). Contested compliance: Interventions on the normative structure of world politics. *European Journal of International Relations,* 10(2), 189–234.
Wiener, A. (2007). The dual quality of norms and governance beyond the state: Sociological and normative approaches to "interaction". *Critical Review of International Social and Political Philosophy,* 10(1), 47–69.
Wiener, A. (2008). *The invisible constitution of politics. Contested norms and international encounters.* Cambridge: Cambridge University Press.
Wiener, A. (2009). Enacting meaning-in-use: Qualitative research on norms and international relations. *Review of International Studies,* 35(1), 175–193.
Wiener, A., & Puetter, U. (2009). The quality of norms is what actors make of it. *Journal of International Law and International Relations,* 5(1), 1–16.
Zangl, B., & Zürn, M. (1996). Argumentatives Handeln bei internationalen Verhandlungen. Moderate Anmerkungen zur post-realistischen Debatte. *Zeitschrift für Internationale Beziehungen,* 3(1), 341–366.
Zehfuss, M. (1998). Sprachlosigkeit schränkt ein. Zur Bedeutung von Sprache in konstruktivistischen Theorien'. *Zeitschrift für Internationale Beziehungen,* 5(1), 109–137.
Zhang, M. (1995). *Major powers at a crossroads: Economic interdependence and an Asia Pacific security community.* Boulder: Lynne Rienner.

CHAPTER 2

Security Community Disintegration: An Analytical Framework

In this chapter, I develop a framework for studying normative change in a security community. In this book, it is argued that security communities are normative communities. Hence, these communities should cease to exist when its norms are no longer followed and when collective meanings are no longer meaningful. This process involves normative change understood here as the degeneration of established community norms. The scope of normative change is expected to determine whether security community disintegration is 'successful' or not.

According to Deutsch, political integration is a multidimensional process.[1] This means that the framework needs to be able to reconstruct the social realities of (dis)integrative processes at various levels (Deutsch 1954, p. 61). In order to capture processes of normative change in a security community, it is thus necessary to study these processes across levels of analysis. From this, two implications may be deducted that carry relevance for this chapter. First, a disintegration framework will be more plausible if it addresses a set of potentially interrelated conditions and mechanisms related to normative change. Second, a framework to trace disintegrative processes needs to take into account not only normative structures of peaceful change but also, more importantly, the perceptions, beliefs, and interpretations by relevant actors that make these structures meaningful (Deutsch 1961, p. 47).

For this purpose, this chapter is divided into four main parts. First, I explain the normative structure of a security community. In the second part, I conceptualize the nature of agency in a security community framed as norm leaders and norm challengers. In the third part, I outline three dimensions of change (external, social and internal, normative) leading to security community disintegration. Finally, I merge these insights into a dynamic model to analytically trace the path of disintegration in a security community in the subsequent case studies.

Which Norms Change? The Normative Structure of a Security Community

Actors in IR are subject to a variety of identities, norms, and belief systems. Unless one clearly conceptualizes the normative structure that is relevant to a particular group of actors, the empirical findings will ultimately remain indeterminate (Foot and Walter 2013, p. 334). In other words, the normative structure within which normative change takes place needs to be specified first because some norms may be more legitimate and persuasive than others, while some norms may be less important or even irrelevant (Kowert and Legro 1996, p. 486; Legro 1997, p. 31; Müller 2013, p. 14). I will refer to this structure as the normative order of a pluralistic security community.

A normative order may be defined as the 'set of standards and values legitimizing the basic structure of a society (or the structure of inter-, supra-, or transnational relations), the exercise of political authority, and the distribution of basic goods' (Forst and Günther 2011, p. 15, my own translation). This definition can also be applied to a pluralistic security community. In a security community, collective behavioral standards and norms are translated into shared meanings and interpretative frames that provide mutual knowledge about community membership and define the group as 'we' (Adler and Barnett 1998, p. 57). The normative order of a security community can thus be said to be legitimized by and embedded in narratives and counter-narratives, reproduced or contested through symbols, rituals, institutions, and memories that make the normative order 'real' in the eyes of its members (Forst and Günther 2011, p. 18; Ikenberry and Kupchan 1990, p. 289; see also Ikenberry 2001; Wiener 2008). From this perspective, a normative order serves as a 'quasi-constitution' in the sense that it defines and constitutes the 'way of life' of a particular security community (Adler and Barnett 1998, p. 58; Kacowicz and Bar-Siman-Tov 2000, p. 32). The remainder of this section specifies the substantive content of the normative order of a security community.

Karl Deutsch and his associates identify three essential conditions for a pluralistic security community. The first condition involves the *compatibility of major values* among the members. These values become most effective when they are not merely invoked in abstract terms but when they are incorporated and reproduced through common institutions and norms of appropriate behavior in a way that people grow attached to them. As a result of this nexus of values, institutions, and normative behavior, security communities may eventually develop a 'distinctive way of life'[2] that sets them apart from other areas and regions including the one they previously inhabited (Deutsch et al. 1957, p. 48). The development of such a 'way of life' is of course closely related to the social construction of a collective identity, a sense of community, or 'we-feeling' (Adler and Barnett 1998, p. 46).

The second condition is *mutual predictability of behavior*. Through a process of social learning, the normative behavior of community members gradually align in a way that enables them to anticipate or even predict one another's actions as opposed to 'the alleged treacherousness, secretiveness, or unpredictability' of outsiders (Deutsch et al. 1957, pp. 56–7). Actors in IR may learn new behavior by observing and responding to their social environment. If actors experience positive, desired outcomes, then they are more likely to model, imitate, and adopt that behavior (Levy 1994; Risse et al. 1999). In a security community, members eventually develop mutual trust because the nonviolent normative behavior of their fellow members reflects their own (Deutsch et al. 1957, p. 6). As a result, members are socialized through the social learning of nonviolent behavior as a psychological fact. At the same time, these actors unlearn their previous social behavior by restraining and eventually eliminating social patterns of violent actions among each other (Deutsch et al. 1957, p. 37).

The third essential condition for the formation of a pluralistic security community is *mutual responsiveness*. The members of the community must be capable of responding to each other's needs, messages, and normative actions in a way that enables them to resolve their conflicts peacefully. Critically, this requires the presence of unbroken and effective channels of communication both horizontally among the political governments and societies and vertically between domestic political elites and their constituents (Deutsch et al. 1957, p. 51). It is important to add that these channels of communication run both ways.

Building on these conditions, it is possible to analytically reconstruct the normative order of a pluralistic security community as a set of three fundamental norms or 'meta-norms' (Wiener 2008, pp. 66–7; Sandholtz and Stiles 2009, p. 17) that are tied together through intersubjective structures, meanings, institutions, and practices.

Norm of Common Values

A pluralistic security community rests on a consensus on its main values. However, the spatial localization[3] of these normative values may vary significantly. It is thus necessary to distinguish between primary (or 'major') and secondary (or 'minor') values (Deutsch et al. 1957, p. 123). Primary values are 'those that rank the highest within a particular perspective, whereas secondary values are those that rank lower within that same perspective' (Rosenfeld 1998). One important element in the category of primary values is, for example, a 'basic political ideology' (Deutsch et al. 1957, p. 124).[4] In addition to these primary values, there are secondary values, which are contested, and represent either different approaches to cope with individual and societal risks and/or are historically and culturally constructed (Ruggie 1983).

To be sure, these secondary values are certainly part of the overall normative framework shaping mutual trust and collective identity. A pluralistic security community does not imply absolute congruence of values. Deutsch and his associates (1957, p. 126) make this point very clear: 'There is a tendency in popular thinking to consider too many values as incompatible with each other. The public is apt to become upset about a seemingly incompatible value that may actually be irrelevant to the formation of a security-community.' Instead, a security community presupposes coherence of primary values and, at the same time, the desecuritization or even depoliticization[5] of secondary value differences (Wæver 1995, p. 46; Deutsch et al. 1957, p. 125). A pluralistic security community is not a regional melting pot but a heterogeneous community of states and societies bracketed by a dynamic consensus on primary values (one could speak of a value cluster) that allows for certain domestic variations and adaptations (Koschut 2010, p. 56). Secondary values, by contrast, are derivatives and must always reflect and meet the meaning of primary values. Peaceful conflicts over secondary values are thus not a sign of a security community's weakness or decay as long as its primary values remain uncontested. In fact, these conflicts can be said to be constitutive to the emergence of a security community since without such conflict the presence of institutional cooperation and value coordination would hardly be required (Keohane 1989).

The presence of contested secondary values grants importance to clearly defined primary values. Primary values are thus usually written down in foundational documents and treaties, constantly reiterated through symbols, rituals, and speech acts, and often contrasted against outside values (Deutsch et al. 1957, p. 123). In sum, a pluralistic security community is characterized by a multitude and diversity of secondary values at the domestic (member-state) level. At the regional (community) level, it requires a consensus over the primary values of the community.

Norm of Multilateral Practice

The ability of members to predict the behavior and performance of other members characterizes a pluralistic security community as a 'community of practice'[6] (Adler 2005). In a security community, the peaceful resolution of conflicts of interest through diplomacy and negotiation becomes the norm while war or physical coercion among its members becomes a taboo. This collective knowledge is rooted in a normative understanding of multilateralism, which involves a strong or 'thick' type of multilateralism. Thick multilateralism is more than 'the practice of coordinating national policies in groups of three or more states' (Keohane 1990, p. 731) but rather submits to certain normative principles (Ruggie 1993). Thick multilateralism thus transcends the instrumental logic of egoistic and utility-maximizing behavior (which would be weak or 'thin' multilateralism) and instead refers to the practice of self-restraint and peaceful conflict resolution (Adler 2001, p. 146; Adler and Greve 2009, p. 71).

The norm of multilateral practice also involves collective defense. The fact that the members of a pluralistic security community maintain peaceful relations among each other does not mean that its members will not fight wars against non-members. Security communities often develop a collective identity in order to distinguish themselves from a particular Other (Wendt 1999; Risse-Kappen 1996; Owen 2000; Diez 2004). Defining a community in such a way enables members to distinguish between members and non-members. Disconnecting the normative Self from a normative Other can thus be understood as an act of identity building necessary for developing and maintaining a pluralistic security community. Any outside threat—defined in terms of a perceived risk or harm to the distinctive 'way of life' of the security community—should thus trigger a collective response (Deutsch et al. 1957, p. 48; Adler and Barnett 1998, p. 56; Wendt 1999, p. 298). In sum, a pluralistic security community involves a normative (as opposed to an instrumental or strategic) understanding of security multilateralism based on peaceful conflict resolution and the practice of self-restraint on the inside. On the outside, it includes the use of force against outsiders based on collective defense.

Norm of Meaningful Communication

Even though the norm of multilateral practice implies the primacy of self-restraint and collective action, unilateral actions and conflicts of interests are still possible as members of a pluralistic security community maintain state sovereignty. This adds significance to the norms of communication and consultation among members of a pluralistic security community. In fact, Karl Deutsch (1966, p. 77) places communication at the center of any social community: 'Communication is the cement that makes organizations. Communication alone enables a group to think together, to see together and to act together.' Hence, a pluralistic security community is also a community of communication (Risse 2010; Müller (2006)).

A community of communication establishes a common 'communicative space' in which issues of common concern are debated and conflicts of interests are resolved within shared meaning structures and interpretative frames (Risse 2010, p. 109). For the purpose of maintaining a security community, this involves, above all, shared conceptions about security threats, similar security perceptions and responses, and common security discourse involving shared conceptual vocabulary and symbols (Koschut 2010, p. 58). This, in turn, requires that community members recognize each other as legitimate speakers and establish common reference frames for communication (Risse 2010, p. 109). Critically, the norm of communication involves not simply informing other members about imminent actions or policies but includes the permanent exchange of values, beliefs, interests, and perceptions (Kitchen 2009). The purpose of such 'thick' communication (Koschut 2010, p. 58) is to limit unilateral actions and resolve conflicts of interests.

This normative understanding of communication implies responsiveness. Responsiveness is the willingness to listen to and be persuaded by others (Deutsch et al. 1957, p. 165). In a security community, collective actions aim not at physical coercion, instrumental calculations, and strategic incentives but at consensus building (Risse 2000; Müller 2006). This is a matter of giving attention to the needs of participating members within an integrated regional area (Deutsch et al. 1957, p. 129). In sum,

Table 2.1 Normative order of a security community

Common values	Multilateral practice	Communication
Primary values	Peaceful conflict resolution	Consultation
Secondary values	Collective defense	Responsiveness

a pluralistic security community is characterized by the willingness among its members to be convinced by the better argument and thus generally follow the logic of communicative action (Habermas 1981; Risse 2000). It rests on the norms of genuine and timely consultation and mutual responsiveness (Table 2.1).

Application to Cases

Security community norms—common values, shared multilateral practices, and meaningful communication—represent and embody Karl Deutsch's essential conditions for building and maintaining a security community. Moreover, in line with Deutsch's assumptions on integration as a multidimensional process, the normative order of a security community combines three general dimensions: a cognitive one describing what its members are 'believing' (common values); a practical dimension showing what its members are 'doing' (multilateral practices); and a discursive dimension tracing what its members are 'saying' (meaningful communication). It is the interdependence and compatibility of these three dimensions through which shared meanings are generated and established.

This three-dimensional intersubjective meaning structure (understood as the normative order of a security community) may appear broad and underspecified at first. Yet, this has been done so deliberately. As Katzenstein (2005, p. 13) and others (see, e.g., Acharya 2004) remind us, regional orders and identities vary greatly according to their institutional forms and cultural belief systems. For analyzing security community disintegration across different regions and time periods it is thus necessary to construct a normative order that explicitly allows for distinctive institutional forms as well as variations in spatial, cultural, sociopolitical, and historical contexts. In the subsequent empirical cases, I will further specify the collective norms of each security community within its respective regional and historical framework by reconstructing the normative order of each security community based on its treaties and other legal documents as well as explanatory reports and historical records.

In this section, I outlined the normative structure of a security community. In the following section, I conceptualize the nature of normative agency in the process of security community disintegration as the interplay between norm leaders and norm challengers.

Whose Norms Change? Normative Agency in a Security Community

The ability of a security community to develop and maintain its normative order requires agency. Normative orders spelled out in treaties, conventions, resolutions, reports, or summit statements cannot 'do' anything unless they are enacted by purposeful agents (Simmons 2013, p. 54). Who are these agents?

Karl Deutsch et al. (1957, p. 5) defined a security community as 'a group of people which has become integrated'. But this raises a central question: Are normative discourses, language, symbols, practices, and institutions equally shared among *all* people in the *same* way? Or are some individuals and groups perhaps more active and engaged in these community-building activities and norm-following behavior than others? Indeed, empirical evidence indicates that there is a need to differentiate. For example, it seems perfectly normal to see a flag of NATO or the EU in front of a state building or public office but one rarely finds the same symbol in an allotment garden or someone's private front yard. Moreover, the presence and activity of so-called 'Eurosceptics' and anti-EU populism looms large in some member states while less so in others. Also, while NATO enjoys strong public support in virtually every member state, there also exist transnational and domestic anti-war movements and peace networks who define 'peaceful change' in a very different way than NATO's official summit declarations. In fact, these groups openly challenge the collective norms (e.g., the mutual defense clause) of the transatlantic security community. To sum up, a significant portion of the politically relevant strata may live in a security community but it can hardly be claimed that each and every one of them identifies with that security community to the same degree or follows norms of appropriate behavior in the same way. While some agents will promote a certain image of security community, other agents may advocate conflicting interpretations and meaning frames of the same security community (Risse 2010, p. 49; Fligstein 2009, p. 133).

This is not a trivial question. What many people perceive as the 'natural order' of a security community is, as outlined above, a carefully constructed set of collective meanings tied to a particular set of institutionalized norms. If a significant portion of people living in a particular security community were to 'unlearn' that stable peace is linked to the maintenance of these institutionalized norms, the normative order of peaceful change would cease to exist (McNamara 2010, p. 165; see also Wendt 1992). This is why it takes agency to meaningfully link these normative expectations of peaceful change to the existence of a pluralistic security community and defend it against competing meaning frames. As Karl Deutsch et al. (1957, p. 113) point out: 'proponents of union (security community) had to make the union issue paramount in politics. They had to link the remaining urgent local pressures and issues to it; and they had to present eventually the practical approach to union in terms of a single political plan. Eliminating rival plans was crucial.'

Hence, awareness of what it means to be a member of a particular security community enables people to reproduce but also to contest the normative order of that community. For example, some members with few transnational interactions and low levels of attachment to European integration may tend to question the relevance of the EU by focusing on short-term gains of increased political independence (Risse 2010, p. 49). This may become an attractive option for some member states during times of crisis as the Euro crisis exemplifies. In this crisis, the 'Eurosceptics' shifted the discursive focus away from peaceful integration by framing the meaning of the EU as an overblown bureaucratic institutional body and by mobilizing nationalist sentiments instead (Kleger and Mehlhausen 2013). Moreover, certain meaningful symbols of peaceful change like the common currency were discredited by such counter-narratives. For example, Dirk Müller, a popular German pundit advocates such a counter-narrative: 'The euro isn't bringing us peace,' he says. 'In fact, the euro is the spirit of discord.'[7] These counter-narratives can have deep material effects. In the 2013 German national election, the recently founded 'Eurosceptic' party AfD collected a significant portion of the votes. To counter this weakening of the European normative order, 'Europhile' political elites and ordinary citizens attempted to shift the narrative back to the meaning of the EU as a regional pacifier by invoking symbols and memories linked to a war-torn European history (Kleger 2008; Kaelbe 2009; Risse 2010). The 2012 Nobel Peace Prize, which was awarded to the EU, is a case in point. In sum, as this micro-level account illustrates, collective meanings (making sense of what is) are tied to collective norms (expectations about proper behavior) in a security community through agency.

Norm Leaders and Norm Challengers

In this book, I argue that the nature of agency in a security community can be framed as a conflict over collective meanings and interpretations between norm leaders and norm challengers.[8] As Martha Finnemore and Kathryn Sikkink (1998, p. 900) remind us, norm leaders are responsible for promoting and enforcing an established normative order. In this sense, norm leaders can be said to 'govern' and 'manage' a security community through political socialization and social control including the teaching of community norms and the sanctioning of inappropriate behavior at the level of intergovernmental and transnational institutions, networks, and other forms of interaction (Avant et al. 2010, p. 2; Deitelhoff 2009, p. 252; Johnston 2007, p. 124; Rublee 2008, p. 426). Norm leaders also act as gatekeepers and, if necessary, may erect 'firewalls' and structural barriers (e.g., press censorship) to prevent the spread of ideas and norms that they deem as harmful to the security community (Solingen 2012, p. 631).

Individual norm leaders are bound together as a norm regime[9] that promotes and protects the established normative order of a security community. A norm regime, however, is not to be equated with state governments or political elites. Norm regimes may be predominantly made up of these actors because a lot of transactions and communications in a security community happen at the intergovernmental level (Lantis 2011). Nevertheless, Deutsch's definition of a security community as a 'group of *people*' suggests a much broader concept. Thus, while emphasizing the role of state actors (policymakers, diplomats, public employees, and staffers) the norm regime of a security community involves, in principle, actors from all levels of society such as interest groups, political parties, business leaders, researchers, and ordinary citizens that are able to form people-to-people ties (Deutsch et al. 1957, p. 88).

Norm leaders are conceptually linked to norm challengers. Norm challengers are actors who are dissatisfied with the existing normative order and actively try to change it (Finnemore and Sikkink 2001, pp. 400–1; see also Sunstein 1996). Norm challengers have been central, for example, to analyze the impact of non-state actors both within and beyond states on the promotion of human rights (Risse et al. 2013) or the role of state actors in multilateral arms control (Müller and Wunderlich 2013). Dissatisfied with the normative status quo, norm challengers bring their concerns to public attention, developing as well as articulating alternative normative concepts and ideas, and mobilizing followers as well as material support for their cause (Braveboy-Wagner 2009, p. 13). In the words of Emma Sjöström (2010, p. 180), they are 'actors who break away from the established (...) (and) advocate alternative ideas about appropriate behavior'. This conceptualization of agency is supported by Karl Deutsch and his associates (1957, p. 196): 'In all the cases we studied, the victorious party (...) stood for something new in the way of social institutions and individual opportunities, and not for a mere defense of a status quo.' For reasons of analytical clarity, I use the term 'norm challenger' instead of 'norm violator' here because violating a norm per se does not necessarily imply a motivation to contest or overthrow an existing normative order (Nyhamar 2000; Acharya 2011). Accordingly, norm challengers are understood here as actors who seek to replace the normative order as a whole. The term norm violator, by contrast, does not presuppose such an intention.

To sum up, while norm leaders emphasize the normative status quo, norm challengers advocate normative change. Norm leaders and challengers are thus conceptual antipodes. Norm challengers will contest the established normative order of a security community and dispute the authority of norm leaders to define meanings of peaceful change while norm leaders will resist these efforts in order to preserve the normative status quo. To be sure, both concepts may overlap sometimes and may, at different times, even apply to the same group of individuals. For example, a group of norm challengers may turn into a norm regime once it has acquired the authority to define alternative meanings and to set the normative standards. Likewise, norm leaders may become norm challengers if they are dissatisfied with established community norms and become more open to its reinterpretation and redefinition (Deutsch et al. 1957, p. 89; see also Sikkink 2013). Hence, the conceptualization of linking collective meanings to the normative order in a security community at the actor level can be generally framed as an ongoing conflict between (marginalized) norm challengers as 'agents of social change' (Björkdahl 2002, p. 45) and (established) norm leaders as proponents of the status quo.

The presence of this ongoing conflict over norms and meanings resonates well with Karl Deutsch's conceptualization of pluralism as the strength and defining feature of a security community. Deutsch was well aware that social interaction is not per se conducive to integration but will ultimately generate conflict (Deutsch 1969). In a security community, pluralism produces and incorporates a variety of self-images, of opinions, and supposed truths that are ultimately reflected in a plurality of interests

(Deutsch et al. 1957, pp. 10–2). In other words, the presence of norm challengers in a security community is not per se a sign of weakness or decay but rather an essential component of a security community that is 'alive and kicking'.

As a result, in a security community, norms and identities are not fixed or static but there is an ongoing 'war of interpretations' (Nietzsche 1958, pp. 1078–9). Norm contestation and competition are thus a necessary component of any security community. The key question then becomes who has access to norm contestation and who are the involved stakeholders (Wiener 2008). To this end, it has been argued here that, in a security community, norm challengers will seek windows of opportunities (e.g., external 'shocks') to introduce and promote new ideas that contest collectively shared norms and meanings. Given that these external 'shocks' are unavoidable in international politics, the survival of a security community (and of the collective normative order within it) ultimately rests on the ability of norm leaders to develop integrative capabilities through norm socialization and the sanctioning of norm violations as well as to effectively deal with or incorporate new ideas introduced by norm challengers or engage in norm innovation, or—in the case of a degenerated normative order—norm repair.

Core States

It should be pointed out that inside the norm regime of a security community, norm leaders are not treated as approximate equals but are woven together in asymmetrical power relationships and implicit hierarchies. The self-image of the security community is formed based on the minority of its 'best' members (core states). These core states perform a norm building function and exercise 'power-over' to sanction potential or actual norm breakers through social control (Katzenstein 2005, p. 22). The concept of core states resonates nicely with Karl Deutsch et al.'s (1957, p. 70) assumption that security communities develop around 'cores of strength' that push and pull for integration. Core states are thus 'states that possess superior material power, international legitimacy, and have adopted norms and practices that are conducive to peaceful change' (Adler and Barnett 1998, p. 44). Cores states exercise power by projecting shared meanings and normative understandings, thereby contributing to 'a sense of purpose' that can have a magnetic effect on other members (Adler and Barnett 1998, p. 424). In this sense, powerful core states play a pivotal role in promoting and defending the normative order of a security community as 'superior' norm leaders (Deutsch et al. 1957, p. 72).

The concept of power deserves further attention. In a security community, it is important to distinguish between 'power' (material power) and 'responsiveness' (non-material power) (Deutsch et al. 1957, p. 40). In analyzing security community formation, Emanuel Adler (1997, p. 335) makes a similar distinction between the material resources to accomplish certain goals (power) and the authority to define collective meanings and norms (knowledge). Material power is thus tied to knowledge and responsiveness. For example, Poland is aware of the superior power of the USA to define meanings in the transatlantic security community but, in stark contrast to Russia, accepts its norm authority not as something to be feared but to be emulated (Adler and Barnett 1998, p. 424). In a security community, the interplay of power and knowledge remains decisive since all members continue to pursue their own interests. These interests, however, acquire constitutive meaning only within common normative structures and rules of behavior. Power thus becomes representational as security communities replace the threat of physical force with the threat to the individual identities of its members since 'preserving the Self mean(s) sustaining the narrative' of the community (Bially Mattern 2001, p. 20).

As a result, core states play an important role in building and maintaining security communities because their political and economic resources as well as social and cultural attraction facilitate the establishment of common institutions, norms, and meanings and promote communication channels and social interaction among the members of the security community (Deutsch et al. 1957; Adler and Barnett 1998). In this sense, core states possess what Deborah Avant, Martha Finnemore, and Susan Sell (2010, p. 13) term as 'capacity-based authority'. Core states promote peaceful integration due to their capabilities and strength (ability to act) *as well as* due to their responsiveness and adaptability to the needs and beliefs of smaller members (ability to respond), the latter being decisive for the community's preservation (Deutsch 1979, p. 183; Deutsch et al. 1957, p. 138).

If we accept the fact that powerful core states contribute to stable normative orders in a security community, the inability or unwillingness of these cores to practice self-restraint, punish norm violators, and facilitate knowledge transfer should undermine their legitimacy in the eyes of other members. As Bruce Russett (1998, p. 386) points out, 'to be tolerated in any hegemonic role hegemons will have to be "nice" ones who provide collective goods as well as coerce recalcitrants. The Deutsch et al. praise for "strong core areas" needs to be seen in this light (…) as holding themselves to the same norms they enforce.' If core states practice unresponsiveness, smaller members will almost certainly come to view the asymmetrical power relationship in a security community as a threat (Sikkink 2013, p. 162; Daase 2003, p. 30).

To sum up, the ability of a security community to develop and maintain its normative order requires agency. Agency in a security community has been framed as an ongoing conflict over collective meanings and interpretations between norm leaders and norm challengers. Norm leaders engage in constant efforts to coordinate their actions to justify and defend the normative order against norm challengers. The superior social status of core states plays a pivotal role in promoting and defending the normative order of a security community but may also undermine it through unresponsive behavior. From conceptualizing the normative structure and agency of a security community, I now move to the task of tracing the process of norm degeneration in a security community.

How Do Norms Change? The Process of Norm Degeneration in a Security Community

The purpose of this chapter is to develop an analytical framework for explaining security community disintegration through norm degeneration. It does not present a theory of disintegration but rather outlines certain conditions under which security community disintegration is likely to take place. As pointed out in the previous chapter, the security community literature is rather silent on this point. Most authors ascribe disintegration to structural factors, such as major systemic transformations in the international system, but this says relatively little about the actors and processes involved. From a Constructivist perspective, explanations that center on exogenous structural factors remain limited because they tend to eclipse the endogenous (de-)construction of collective norms and meanings among members of a security community (Berger 1996, p. 318; Legro 2000, p. 423). The implications and consequences of change in the international system are neither accidental nor inevitable—like a natural disaster that hits without warning—but are significantly shaped and perceived through agency at the regional and domestic level (Foot and Walter 2013, p. 330; Müller (2006), p. 8, 2013, p. 351). A more promising approach is thus to combine these factors in a holistic framework that includes an external dimension but, more importantly, accounts for what happens inside the security community itself. Such a holistic framework for studying norm dynamics is presented by Paul Kowert and Jeffrey Legro (1996, p. 470). They analytically distinguish between three levels of normative interaction: ecological, social, and internal processes. The model developed in this chapter builds on their framework to explain the process of norm degeneration in a security community. It is thus necessary to briefly outline Kowert and Legro's assumptions.

Ecological processes describe 'the patterned interaction of actors and their environment'. Under these processes, actors interact with an external environment that is either stable or rapidly changing or that appears, in the eyes of the actors involved, ambiguous. A stable international environment is expected to be conducive to norm maintenance (Finnemore 1996; Price and Tannenwald 1996). On the contrary, external 'shocks' or crises may be conducive to normative change (Berger 1996, p. 331; Kowert and Legro 1996, p. 470; Finnemore and Sikkink 1998, p. 909). Given that most scholars agree on the fact that major external change affects security community cohesion in a negative way, most significant to the study at hand are settings in which actors are confronted with 'a rapidly changing environment'. The problem here lies in the definition. At what point can we speak of rapid structural change or external 'shocks' as opposed to incremental and 'normal' change in the international system? While part of the answer lies in the social perception of the actors involved, a working definition of rapid structural change is employed here that defines this type of high-level change as altering the properties of an entire regional system and not just particular alterations (Holsti 1998, p. 10).

The second level of Kowert and Legro's framework involves social processes. Social processes are normative interactions among the actors themselves. Such processes deal with norm diffusion, in-group/out-group differentiation, and social roles (Kowert and Legro 1996, p. 474). There is an abundant literature on these types of processes so there is no need to reiterate them here.[10] What concerns us here is the question of how these social roles and inside/outside configurations among members of a security community become contested and possibly redefined to result in a weakening of existing security community norms. Here, a variety of mechanisms and actors driving social processes of norm contestation in one direction or the other need to be taken into account. On agency, some scholars, for example, highlight the role of transgovernmental networks and transnational groups (Risse-Kappen 1996; Keck and Sikkink 1998;

Farrell 2001). Others underline the importance of international organizations (Finnemore 1993, 1996) and domestic alliances (Herman 1996; Gurowitz 1999; Davis 2000). Regarding mechanisms, most Constructivist scholars emphasize diverse strategies such as learning (Adler 1997), arguing and persuasion (Risse 2000), naming and shaming (Liese 2006), or the power of language (Bially Mattern 2001). What is also of relevance for the disintegration of security community is the interplay between these different social mechanisms.

Finally, internal processes describe normative interactions that occur inside political actors. According to Kowert and Legro (1996, p. 477), these processes involve self-perception ('Who am I?'), distinctions between Self and Other, use and interpretation of language as well as strategic social construction (Finnemore 2003). The study at hand deals with state actors and their societies as members of a pluralistic security community. Internal processes should thus involve normative interaction and sense making within and between different sets of groups and individuals that may question established security community norms at the domestic level (Armstrong 1993; Sandholtz and Stiles 2009; Müller and Wolff 2006).

To sum up, Kowert's and Legro's assumptions imply that the normative order of the security community may be weakened through normative interaction at three levels of analysis: between the members and their external environment, between the members themselves, and within the domestic setting of the members involved. As outlined earlier, the security community literature assumes that normative change in a security community may lead to its disintegration (if at all) based on major external change. This book shares the basic assumption that external change plays an initiating role in the disintegration of security communities. However, it is argued that the story does not end there. Building on Kowert and Legro's framework, this book assumes instead that ecological processes are only the starting point in a sequence involving also social and internal processes of normative interaction that undermine established security community norms. It is important to point out that this book does not make the argument that major external change must always or automatically result in the weakening of security community norms. In principle, there may also be instances where external 'shocks' may, at least initially, reinforce existing normative orders by bringing its members closer together (Kowert and Legro 1996, p. 474; Müller et al. 2013, p. 142).

Helpful as it is, Kowert and Legro's framework does not tell us much about the processes connecting levels of normative interaction. To answer this challenge, I begin by building deductively on what we know about security community development. Emanuel Adler and Michael Barnett (1998), for example, outline three conditions that have to be met for security community formation. First, there needs to be a trigger that sets off the process of community formation. According to Adler and Barnett, this is due to changes in the external environment that provide windows of opportunity for actors to develop new interpretations of social reality (tier 1). Second, internal transformations in structure (power and knowledge) as well as process (transactions, organizations, and social learning) occur (tier 2) that provide the conditions conducive for the development of mutual trust and collective identity as necessary conditions for security community (tier 3). In short, Adler and Barnett frame the development of security community as an outside-in process: an external stimulus sets off internal and social changes that, in turn, alter the way actors perceive each other as well as their relationship.

It is plausible to suggest that similar conditions may also lead to the unraveling of a security community. In their brief remarks on security community disintegration, for example, Adler and Barnett (1998, p. 58) note that 'the same forces that "build up" security communities can "tear them down". Therefore, many of the same social processes that encourage and serve to reproduce the security community are also associated with its decline.' As noted in the previous chapter, Adler and Barnett do not provide a detailed account as to how this might take place. If we take their idea seriously, however, it is possible to construct a framework for security community disintegration that mirrors the outside-in process of security community formation. Building on Kowert's and Legro's three-level framework of normative interaction as well as Adler and Barnett's three-tier model of security community formation, I suggest that the path of security community disintegration is similar to its formation but under opposing signs: external change sets off social and internal change that leads to the degeneration of community norms (normative change) (see Fig. 2.1). I now explain the components along this path in greater detail.

External Change

Security communities do not exist in a vacuum. Its members not only interact and maintain relationships with the 'outside world' but, as argued earlier, even frame their identities in part based on outside subjects.

External change

Rapid and far-reaching changes in the international environment (external 'shocks')

↓

Social and internal change

Persuasiveness of new ideas
Disruption of symbolic interaction
Institutional failure
Social unlearning

↓

Normative change

Lack of norm iteration and enforcement
Degeneration and replacement of collective norms
Undermining of mutual trust and collective identity

↓

Breakdown of dependable expectations of peaceful change

Fig. 2.1 The disintegration of security communities

Mutual acceptance and rigorous observance of formal or informal rules, principles, and norms make up the social structure of security communities (Holsti 1967, p. 479). Yet, its members may over time develop new interpretations of social reality as they confront major changes in their external environment (Bellamy 2004, p. 21; Acharya 2001, p. 37). These changing ideas, belief systems, and ideologies can then undermine the way actors define themselves as well as others and eventually alter the normative framework for meaningful communication, multilateral practice, and common values within a pluralistic security community. Hence, security communities that fail to adapt to major external change may eventually walk down the path of disintegration. It should be pointed out again that major external change is not viewed here as the cause of norm contestation and degeneration but merely creates the 'opportunity structure' for normative change to take place (Müller 2013, p. 346).

Such major external change includes 'great events' (Holsti 1982, p. x) or 'systemic shocks' such as revolutions, major wars, or the collapse of large communities or empires (Adler and Barnett 1998, p. 58; see also Tilly 1995, p. 13; Müller (2006), p. 8; Kupchan 2010, p. 67). In addition to these rapid changes, long-term systemic power shifts or gradual technological innovations (e.g., the industrial or information revolution) as well as significant demographic changes or migration patterns might also contribute to norm degeneration since they 'move people to reconsider who they are and with whom they want to associate' (Deutsch 1953; see also Tilly 1995). However, since these gradual transformations occur slowly and mostly in the background of day-to-day politics their impact is felt only incrementally, and thus, does not develop the same thrust and 'shock waves' as rapid and fundamental external changes.

Finally, it should be pointed out that even though this book deals with external change as a structural condition for normative change, the impact of external actors on the cohesion of a pluralistic security community cannot be denied. For example, the role of Russia, following the disintegration of the Soviet Union, has undoubtedly slowed down the process of expanding the transatlantic security community to the Baltic region as many Western European countries take Russian security interests into consideration (Väyrynen 2000). In the case of the Ukraine, this (along with domestic public opinion in the Ukraine) has actually resulted in a temporary freeze of the country's accession process to NATO and violent conflict. These examples show that external actors can affect the process of peaceful integration in a negative way if their interests, norms, and identities are relevant to the members of a pluralistic security community. However, these examples arguably also represent structural constraints on norm dynamics in a security community, as their impact and relevance can be ultimately traced to a 'systemic shock': the demise of the Soviet Union.

To sum up, external change provides a window of opportunity for disintegration to occur because it forces members of a security community to critically reflect on their collective norms and identities. In other words, given the presence of major external change, members can be expected to 'check' if their meaning structures and interpretative frames of collective normative understanding are still compatible with and 'fit' the changing external environment or, alternately, need to be adapted and changed (Avant et al. 2010, p. 3). For example, as I will later show, the end of the Cold War forced NATO member states to reconsider the meaning of their collective identity because an important part of this identity—the common enemy—had disappeared (Adler and Barnett 1998). Major external change needs to be rapid and fundamental to provide a window of opportunity for security community disintegration to occur.

Social and Internal Change

While rapid and fundamental external change sets the stage for normative change in a security community, it is not sufficient to set this process in motion. This requires agency and the presence of social and internal changes (Legro 2000). I have already dealt with the role of agency above. In this section, I focus on the various social and internal mechanisms that arguably contribute to the degeneration of security community norms.

The presence of external change may stimulate the development of a crisis situation in which established community norms are openly questioned or even contested. However, a mature security community should, in principle, be able to resolve such situations peacefully because a security community, which only functions in the absence of a crisis would be pointless. Each crisis, then, represents a turning point that may either lead to its resolution or, if it persists, may ultimately result in the demise of the security community. For example, major external change may compel individual member states as well as domestic or transnational groups to seek more freedom of action. As a result, members may begin to openly question collectively shared norms as these are perceived to inhibit their room for maneuvering in the international system. In the end, community norms may either degenerate or are repaired depending on the social and internal mechanisms and the agents involved.

To sum up, while external change provides a window of opportunity for norm contestation within a security community, social and internal change (along with agency) can be expected to influence the outcome of such contests. Below, I will outline four mechanisms of social and internal change and explain why these are assumed to drive the process security community disintegration: the persuasiveness of new ideas, the disruption of symbolic interaction, institutional failure, and social unlearning.

The Persuasiveness of New Ideas

The persuasiveness of new ideas is an important driver in shaping the process of norm degeneration since it introduces an alternative frame to established normative understandings and meanings. In a security community, these normative understandings and meanings are based on an ideational reality—a social construction of peaceful change that exists only because members believe in it and act accordingly (Schmitz and Sikkink 2002, p. 517). This ideational reality may be subject to reinterpretation when established ideas lose traction while new ideas gain ground.

Such processes of ideational diffusion remain incomplete, however, unless one considers potential counterfactuals. As Thomas Risse (Risse-Kappen 1994) reminds us: 'ideas do not float freely' in world politics. Thus, awareness of which ideas do or do not diffuse and why or why not is crucial to understanding social and internal change within a security community. To this end, Ethel Solingen (2012) proposes the concept of 'firewalls' to capture instances of ideational non-diffusion such as state censorship, literal electronic firewalls, or fences against immigration. In addition, structural barriers such as the wealth generated by natural resources, intelligence, surveillance, or the suppression of domestic protest may also prevent new ideas from taking hold in a security community (Solingen 2012, p. 633). Hence, firewalls and structural barriers—anything that keeps ideas from flowing, diffusing, or gaining effectiveness—can guard against the persuasiveness of new ideas or, at the very least, delay and dilute their impact within a security community.

The blocking of new ideas, however, may also backfire. The power of ideas ultimately depends on their persuasiveness. What makes an idea persuasive is its ability to relate to current political and economic problems (Hall 1989, pp. 9–10). People tend to seek independence from any government, country, or group of states that do not respond to their messages and needs in the way people expect them to (Deutsch 1979, p. 202). A lack of such ideational responsiveness, resulting from firewalls and structural barriers, may disrupt open communication channels and lead to a decoupling of collective memories, habits, and institutions in a security community. As Charles Kupchan (2010, pp. 12–3) notes, 'narratives of opposition prompt societal separation (…) ultimately awakening geopolitical competition. And it is the absence of the key causes of stable peace—institutionalized restraint, compatible social orders, and cultural commonality—that explains (…) failure.' These new ideas often emerge from the domestic arena in response to external transformations such as dramatic changes in the material and social environment (Odell 1982; Kowert and Legro 1996). Another way to introduce new ideas and normative meanings to the security community is the admission of new member states. These new members may also bring in new ideas that may contest existing ones. For example, in contrast to some of the founding EU members (e.g., France), the new EU members of the former Eastern bloc have strongly advocated a 'NATO-first' approach to European Defence and Security Policy (Král 2009, p. 8).

The link between the breakdown of pluralistic security community, on the one hand, and the persuasiveness of new ideas, on the other hand, correlates with Karl Deutsch's observations about the disintegration of amalgamated security communities. For example, in the run-up to the French revolution, the absolutist state failed to respond to rising demands for reform raised during the Enlightenment, which facilitated normative change and resulted in the violent breakdown of the French monarchy (Deutsch 1954, p. 20). According to Deutsch, the persuasiveness of new ideas of equality, citizenship, and inalienable rights played a decisive role in that process. If the persuasiveness of new ideas can reshape the norms and identities of actors in an amalgamated security community, it appears plausible that the persuasiveness of new ideas could play a similar role in the process of pluralistic security community disintegration. As I will explain in more detail below, members of a security community acquire collective knowledge and establish shared normative understandings through social learning. Conversely, the same actors may 'unlearn' this social behavior when established or 'old' ideas lose influence and persuasiveness as they no longer fit normative expectations. Members of a security community may then begin to develop new interpretations and meanings of regional security that may or may not be compatible with each other. In the latter case, this may promote a weakening of mutual normative understandings, a revision of previously existing images of Self and Other, and ultimately, the unraveling of the security community as an ideational reality.

To sum up, it can be argued that peaceful change requires a process of active teaching and ideational recognition as other actors also set the agenda and shape member states' norms and identities (Finnemore 1996, p. 12). Conversely, the interruption of these processes due to the introduction and persuasiveness of new ideas may ultimately result in reinterpretations and degeneration of formerly accepted normative meanings that, in turn, may be conducive for security community disintegration (Wiener and Puetter 2009, p. 7).

Disruption of Symbolic Interaction
It should be clear by now that a security community is built on social interaction. This is also evident in Karl Deutsch's general definition of (security) communities as 'a group of people characterized by the existence of

a significant amount of transactions among them' (Deutsch 1954, p. 33). Yet, as Charles Taylor (1971, p. 122) reminds us, these transactions do not 'create' a community unless its members attach meaning to them. Consequently, Deutsch extends his definition of community to include 'a group of people whom one understands and by whom one is understood' (Deutsch 1970, p. 96). In a similar way, Herbert Mead (1934, pp. 113 and 156) defines communication within a community as a process of mutual responsiveness about the meaning of specific interaction that involves the ability 'to take the role of the other' in a shared 'universe of discourse', a concept which is also prevalent in Peter Berger and Thomas Luckman's (1966, p. 22) notion of collective action and language that creates meaning in an 'intersubjective world'. While these approaches differ in their theoretical viewpoint, they all share the basic assumption that members of a community live in a symbolic world of shared meanings.

Symbols may be defined as 'orders to recall something from memory' (Langer 1942, p. x). They represent meanings and acquire motivational significance for collective behavior (Herman and Reynolds 1994). Deutsch equally underlines the importance of symbolic interaction in a security community: 'By noting which symbols are frequently associated with each other, we may learn something about the context in which political messages are perceived, remembered, and recalled on later occasions' (Deutsch 1979, p. 201). Symbolic interaction contributes to identify political meanings in a given situation. Empirically, symbols are traceable in different forms such as abstract symbols (words, ideas, slogans), pictorial symbols (codes of arms, flags), personal or human symbols (heroes, leaders, saints, prophets), or symbolic places (capital cities, historic sites, national shrines, centers of pilgrimage) (Deutsch 1979, p. 202).

Symbols perform a representational function by designating a certain group to form collective memories, experiences, and emotional attachment (Wendt 1999, p. 335; McNamara 2010, p. 165). For example, what it means to be an American evokes a certain conceptual idea of 'we-feeling' only among those that can relate to it. Those that identify themselves as 'Americans' share a distinct pattern of collective attachment that is manifested in recurring rituals such as Fourth of July celebrations, presidential inaugurations, and the pledge of allegiance as well as worshiping places and objects with symbolic significance such as the Declaration of Independence or the Lincoln Memorial (Bellah 1967). More negative examples that show that the process of binding people together often works in tandem with pernicious representations of Others include the Nazi efforts to install collective meanings through a variety of resentment and hate strategies and the extensive use of collective symbols and rituals.

Symbols play an important role in solidarity rituals at the intergovernmental and transnational level such as speeches, summits, ceremonies, youth exchanges, or festivals that all contribute to maintaining a security community (Koschut 2014a). A ritual is understood as 'the performance of more or less invariant sequences of formal acts and utterances not entirely encoded by the performers' (Rappaport 1999, p. 22). Rituals involve the physical assembly of the members of a social group, their awareness and focus on a common object or action, and the sharing of similar emotions through their expression and discourse toward these objects or action (Collins 1998). Such symbolic rituals produce so-called 'high-order meanings' that lead to mutual identification between Self and Other (Rappaport 1999, p. 71). Rituals thus function as mechanisms to synchronize individual discourse and practice, to define social roles and status, commit members to future actions, and sharpen the boundaries between insiders and outsiders. In a Durkheimian sense, the symbolic meaning of a particular object or person acts as a prism that concentrates the particular meanings of individual group members into a collective bundle of shared meanings.

In a security community, the density of political, economic, and societal transactions is thus a mere background condition to political integration. In order for these transactions to create collective meanings, there needs to be a common purpose undergirding them that transcends cooperation in issue areas and that is communicated between relevant audiences through symbols, rituals, and other types of meaningful behavior (Deutsch et al. 1957). In other words, the bundle of shared transactions in a security community becomes meaningful (in the sense of community-building behavior and collective identity) through symbolic interaction (Adler and Barnett 1998, p. 417). In the EU, for example, common market policies and a common European currency have been associated not only with economic benefits and prosperity but also with security and peace. As a result, the euro has become a symbol for peaceful European integration. Its survival or decline can be thus meaningfully linked (rightly or wrongly) to the survival and decline of the security community as a whole. Symbolic interaction, understood as meaningful exchange among a group of actors, represents the cornerstone of any security community (Adler and Barnett 1998, p. 416; see also Kitchen 2009).

If we accept the fact that meaningful interactions of a symbolic and ritualized nature can alter perceptions and norms of appropriate behavior in a way that leads to peaceful change, it seems plausible to suggest that a similar process may also apply to disintegration. Experiments in social psychology have shown, for example, that friendly and cooperative behavior frequently motivates others to behave friendly and cooperative as well. In IR, Constructivists have equally shown how symbolic interaction and reciprocity can lead to community building and the reproduction of a shared normative order because states will base their behavior on the meaning that this structure has for them (Wendt 1999, p. 328).

Conversely, the disruption of symbolic interaction can lead to norm degeneration. As pointed out above, members of a security community create meanings of objects and events inside the community but also respond to external transformations on the basis of the subjective meanings that these exogenous changes have for them. In other words, members can alter meanings but are equally influenced by changing meanings themselves (Herman and Reynolds 1994, p. 1). It is thus important to think about external change not as an objective fact but as a social construction interpreted and construed by as well as impacting on members of a security community. The presence of a significant external stimulus may motivate members to act in a certain way based on shared normative meanings.

If members of a security community do not respond 'in-kind' because external change does not fit pre-existing collective meanings, the nature of their symbolic interaction may change and be interrupted facilitating misperception and incomprehension. In the worst case, members of a security community may begin to construct diverging interpretations of the new situation introduced by external change. They may then find new ideas more persuasive initiating a vicious spiral of reciprocal retaliatory behavior. Disrupted symbolic interaction can then undermine meaningful interaction in a security community if individual members articulate and habituate new understandings of normative meanings and engage in alternative symbolic and ritualized interaction that do not resonate with other members.

In sum, it seems reasonable to argue that new meanings constructed in response to major external change and facilitated by the introduction of new ideas may disrupt symbolic interaction. This, in turn, may invite an overemphasis on individual and alternative meanings while deconstructing collectively established meanings within the security community.

For example, following the end of the Cold War, the people in the former Yugoslavia started to define each other along divisive ethnic categories and nationalist ideologies while discarding prior symbolic rituals and slogans of Yugoslavian 'brotherhood and unity' (Stipe 2004, p. 246).

Institutional Failure

Security communities develop common institutions in order to facilitate the communication and coordination of interests among its members (Adler and Barnett 1998, p. 54). In a legal way, this describes the 'mutual acceptance and rigorous observance of certain rules of international law and bilateral treaties when collective objectives of the units are not in harmony' (Holsti 1967, p. 479). However, its political meaning goes beyond simply 'following the rules' and is based instead on a 'strong' or 'thick' type of multilateralism. As explained above, thick multilateralism transcends the instrumental logic of egoistic and utility-maximizing states and instead refers to the practice of self-restraint and the social construction of collective identity (Adler 2001, p. 146; Adler and Greve 2009, p. 71). This grants importance to the formal establishment of regional organizations and institutions.

Adler and Barnett (1998, pp. 418–9) list six roles that regional organizations perform in the formation and consolidation of a security community. First, regional organizations enable members to monitor international agreements. Second, regional organizations highlight areas of mutual interests. Third, regional organizations constitute, articulate, and spread collective norms. Fourth, regional organizations transport 'symbolic legitimacy' as multilateral forums that are capable of handling regional security. Fifth, states and societies imagine and seize common regional spaces through regional organizations. Finally, regional organizations shape and transform the identities of its members.

As most scholars would probably agree, regional organizations form an important component in the development of the normative order in a security community since they 'promote the diffusion of meanings from country to country, may play an active role in the cultural and political selection of similar normative and epistemic understandings in different countries, and may help to transmit shared understanding from generation to generation' (Adler and Barnett 1998, p. 44). Furthermore, as Katharina Coleman (2013) shows, the institutional setting in which actors interact is also of critical importance for norm emergence and compliance. Other scholars also share the understanding that organizational platforms are important for the development and enforcement of norms based on monitoring, communicative action, as well as shaming and blaming strategies (Finnemore 1993, p. 595; Finnemore and Sikkink 1998, p. 899; see also Deitelhoff 2009).

One effect of such close linking of security community norms to regional organizations is obvious: If regional organizations are so intimately tied to security communities that the two become virtually indistinguishable, the fate of the security community rests in part on the survival of that regional organization. NATO, for example, is often used as a synonym for the transatlantic security community even though the two are not the same.[11] Thus, when regional organizations loose legitimacy in the eyes of their members because they no longer provide the social role of monitoring and promoting regional norms, mutual interests, or shaping the identities of their members as part of a regional community, this may, in turn, also destabilize the security community.

Such institutional failure is not confined to the regional level. As Thomas Risse and Tanja Börzel (2013, pp. 83–4) point out, commitment and compliance to regional norms require the institutional and administrative capacity of member states to enforce norms and punish norm violations at the domestic level. Any increase in the political participation of previously politically passive groups may thus significantly affect a pluralistic security community from below as new hopes, claims, needs, pressures, and expectations have to be accommodated within the existing institutional framework. If domestic institutions fail to adapt their integration capabilities in time, the subsequent societal disappointment and frustration may even produce organized radical or populist movements that contest domestic norms, undermine domestic stability, and inhibit member state capacity to practice self-restraint vis-à-vis other member states. This development may be facilitated by an increase in ethnic and/or linguistic differentiation (Deutsch et al. 1957, p. 62; Hagan 2000, p. 43; Kupchan 2010, p. 409). In some exceptional cases, a political election may also result in a significant increase in political participation and domestic normative change. For example, the election of Jörg Haider and his right-wing FPÖ into the Austrian national government in 1999 led to EU sanctions against one of its members.

Finally, many of the norm dynamics described above may also take place at the transnational level through epistemic or transversal communities. Such transnational normative change can significantly affect the security community if significant groups of individuals within and across states establish domestic norms that are incompatible with security community norms at the regional level (Koschut 2014b). The negative impact of transnational actors on the normative order of a pluralistic security community can be witnessed, for example, at the border between Mexico and the USA where illegal migration and criminal activities make it easier for US officials to argue in favor of more border patrol and tighter security measures and to invoke the Othering of Mexican drug cartels and migrants thereby introducing a divisive element into the North American security community.[12] Even the US-Canadian relationship, a textbook example of a pluralistic security community, has recently come under significant pressure as many US policymakers argue that transnational terrorists might exploit the virtually uncontrolled border between the two countries in order to harm the USA (Haglund 2007).

Related to the bottom-up norm dynamics involving domestic and transnational institutions is the top-down process of introversion and seclusion by governments and political elites resulting from routine processes, lack of outside pressures, or lack of innovative ideas (Deutsch et al. 1957, p. 63). The degradation and decay of such integrative capabilities resulting from the closure of political elites may eventually lead to an excessive delay of social, economic, or political reforms, create barriers to societal communication links, or even worse, result in domestic violent repression leading to a decrease in the legitimacy of political leaders that may, in turn, undermine relations with other members of the pluralistic security community (Eberwein 1995, p. 352).

Finally, institutional failure resulting from political instability or even civil war may also undermine the promotion and enforcement of norms of appropriate behavior necessary in a security community. One reason for this is that institutional failures at the domestic level often interact with the regional level in a negative way. Moreover, the absence of large-scale domestic violence is a significant condition for maintaining dependable expectations of peaceful change among a group of states and people (Deutsch et al. 1957, p. 63). Expectations of domestic violence or civil war may create negative spillover effects such as cross-border violence, possible destabilization of neighboring countries and the formation of uncertainty, tension, and mistrust among states and societies (Nathan 2006, p. 280). In sum, institutional failure at the regional, transnational, and domestic level can be said to contribute to norm degeneration and security community disintegration.

Social Unlearning

The concept of social learning is based on the assumption that states learn to act in a certain way through social interaction and communication with others (Bandura 1977; Nye 1987; Levy 1994). Social learning constitutes an important element in the development of security communities as it builds the capacity of social actors necessary to develop common norms, mutual trust, and collective identification. According to Emanuel Adler and Michael Barnett (1998, p. 422), it describes 'an active process of redefinition or reinterpretation of reality on the basis of new causal and normative knowledge'. Social learning also promotes the diffusion of collective meanings and norms between members, which helps explain how community norms are institutionalized and internalized in a security community (Adler and Barnett 1998, pp. 44–5; see also Wendt 1999; Risse 2000; Kacowicz and Bar-Siman-Tov 2000; Checkel 2001). The institutionalization and internalization of community norms requires a process of active teaching and social recognition as other actors also set the agenda and shape members' norms and identities (Finnemore 1996, p. 12). In short, the norms and ideas that 'jump from mind to mind' (Adler 2005, p. 20) within and through a security community influence the social processes among its members and shape a collective learning process that constitutes the normative understanding of what it means to be a member of this particular community (Adler and Crawford 1991, p. 49).

This social-constructivist understanding of learning is based on the theory of cognitive evolution which holds that certain norms and ideas are 'politically selected' and thus become 'taken for granted' and 'naturalized' while 'competing ideas and practices are delegitimized' (Adler and Crawford 1992; see also Adler 2005).[13] Social learning can thus be viewed as a significant factor in the process of building a security community as well as maintaining it (Adler and Barnett 1998, p. 43). As Deutsch and his associates (1957) argue: 'peaceful change does not seem assured without a continuous learning process.' However, if social actors are able to form security communities by 'changing their beliefs' and 'normative expectations' through social learning (Adler and Barnett 1998, p. 43), then 'the same forces that "build up" security communities can (also) "tear them down"' (Adler and Barnett 1998, p. 58). In other words, social learning may not only be conducive to the evolution of security community but may also lead to its demise. For reasons of analytical clarity, I will refer to the latter process as social *un*learning.

Social unlearning involves the rejection and overwriting of previous knowledge. It is not simply about temporarily 'forgetting' or adapting previous knowledge but entails the irrevocable tearing down of previously held beliefs, norms, and identities to open alternative development paths (Pateman 2002, p. 82). In a metaphorical sense, a dilapidated building that is unsafe for people to live in must be demolished before a new building can be constructed in its place. The unlearning of collective norms in a security community involves a similar pattern. Karl Deutsch and his associates (1957, p. 85) describe it as a 'double-process of habit-breaking (through) the presence of some external challenge (and) an emerging way of life'.

Yet, cognitive patterns—like old habits—are hard to break. People who try to quit smoking or attempt to lose weight will attest to this. This is because habits can become part of an agent's identity, thereby reiterating and reinforcing norms of appropriate behavior (Butler 1990, p. 140). Once such habitual norms are internalized they tend to become 'unreflective' in the sense that people no longer think consciously about what they are doing (Dewey 1922, p. 121). In a security community, habitual norms can be said to be a strong promoter of the status quo. As Ted Hopf (2010, p. 553) points out: 'The logic of habit expects far fewer instances of perceived conflicts of interest in the first place, thereby greatly reducing any opportunity for considering violence as a response. Hence, security communities are far more stable.' Even though Hopf's assumptions on the stabilizing role of habitual norms in a security community differ in some ways from the concept of social learning presented here it nevertheless reinforces the notion of the persistence of internalized norms in a security community.

However, habits *can* be broken. As Ted Hopf (2010, p. 543) points out, the most likely source stems from 'high-impact exogenous events' because they disrupt the reiteration of norms through performed habits. Again, this resonates nicely with the argument raised above that major external change is the starting point for security community disintegration to occur. By forcing members to reevaluate existing collective norms and identities, major external change motivates members to reflect on their seemingly 'unreflective' habitual norms, to pause for a moment, and (possibly) to become aware of a need for change in the security community's 'way of life'. As an analogy, consider a high-impact external event like a close relative dying of lung cancer which may motivate a person to internally pause and reflect on his or her own smoking habit potentially resulting in a redefinition or rejection of previously held social identities and norms such as 'smoking is cool' or identifying with smoking icons as a symbol of freedom and maturity. From this perspective, social unlearning can be understood as a strategy to cope with rapid external change and uncertainties (Bauman 2004). Social unlearning hence creates awareness of the fact that 'the very habits that have served us so well in stable times might actually become impediments to social success, even to social survival' (McWilliam 2005, p. 5).

Such cases of social unlearning can also be found in international politics. Take, for example, West and East Germany's break with their collective Nazi and Wilhelminian past after World War II, which resulted in a virtually complete renunciation of previously held collective norms and identities. A similar replacement of past norms and identities with 'Western' norms and identities can be found in most Eastern European countries after the dissolution of the Warsaw Pact (Rothschild and Wingfield 2000). Given the centrality of social learning in security communities outlined above, it is entirely plausible to suggest that similar processes may also be at work in cases of norm degeneration. This implies two things. First, established and internalized norms of peaceful change can be 'unlearnt' which significantly contributes to security community disintegration. Second, social unlearning implies that collective norms are not simply 'lost' or forgotten. Rather, social unlearning involves an active process of reinterpretation, redefinition, and ultimately, rejection and removal of 'old' collective norms.

Thus far, I presented two levels of norm degeneration in a security community: First, external change as a window of opportunity and a stage-setter. Second, social and internal change which alters meaning structures. In the next section, I turn to the final level of this process: how normative change is linked to security community disintegration.

Normative Change

Security communities are socially constructed by mutual trust and identity. Both are reinforced through collective norms (Adler and Barnett 1998, pp. 45–6). Trust in a security community rests on a shared normative belief that actors develop through social interaction and experience despite a state of uncertainty (Misztal 1996, p. 18; Bengtsson 2000, pp. 94–6). Torsten Michel's (Michel (2012) has been changed to Michel (2013) as per the reference list here and in other occurrence. Please check if okay.2013, p. 18) conception of trust is helpful here. He distinguishes between trust as a normative disposition, which *precedes* cooperative behavior, on the one hand, and strategic trust, on the other hand (which he calls 'reliance'), which *follows from* cooperative behavior. A similar account is presented by Ken Booth and Nicholas Wheeler (2008, p. 229) who distinguish between functional 'trust-as-predictability' and normative 'trust-as-bond'. The latter conception of trust represents a normative disposition: 'Trust emerges here as a moralistic disposition which guides and influences behavior by structuring our engagement with the world' (Michel 2013, p. 18). This conception of 'trust-as-bond' undergirds the argument presented in this book about the binding role of norms in a security community and has significant implications for processes of disintegration.

Mutual trust-as-bond in a security community is a judgment based on decades of experiences and interactions. It is based on, but ultimately runs deeper than, international legal treaties, conventions, or organizations. Rather, it involves the construction of a normative order of 'peace norms' or a 'Code of Peace' (Jones 1991). This normative order, as presented in this chapter, consists of a set of 'meta-norms' that have achieved a high level of formality, a low level of contestation, and are supported through conventional and ritualized iteration. As pointed out above, the normative order thus serves as a 'quasi-constitution' in the sense that it constitutes a security community (Adler and Barnett 1998, p. 58; Kacowicz and Bar-Siman-Tov 2000, p. 32). Fundamental changes in the collective normative order can thus be expected to place significant psychological burdens on the cognitive structure of the community because it undermines mutual trust.

Recent literature on norm degeneration is insightful here. Diana Panke and Ulrich Petersohn (2012), for example, argue that norm degeneration occurs whenever there are (a) violations of a particular norm and (b) other actors who fail to enforce compliance. The absence of such sanctions will then trigger non-compliance cascades as other actors also begin to break the norm leading to an either incremental or rapid disappearance/substitution of the original norm. It has been suggested here that such degenerative processes of normative change also take place in a security community. As pointed out above, collective norms reduce the level of uncertainty in a security community by prescribing certain types of behavior while prohibiting actions that violate the normative order. In this sense, norm compliance is a necessary condition for trust in a security community because trust rests on an individual assessment or belief that others will behave within the framework of normative expectations (Adler and Barnett 1998, p. 46). Thus, when norm degeneration occurs due to unpunished norm violations (lack of social control), it is likely to lead to an undermining of trust in a security community.

Like trust, collective identity in a security community is also associated with the quality and duration of normative interactions. Normative behavior is bound by collective understandings about meanings that, in turn, reinforce the collective identity of the community (Adler and Barnett 1998, p. 426; Finnemore 1996, p. 28). They also make the community more 'real' in the minds of policymakers and people by strengthening its psychological existence (Castano 2004; Risse 2010). As pointed out above, this involves active teaching beyond the point of norm internalization (Risse et al. 2013, p. 15). In other words, maintaining the collective identity of a security community is a perpetual process of continuous 'life-long learning', iteration, and invocation of community norms. Socialization and social control via normative agents become central to maintaining the normative order. Hence, security communities can be understood as 'schools of learning' with its members (especially the core states) acting as norm educators and enforcers to maintain a sense of community (Johnston 2007, p. 126; see also Finnemore 1993).

Without such efforts, collective identities may fade and are no longer connected to material structures and norms of appropriate behavior in any meaningful way. For example, Harald Müller (2006) shows that even though the Hanseatic League (a medieval confederation of merchant guilds and their market towns) dissolved in 1669, the Hanseatic colors (red and white) and the League's name still appear in numerous modern-day references and memories all over Northern Germany and the Netherlands. However, these symbols are identity shells or relics that no longer carry substantial meaning that would result in normative action. Thus, when norm degeneration takes place due to the absence of constant norm iteration (interruption of socialization processes), it is likely to lead to a weakening of collective identity in a security community.

To sum up, interruptions of socialization processes (norm iteration) together with a lack of social control (norm enforcement) provide necessary conditions for normative change in a security community because they undermine mutual trust and collective identity, which are pivotal for maintaining a 'we-feeling'. The process of security community disintegration thus can be said to follow an outside-in logic similar to its formation process but under opposing signs: major external change ('shocks') sets off social and internal change in a security community through the persuasiveness of new ideas, the disruption of symbolic interaction, institutional failure, and social unlearning that, in turn, lead to a lack of norm iteration and norm enforcement which undermine identity and trust (normative change).

A Model for Security Community Disintegration

Having conceptualized the normative constitution, means, and protagonists involved in the unraveling of security communities, I now attempt to integrate them in a dynamic model to analytically capture the path of security community disintegration. This model will then be applied to the empirical cases.

My understanding of the development of security communities can be summarized as cyclical. This cyclical interpretation is based on the notion that security communities undergo an evolutionary pattern similar to biological life cycles that involve different consecutive stages in the development of a particular species (birth, growth, maturity, aging, decline, and death). This cyclical approach reflects the assumption put forward in the introductory chapter that the development of dependable expectations of peaceful change in a security community is not a linear progressive process but may also involve norm regress.

The following four-stage model is meant to be neither exclusive nor conclusive. As pointed out above, this book does not claim to provide a general theory that is able to explain security community disintegration completely. Such an undertaking would be an almost impossible task given the diverse set of actors, regions, cultures, and levels of integration involved in security community development across the globe. It should also be pointed out that the model will only be applied to cases in which a mature pluralistic security community *already* existed. It does not take into account security communities that did not make it or never actually 'took off'. What the model does provide is a comprehensive analytical framework for security community disintegration that relies on and traces norm dynamics. In this sense, the model should be viewed as incorporating a set of theoretical building blocks that are open to further empirical observation and refinement.

The model outlines a chronological framework that is structured along four consecutive stages. The results of each stage run down to the next and set the parameters for normative interaction during the following stage. This transition from one stage to the next need not necessarily occur through dramatic shifts in behavior but may also resemble a gradual process. Moreover, the model involves different features at each stage, which allows for a clear analytical differentiation of each stage during the disintegration process. It describes a sequential and cumulative historical process: each step builds on past ones. However, this model of disintegration is not strictly linear but, in principle, permits actors to revert to previous stages. What is more, while some life-cycle models prescribe a fixed minimum amount of time for each stage, this model includes no such time constraints. Finally, it is important to point out that the model presented here by no means exhausts all possible directions that the path of security community disintegration may take. Security communities may still evolve and dissolve in distinct and different ways as the political, cultural, and historical conditions can vary from case to case. Hence, the following model pretends to be neither teleological nor definitive. It describes one possible (but no less probable) path for the disintegration of pluralistic security communities.

Stage 1: Dysfunction

In sociological theory, the concept of dysfunction refers to the deviance from collective norms. Borrowing from Robert Merton (1949, p. 238), we may also define this state of dysfunctional integration as 'malintegration'.[14] Malintegration is initiated by major changes in the external environment because such changes offer a window of opportunity for norm challengers to introduce new ideas. According to Martha Finnemore and Kathryn Sikkink (1998), the introduction of new ideas serves as a prerequisite for norm building and is facilitated, for example, through external crises or revolutions. Similar conditions can be used to explain dynamics of norm degeneration (Rosert and Schirmbeck 2007, p. 281; see also Heller et al. 2012).

In response to external 'shocks', norm leaders of a security community try to make sense of the transformed external environment. The altered situation feeds confusion and temporary ambiguity, perhaps even an identity crisis. In this environment, old ideas may lose traction while new ideas may gain ground because, in the eyes of a growing political strata, the latter may appear more persuasive or better relate to current political and economic needs and problems. These new ideas are introduced and actively promoted by norm challengers seeking to change the established normative order. As a result, diverging meanings and interpretations may spread and initiate domestic normative shifts or even revolutions. Changing domestic norms in some member states may become incompatible with the existing normative order of the security community resulting in norm contestation. Also, one or several norm leaders may increasingly deviate from the collective norms of social behavior in a way that is regarded by other norm leaders of the security community as abnormal, inappropriate, or simply 'bad' behavior. While these members still view each other as part of a security community they may sporadically seek to instrumentally and unilaterally advance their interests without taking the interests of other members into account, thereby overemphasizing individual meaning frames. Superior norm leaders (core states) may display an occasional lack of normative understanding and mutual responsiveness toward smaller members while, at the same time, expressing sympathy toward non-members. Possibly, their behavior may exhibit a sense of contempt and hostility, which is displayed in their language, symbols, and general discourse. In sum, normative discourse and practices increasingly deviate from the collective normative order taking the security community 'off track'.

At this stage of dysfunction or malintegration, however, the security community is still largely intact, as its members do not consider threatening each other with the use of military force and continue to trust each other. However, security cooperation as well as other forms of societal and economic interactions and exchange may suffer as a result of continuing and escalating norm contestation. This may also have a negative impact on the smooth functioning of regional organizations and symbolic interaction such as the interruption of joint meetings or even the temporary exclusion of members from participating in institutional forums.

The interruption of norm iteration and occurrence of norm violations, however, do not (yet) seriously undermine the level of mutual trust and collective identity. Certainly, norm challengers, scenting the winds of change, will increase the pressure by advocating and specifying a 'new' normative order. Yet, norm leaders of the security community will still find ways to defend the established normative order and accommodate or adapt accordingly. In most cases, norm leaders will probably erect structural barriers and 'firewalls' to prevent the diffusion of new ideas. In cases of excessive norm violations, norm leaders will usually not hesitate to sanction inappropriate behavior. Hence, the normative order may be occasionally disrupted but it is likely to quickly jump back into balance. At this point, a reversal of the path toward disintegration is still possible. A good metaphor is heart arrhythmia. The heart pulse may be beating too fast, too slow, or irregular which causes problems for the body's basic functions and performance, but its negative effects may still be contained as long as adaptive measures such as medication or changes in life style are taken.

Stage 2: Decline

If norm leaders fail to adapt to major external changes and fail to act responsively, however, norm challengers will gain in strength and legitimacy. Borrowing from Karl Deutsch et al. (1957, p. 83), this stage could be described as 'a period in which small, scattered, and powerless movements of this kind change into larger and more coordinated ones with significant power behind them'. As a result, the security community may enter a stage of decline. The unresponsiveness of norm leaders can be due to a number of reasons. First, norm leaders may simply fail or be unable to recognize major changes in their environment or confuse their causes and effects. Second, norm leaders may simply lack sufficient resources to effectively respond to these changes in their external environment. Finally, norm leaders may simply refuse to adapt to change either because they seek specific material benefits or because they view ideational differences and mutual perceptions as irreconcilable. In some rare cases, they may even find new ideas more persuasive.

The stage of decline thus resembles a transition phase between a dysfunctional security community and the subsequent denial among norm leaders inviting institutional failure and the disruption of symbolic interaction. At this point, a cascade of unpunished norm violations often also sets in as institutional failure facilitates the deterioration of norm compliance among member states. Norm challengers are now able to mobilize growing support and are thus increasingly successful in promoting an alternative normative order. Core states may begin to violate community norms as they either respond to domestic normative change or see the need for greater freedom of action due to the changing external environment. As a result, the normative order of the security community becomes increasingly difficult to maintain and the path toward disintegration harder to reverse (albeit still not impossible). As Zygmunt Bauman (2001, p. 48) notes, 'the decline of community is in this sense self-perpetuating; once it takes off, there are fewer and fewer stimuli to stem the disintegration of human bonds and seek ways to tie again what has been torn apart.'

Stage 3: Denial

Norm leaders can be expected to retreat into denial once the cascade of norm violations becomes intolerable, and the normative order grows to be difficult to justify and defend against norm challengers. Denial may take two forms. Pursuing an ostrich-like policy, norm leaders may simply refuse to acknowledge the degenerated state of security community norms and carry on 'business-as-usual' (defensive denial). Alternatively, they may attempt to increase the level and scope of integration by proposing new organizational structures, inviting new members, or by initiating wars abroad in order to compensate and distract from the growing lack of mutual responsiveness and self-restraint within the community (offensive denial or overjustification). Most importantly, in the latter case, the norm leaders of the security community may bribe norm challengers with symbolic or material concessions while, at the same time, refuse to acknowledge that their behavior contradicts their normative beliefs. This puts norm leaders in a state of cognitive dissonance, which results in further contempt and discomfort among norm leaders (Jervis 1976, p. 404; see also Festinger 1962).

A state of cognitive dissonance (acting contrary to one's own beliefs) is thus likely to further erode the normative order. As Ryan Goodman and Derek Jinks (2013, p. 108) have shown, material inducements or outside pressures can 'crowd-out' social mechanisms of norm compliance through overjustification. Overjustification occurs when rewards or pressures interfere with self-perception.[15] Member states may then unlearn that norm abiding behavior is considered an extension of their identity as part of the community (intrinsic motivation) and instead attribute this behavior to the presence of material incentives, external threats, or punishments (extrinsic motivator). This is particularly problematic since this altered perception via social unlearning introduces a new behavioral logic that is based on cost–benefit calculations and no longer on norms of appropriate behavior (Milburn and Conrad 1996, p. 227). As Alex Wendt (2003, p. 1047) underlines: 'if instrumental rationality instantiates an individualistic view of the Self, then by acting on that basis institutional designers may unintentionally reproduce that mode of subjectivity and thereby make it more difficult to create a genuine sense of community.' Overjustification may then strengthen a sense of self-determination while weakening the sense of community. For example, norm leaders may perceive an increase in the level and scope of integration as a threat to their autonomy as sovereign states (a key hallmark of a pluralistic security community), which invite more institutional failure and further disruption of symbolic interaction. These norm leaders may increasingly focus on material changes introduced by other members (especially by more powerful core states) such as new organizational structures or the invitation of new members which they perceive as an unjustified form of influence and control (Goodman and Jinks 2013, pp. 108–13).

These social and internal changes resulting from cognitive dissonance and overjustification can have detrimental effects. A state of denial may unintentionally produce a 'crowding-out-effect' that induces community members to depart from the logic of appropriateness and increasingly follow the logic of consequence. As a result, meaningful social interaction may also continue to decrease. As a result, community discourse may turn hostile. For example, its members may use common institutions and platforms to discursively attack each other instead of resolving their conflicts or they may even refrain from participating in them at all. At this stage, symbolic interaction is not only disrupted but also begins to enter a spiral of reciprocal retaliatory behavior. In the end, norm leaders begin to socially unlearn community norms by rejecting previous knowledge and by transforming modes of social behavior from the logic of appropriateness to the logic of consequence. To sum up, the stage of denial represents a critical juncture in the process of security community disintegration as norm leaders come to see each other less as members of a community but increasingly as rivals and competitors. If these perceptions persist, the shared normative meanings and social reality of security community are deconstructed.

Stage 4: Disintegration

At the stage of disintegration, the normative order among members of the security community breaks down. To use an earlier metaphor, the heart of the security community stops beating. Taking insights from the study of security community emergence, we would expect, mirroring Deutsch's theory of integration, a 'take-off point' (or, to stick with the figure of aviation speech, a 'touch-down point') that signals the disintegration of security community. Such a 'crash-landing' of the security community should involve normative change. The key question is of course: how do we know when such a 'landing' has occurred?

Karl Deutsch defined the process of integration as 'the crossing of a threshold, from a situation where war between the political units concerned appeared possible and was being prepared for, to another situation where it was neither. It was the crossing of this threshold, and with it the establishment of a security-community, that we called integration' (Deutsch et al. 1957, p. 32). Based on Karl Deutsch's conception, the point of breakdown of the normative order of a security community can thus be defined as a situation where war between members appears possible (or even likely), is actively being prepared for and advocated, or actually occurs.

Once a security community reaches this stage, the normative order can be said to have collapsed, as there is hardly anyone left with the willingness and capacity to actively enforce and defend it. Norm leaders no longer view each other as members of the same community. What is more, they now enter a state of 'chronical anomy' (Durkheim 1897, p. 290) in which norm leaders cease to 'govern' the security community by defining collective meanings and norms. Instead, norm challengers may now establish and consolidate a new normative order as formerly established institutions and norms break down or continue to exist only on paper. When previously inappropriate forms of social behavior spread and take hold, social unlearning becomes indisputable (Peters 1993, p. 140). Previous knowledge is overwritten, collective meanings redefined, and established norms replaced by 'broad political movements, of governments, or of major interest groups, (...) organized mass persuasion and mass response, or else of the organized persuasion of large parts of the political elites' (Deutsch et al. 1957, p. 84). Having previously identified with each other as Self, members now turn into Others. Most importantly, the threat or use of physical force is now reintroduced as an appropriate means to promote self-interest against the interests of other members and to resolve conflicts of interests. Former norm leaders may be able to temporarily prevent violent conflict among them by maintaining a no-war community or an 'adversarial peace'.[16] However, their social interaction no longer follows the logic of appropriateness but is based on instrumental cooperation. War is expected to break out anytime and arrangements are undertaken to prepare for that.

From this perspective, the most likely outcome resulting from the breakup of a security community is war or, at least, some form of organized mass violence. This assumption can be based on disintegration theory in sociology. According to this theory, disintegration among individuals and groups within a social community typically leads to disorientation, which facilitates violent behavior (Imbusch and Heitmeyer 2008). Since security communities are socially constructed in the sense that people identify with each other and share collective norms linked to shared meanings, a similar social pattern can also be attributed to the disintegration of security communities.

As the normative order of a security community disintegrates, former meaningful links are cut off and its members reenter a state of uncertainty and disorientation, which evaporates mutual trust and collective identity. To be sure, common symbols and identity relics may persist even after the disintegration of security community. However, this phenomenon can be easily explained since most collective symbols and identities emerge from or relate to effective political symbols and identities of previous communities (e.g., the Union Jack, see Deutsch 1979, p. 213). However, in the absence of iteration and enforcement these symbols and identities are no longer linked to meaningful norms of appropriate behavior.

In the end, it should be noted that the path that traces security community disintegration outlined above should not be viewed as deterministic. To be sure, once a security community has entered the stage of disintegration, the process of norm degeneration is likely to become irreversible. However, norm leaders may still be able to repair degenerated norms before a security community reaches the stage of disintegration. The following empirical cases represent examples of such alternative outcomes. In the case of the German Confederation, the pluralistic security community eventually dissolved and was replaced a few years later by the amalgamated security community of the German nation-state. In the case of NATO, the pluralistic security community, following severe damage to the normative order during the crisis over the Iraq war in 2003, did not dissolve but remains 'alive and kicking' because its members were able to repair degenerated norms. What explains this variation? The answer, it has been argued, lies in the relative scope of normative change within these security communities. To determine and compare the scope of normative change in each security community, the next two chapters will outline a detailed narrative by applying the model outlined above to the empirical cases.

Notes

1. This statement is not a contradiction to my argument raised in the previous chapter, which claims that changing individual norms and ideas about the intragroup relationship may serve as the *primary* explanation for the disintegration of pluralistic security communities. As already pointed out, I certainly do not claim that norms and ideas can be expected to explain the process of security community disintegration *completely*.

2. Deutsch and his associates (1957, p. 48) define a distinctive way of life as 'a set of socially accepted values and institutional means for their pursuit and attainment, and a set of established or emerging habits of behavior corresponding to them'.
3. By localization is meant 'the active construction (through discourse, framing, grafting, and cultural selection) of foreign ideas by local actors, which results in the former developing significant congruence with local beliefs and practices' (Acharya 2004, p. 245).
4. Ideology may be understood as 'a set of closely-related beliefs or ideas, or even attitudes, characteristic of a group or community' (Plamenatz 1970, p. 15) or, in other words, 'the whole outlook of a social group (…) its total *Weltanschauung* (or *mentalité*) as conditioned sociologically by the group's political orientation, and temporally by its location in the ongoing historical process' (Mannheim 1936, pp. 57 and 125). For a detailed discussion of the concept, please refer to Mullins (1972), Howard (1989), and Gerring (1997).
5. According to Karl W. Deutsch, depoliticization means that an issue is made non-political and taken off the political agenda.
6. This conception of a security community as a community of practice shares some significant theoretical and empirical overlaps with Adler's concept of the same name (Adler 2005; Adler and Pouliot 2011). However, while I treat this concept as *part* of the general normative framework of a security community, Adler and other proponents of a practice approach to IR (especially Pouliot 2008, p. 258) treat the logic of practice as ontologically prior to other forms of social action (logic of consequence, logic of appropriateness, logic of arguing) (see also Koschut 2014b).
7. Quoted in: Spiegel Online (2013), The Rise of Fearmongers: Germany's New Eurosceptic Elite, http://www.spiegel.de/international/europe/new-anti-euro-figures-in-germany-offer-vague-ideas-and-fan-fears-a-906675.html, date accessed 14 January 2014.
8. In studying norms, many IR scholars have used the concept of norm entrepreneurship to describe agents that are either supportive *or* in opposition of norm development (Müller and Wunderlich 2013; Nadelmann 1990; Finnemore and Sikkink 1998; Risse et al. 2013). Norm entrepreneurship is thus understood here as a superordinate concept that includes both norm leaders and challengers.
9. The term 'regime' refers here not to the well-known concept in IR (Krasner 1983) but rather to its meaning in Comparative Politics as a form of governance (Merkel 2010).
10. See, for example, Katzenstein 1996; Price 1997; Keck and Sikkink 1998; Tannenwald 1999; Risse et al. 1999, 2013; Checkel 1999, 2001.
11. While NATO forms the core organizational structure for the transatlantic security community, certain NATO members may not be recognized as

members of the security community and vice versa. For example, there continue to be military stand-offs between Greece and Turkey over Cyprus. On the other hand, while Austria is not a formal member of NATO and only recently joined the EU, it certainly can be counted as a member of the transatlantic security community (Bellamy 2004, p. 9).
12. Beginning during World War II, the USA and Mexico developed into a pluralistic security community ending an era of military confrontations and cross-border raids including common institutions like NAFTA. With increasing illegal immigration and drug trafficking from Mexico, however, the incentives for integration and the foundations for mutual trust have severely deteriorated (Gonzales and Haggard 1998, p. 295).
13. Adler defines cognitive evolution as 'a historical process (by which) institutional or social facts may be socially constructed by collective understandings of the physical and the social world that are subject to authoritative (political) selection processes and thus to evolutionary change' (Adler 1997, p. 106).
14. Malintegration exists when 'the main components of the culture are out of balance and the messages emanating from the culture are at odds with the realities of social structure' (Merton 1949, p. 556).
15. Social psychology research has demonstrated how the introduction of an extrinsic motivator (external pressure or reward) can lead to overjustification that 'crowds out' intrinsic motivation (enjoyment in the performance itself). For example, children who enjoyed drawing pictures without expectation of reward lost interest in that activity once a reward for the drawing was introduced but subsequently withdrawn (Lepper et al. 1973).
16. Adversarial peace is characterized by 'sharp ideological differences, intensive propaganda warfare, and mutual perceptions of grave threat and deep distrust, despite a formal peace' (Shamir 1992, pp. 8–9).

REFERENCES

Acharya, A. (2001). *Constructing a security community in Southeast Asia. ASEAN and the problem of regional order*. London: Routledge.
Acharya, A. (2004). How ideas spread: whose norms matter? Norm localization and institutional change in Asian regionalism'. *International Organization*, 8(2), 239–275.
Acharya, A. (2011). Norm subsidiarity and regional orders: Sovereignty, regionalism, and rule-making in the third world. *International Studies Quarterly*, 55(1), 95–123.
Adler, E. (1997). Imagined (security) communities: Cognitive regions in international relations. *Millennium*, 26(2), 249–277.

Adler, E. (2001). The change of change: Peaceful transitions of power in the multilateral age. In C. A. Kupchan, E. Adler, J. M. Coicaud, & Y. F. Khong (Eds.), *Power in transition: The peaceful change of international order* (pp. 138–158). New York: United Nations University Press.

Adler, E. (2005). *Communitarian international relations. The epistemic foundations of international relations*. New York: Routledge.

Adler, E., & Barnett, M. (1998). A framework for the study of security communities. In E. Adler & M. Barnett (Eds.), *Security communities* (pp. 29–66). Cambridge: Cambridge University Press.

Adler, E., & Crawford, B. (1991). *Progress in post-war international relations*. New York: Columbia University Press.

Adler, E., & Greve, P. (2009). When security community meets balance of power. Overlapping regional mechanisms of security governance. *Review of International Studies, 35*(1), 59–84.

Adler, E., & Pouliot, V. (Eds.). (2011). *International practices*. Cambridge: Cambridge University Press.

Armstrong, D. (1993). *Revolution and world order: The revolutionary state in international society*. Oxford: Clarendon Press.

Avant, D. D., Finnemore, M., & Sell, S. K. (2010). *Who governs the globe?* New York: Cambridge University Press.

Bandura, A. (1977). *Social learning theory*. Englewood Cliffs: Prentice Hall.

Bauman, Z. (2001). *Community: Seeking safety in an insecure world*. Cambridge: Polity Press.

Bauman, Z. (2004). Liquid sociality. In N. Gane (Ed.), *The future of social theory* (pp. 17–46). London: Continuum.

Bellah, R. N. (1967). Civil religion in America. *Daedalus, 96*, 1–21.

Bellamy, A. J. (2004). *Security communities and their neighbours. Regional fortresses or global integrators?* New York: Palgrave Macmillan.

Bengtsson, R. (2000). The cognitive dimension of stable peace. In A. Kacowicz, Y. Bar-Siman-Tov, O. Elgström, & M. Jerneck (Eds.), *Stable peace among nations* (pp. 92–107). Lanham: Rowman and Littlefield.

Berger, T. U. (1996). Norms, identity, and national security in Germany and Japan. In P. J. Katzenstein (Ed.), *The culture of national security* (pp. 317–356). New York: Columbia University Press.

Berger, P. L., & Luckmann, T. (1966). *The social construction of reality: A treatise in the sociology of knowledge*. Garden City: Doubleday.

Bially Mattern, J. (2001). The power politics of identity. *European Journal of International Relations, 7*(3), 349–397.

Björkdahl, A. (2002). Norms in international relations: Some conceptual and methodological reflections. *Cambridge Review of International Affairs, 15*(1), 9–23.

Booth, K., & Wheeler, N. J. (2008). *The security dilemma: Fear, cooperation and trust in world politics.* Basingstoke: Palgrave Macmillan.
Börzel, T. A., & Risse, T. (2013). Human rights in areas of limited statehood: The new agenda. In T. Risse, S. C. Ropp, & K. Sikkink (Eds.), *The persistent power of human rights* (pp. 63–84). Cambridge: Cambridge University Press.
Braveboy-Wagner, J. A. (2009). *Institutions of the global south.* New York: Routledge.
Butler, J. (1990). *Gender trouble: Feminism and the subversion of identity.* New York: Routledge.
Castano, E. (2004). European identity: A social-psychological perspective. In R. K. Herrmann, T. Risse, & M. B. Brewer (Eds.), *Transnational identities. Becoming European in the EU.* Lanham: Rowman and Littlefield.
Checkel, J. T. (1999). Norms, institutions, and national identity in contemporary Europe. *International Studies Quarterly, 43*(1), 84–114.
Checkel, J. T. (2001). Why comply? Social learning and European identity change. *International Organization, 55*(3), 553–588.
Coleman, K. P. (2013). Locating norm diplomacy: Venue change in international norm negotiations. *European Journal of International Relations, 19*(1), 163–186.
Collins, R. (1998). *The sociology of philosophies: A global theory of intellectual change.* Cambridge, MA: Harvard University Press.
Daase, C. (2003). Das Ende vom Anfang des nuklearen Tabus. Zur Legitimitätskrise der Weltnuklearordnung'. *Zeitschrift für Internationale Beziehungen, 10*(1), 7–41.
Davis, J. W. (2000). Understanding the domestic impact of international norms: A research agenda. *International Studies Review, 2*(1), 65–87.
Deitelhoff, N. (2009). The discursive process of legalization. Charting islands of persuasion in the ICC case. *International Organization, 63*(1), 33–66.
Deutsch, K. W. (1953). The growth of nations. Some recurrent patterns of political and social integration. *World Politics, 5*(2), 168–196.
Deutsch, K. W. (1954). *Political community at the international level. Problems of definition and measurement.* Garden City: Doubleday.
Deutsch, K. W. (1961). Security communities. In J. N. Rosenau (Ed.), *International politics and foreign policy. A reader in research and theory* (pp. 98–105). New York: Free Press.
Deutsch, K. W. (1966). *The nerves of government, models of political communication and control.* New York: Free Press.
Deutsch, K. W. (1969). *The analysis of international relations* (2nd ed.). Englewood Cliffs: Prentice-Hall.
Deutsch, K. W. (1970). *Politics and government. How people decide their fate.* Boston: Houghton Mifflin.

Deutsch, K. W. (1979). *Tides among nations.* New York: Free Press.
Deutsch, K. W., Burrell, S. A., Kann, R. A., Lee, M., Jr., Lichterman, M., Lindgren, R. E., Loewenheim, F. L., & van Wagenen, R. W. (1957). *Political community and the North Atlantic area. International organization in the light of historical experience.* Princeton: Princeton University Press.
Dewey, J. (1922). *The human nature and conduct. An introduction to social psychology.* New York: Henry Holt.
Diez, T. (2004). Europe's others and the return of geopolitics. *Cambridge Review of International Affairs, 17*(2), 319–335.
Durkheim, E. (1897/2002). *Suicide. A study in sociology.* New York: Routledge.
Eberwein, W. D. (1995). The future of international warfare: Toward a global security community? *International Political Science Review, 16*(4), 341–360.
Farrell, T. (2001). Transnational norms and military development: Constructing Ireland's professional army. *European Journal of International Relations, 7*(1), 63–102.
Festinger, L. (1962). Cognitive dissonance. *Scientific American, 207*(4), 93–107.
Finnemore, M. (1993). International organizations as teachers of norms: The United Nations educational, scientific, and cultural organization and science policy. *International Organization, 47*(4), 565–597.
Finnemore, M. (1996). *National interests in international society.* Ithaca: Cornell University Press.
Finnemore, M. (2003). *The purpose of intervention: Changing beliefs about the use of force.* Ithaca: Cornell University Press.
Finnemore, M., & Sikkink, K. (1998). International norm dynamics and political change. *International Organization, 52*(4), 887–917.
Finnemore, M., & Sikkink, K. (2001). Taking stock: The constructivist research program in international relations and comparative politics. *Annual Review of Political Science, 4*, 391–416.
Fligstein, N. (2009). Who are the Europeans and how does this matter for politics? In J. T. Checkel & P. J. Katzenstein (Eds.), *European identity.* Cambridge: Cambridge University Press.
Foot, R., & Walter, A. (2013). Global norms and major state behaviour: The cases of China and the United States. *European Journal of International Relations, 19*(2), 329–352.
Forst, R., & Günther, K. (2011). *Die Herausbildung normativer Ordnung. Interdisziplinäre Perspektiven.* Frankfurt am Main: Campus.
Gerring, J. (1997). Ideology: A definitional analysis. *Political Research Quarterly, 50*(4), 957–994.
Gonzalez, G., & Haggard, S. (1998). The United States and Mexico: A pluralistic security community? In E. Adler & M. Barnett (Eds.), *Security communities* (pp. 295–332). Cambridge: Cambridge University Press.

Goodman, R., & Jinks, D. (2013). Social mechanisms to promote international human rights: Complementary or contradictory? In T. Risse, S. C. Ropp, & K. Sikkink (Eds.), *The persistent power of human rights* (pp. 103–121). Cambridge: Cambridge University Press.

Gurowitz, A. (1999). Mobilizing international norms: Domestic actors, immigrants, and the Japanese state. *World Politics, 51*(3), 413–445.

Habermas, J. (1981). *Theorie des kommunikativen Handelns*. Frankfurt am Main: Suhrkamp.

Hagan, J. D. (2000). Domestic political sources of stable peace. The great powers, 1815–1854. In A. Kacowicz, Y. Bar-Siman-Tov, O. Elgström, & M. Jerneck (Eds.), *Stable peace among nations* (pp. 36–54). Lanham: Rowman and Littlefield.

Haglund, D. G. (2007). A security community – "if you can keep it": Demographic change and the North American zone of peace. *Nortamérica, 2*(1), 77–100.

Hall, P. A. (1989). *The political power of economic ideas: Keynesianism across nations*. Princeton: Princeton University Press.

Heller, R., Kahl, M., & Pisoiu, D. (2012). The "dark" side of normative argumentation. The case of counterterrorism policy. *Global Constitutionalism, 1*(2), 278–312.

Herman, R. G. (1996). Identity, norms, and national security: The Soviet foreign policy revolution and the end of the Cold War. In P. J. Katzenstein (Ed.), *The culture of national security* (pp. 271–316). New York: Columbia University Press.

Herman, N. J., & Reynolds, L. T. (1994). *Symbolic interaction: An introduction to social psychology*. New York: General Hall.

Holsti, K. J. (1967). *International politics. A framework for analysis*. Englewood Cliffs: Prentice-Hall.

Holsti, K. J. (1982). *Why nations realign: Foreign policy restructuring in the postwar world*. London: Allen and Unwin.

Holsti, K. J. (1998). *The problem of change in international relations theory* (Working paper 26). Vancouver: University of British Columbia.

Hopf, T. (2010). The logic of habit in international relations. *European Journal of International Relations, 16*(4), 539–561.

Howard, M. (1989). Ideology and international relations. *Review of International Studies, 15*(1), 1–10.

Ikenberry, G. J. (2001). *After victory. Institutions, strategic restraint, and the rebuilding of order after major wars*. Princeton: Princeton University Press.

Ikenberry, G. J., & Kupchan, C. A. (1990). Socialization and hegemonic power. *International Organization, 44*(3), 283–315.

Imbusch, P., & Heitmeyer, W. (2008). *Integration – Desintegration*. Wiesbaden: Verlag für Sozialwissenschaften.

Jervis, R. (1976). *Perception and misperception in international politics*. Princeton: Princeton University Press.
Johnston, A. I. (2007). *Social states: China in international institutions, 1980–2000*. Princeton: Princeton University Press.
Jones, D. V. (1991). *Code of peace. Ethics and security in the world of the warlord states*. Chicago: University of Chicago Press.
Kacowicz, A. M., & Bar-Siman-Tov, Y. (2000). Stable peace. A conceptual framework. In A. Kacowicz, Y. Bar-Siman-Tov, O. Elgström, & M. Jerneck (Eds.), *Stable peace among nations* (pp. 11–35). Lanham: Rowman and Littlefield.
Kaelbe, H. (2009). Identification with Europe and politicization of the EU since the 1980s. In J. T. Checkel & P. J. Katzenstein (Eds.), *European identity*. Cambridge: Cambridge University Press.
Katzenstein, P. J. (1996). Introduction: Alternative perspectives on national security. In P. J. Katzenstein (Ed.), *The culture of national security* (pp. 1–32). New York: Columbia University Press.
Katzenstein, P. J. (2005). *A world of regions. Asia and Europe in the American imperium*. Ithaca: Cornell University Press.
Keck, M. E., & Sikkink, K. (1998). *Activists beyond borders. Advocacy networks in international politics*. Ithaca: Cornell University Press.
Keohane, R. O. (1989). *International institutions and state power: Essays in international relations theory*. Boulder: Westview Press.
Keohane, R. O. (1990). Multilateralism: An agenda for research. *International Journal, 45*(3), 731–764.
Kitchen, V. M. (2009). Argument and identity change in the Atlantic security community. *Security Dialogue, 40*(1), 95–114.
Kleger, H. (2008). *Gibt es eine europäische Zivilreligion? Pariser Vorlesung über die Werte Europas*. Potsdam: Universitätsverlag.
Kleger, H., & Mehlhausen, T. (2013). Unstrittig und doch umstritten. Europäische Solidarität in der Eurokrise'. *Politische Vierteljahresschrift, 54*(1), 50–74.
Koschut, S. (2010). *Die Grenzen der Zusammenarbeit. Sicherheit und transatlantische Identität nach dem Ende des Ost-West-Konflikts*. Baden-Baden: Nomos.
Koschut, S. (2014a). Emotional (security) communities: The significance of emotion norms in inter-allied conflict management. *Review of International Studies, 40*(3), 533–558.
Koschut, S. (2014b). Transatlantic conflict management inside-out: The impact of domestic norms on regional security practices. *Cambridge Review of International Affairs, 27*(2), 339–361.
Kowert, P., & Legro, J. (1996). Norms, identity, and their limits. A theoretical reprise. In P. J. Katzenstein (Ed.), *The culture of national security* (pp. 451–497). New York: Columbia University Press.
Král, D. (2009). *Not your grandfather's eastern bloc. The EU new member states as agenda setters in the enlarged European Union* (Comparative policy report). Prague: European Policies Initiative.

Krasner, S. D. (1983). Structural causes and regime consequences: Regimes as intervening variables. In S. D. Krasner (Ed.), *International regimes* (pp. 1–22). Ithaca: Cornell University Press.

Kupchan, C. A. (2010). *How enemies become friends. The sources of stable peace.* Princeton: Princeton University Press.

Langer, S. K. (1942). *Philosophy in a new key. A study in the symbolism of reason, rite, and art.* Cambridge, MA: Harvard University Press.

Lantis, J. S. (2011). Redefining the nonproliferation norm? Australian uranium, the NPT, and the global nuclear revival. *Australian Journal of Politics and History, 57*(4), 543–561.

Legro, J. W. (1997). Which norms matter? Revisiting the "failure" of internationalism. *International Organization, 51*(1), 31–63.

Legro, J. W. (2000). The transformation of policy ideas. *American Journal of Political Science, 44*(3), 419–432.

Lepper, M. R., Greene, D., & Nisbett, R. E. (1973). Undermining children's intrinsic interest with extrinsic reward: A test of the "overjustification" hypothesis. *Journal of Personality and Social Psychology, 28*(1), 129–137.

Levy, J. S. (1994). Learning and foreign policy: Sweeping a conceptual minefield. *International Organization, 48*(2), 279–312.

Liese, A. (2006). *Staaten am Pranger: Zur Wirkung internationaler Regime auf innerstaatliche Menschenrechtspolitik.* Wiesbaden: Verlag für Sozialwissenschaften.

Mannheim, K. (1936). *Ideology and utopia*. London: Routledge.

McNamara, K. R. (2010). Constructing authority in the European Union. In D. D. Avant, M. Finnemore, & S. K. Sell (Eds.), *Who governs the globe?* (pp. 153–181). Cambridge: Cambridge University Press.

McWilliam, E. L. (2005). Unlearning pedagogy. *Journal of Learning Design, 1*(1), 1–11.

Mead, H. (1934). *Mind, self, and society*. Chicago: Chicago University Press.

Merkel, W. (2010). Are dictatorships returning? Revisiting the "democratic rollback" hypothesis. *Contemporary Politics, 16*(1), 17–31.

Merton, R. K. (1949). *Social theory and social structure*. Glencoe: The Free Press.

Michel, T. (2013). Time to get emotional: Phronetic reflections on the concept of trust in international relations. *European Journal of International Relations, 19*(4), 864–890.

Milburn, M. A., & Conrad, S. D. (1996). *The politics of denial*. Cambridge, MA: Massachusetts Institute of Technology Press.

Misztal, B. A. (1996). *Trust in modern societies: The search for the bases of social order*. Cambridge: Polity Press.

Müller, H. (2006). A theory of decay of security communities with an application to the present state of the Atlantic alliance (Working paper). Berkeley: University of California at Berkeley.

Müller, H. (2013). Conclusion: Agency matters. In H. Müller & C. Wunderlich (Eds.), *Norm dynamics in multilateral arms control. Interests, conflicts, and justice* (pp. 141–162). Athens: Georgia University Press.
Müller, H., & Wolff, J. (2006). Democratic peace: Many data, little explanation? In A. Geis, L. Brock, & H. Müller (Eds.), *Democratic wars. Looking at the dark side of democratic peace* (pp. 41–73). Basingstoke: Palgrave Macmillan.
Müller, H., & Wunderlich, C. (2013). *Norm dynamics in multilateral arms control. Interests, conflicts, and justice*. Athens: Georgia University Press.
Müller, H., Fey, M., & Rauch, C. (2013). Winds of change: Exogenous events and trends as norm triggers (or norm killers). In H. Müller & C. Wunderlich (Eds.), *Norm dynamics in multilateral arms control. Interests, conflicts, and justice* (pp. 141–160). Athens: Georgia University Press.
Mullins, W. A. (1972). On the concept of ideology in political science. *American Political Science Review, 66*(2), 498–510.
Nadelmann, E. A. (1990). Global prohibition regimes: The evolution of norms in international society. *International Organization, 44*(4), 479–526.
Nathan, L. (2006). Domestic instability and security communities. *European Journal of International Relations, 12*(2), 275–299.
Nietzsche, F. (1958). Ecce Homo. In K. Schlechta (Ed.), *Friedrich Nietzsche. Werke in drei Bänden* (Vol. 2). München: Hanser.
Nye, J. S. (1987). Nuclear learning and U.S.-Soviet security regimes. *International Organization, 41*(3), 371–402.
Nyhamar, T. (2000). How do norms work? A theoretical and empirical analysis of African international relations. *International Journal of Peace Studies, 5*(2), 27–43.
Odell, J. S. (1982). *U.S. international monetary policy: Markets, power, and ideas as sources of change*. Princeton: Princeton University Press.
Owen, J. M., IV. (2000). Pieces of maximal peace. Common identities, common enemies. In A. Kacowicz, Y. Bar-Siman-Tov, O. Elgström, & M. Jerneck (Eds.), *Stable peace among nations* (pp. 74–91). Lanham: Rowman and Littlefield.
Panke, D., & Petersohn, U. (2012). Why international norms disappear sometimes. *European Journal of International Relations, 18*(4), 719–742.
Pateman, T. (2002). Lifelong unlearning. In D. Barford (Ed.), *The ship of thought. Essays on psychoanalysis and learning*. London: Karnac.
Peters, B. (1993). *Die Integration moderner Gesellschaften*. Frankfurt am Main: Suhrkamp.
Plamenatz, J. (1970). *Ideology*. London: Pall Mall.
Pouliot, V. (2008). The logic of practicality. A theory of practice of security communities. *International Organization, 62*(2), 257–288.
Price, R. (1997). *The chemical weapons taboo*. Ithaca: Cornell University Press.
Price, R., & Tannenwald, N. (1996). Norms and deterrence: The nuclear and chemical weapons taboos. In P. J. Katzenstein (Ed.), *The culture of national security* (pp. 114–152). New York: Columbia University Press.

Rappaport, R. A. (1999). *Ritual and religion in the making of humanity.* Cambridge: Cambridge University Press.
Risse, T. (2000). Let's argue! Communicative action in world politics. *International Organization, 54*(1), 1–39.
Risse, T. (2010). *A community of Europeans? Transnational identities and public spheres.* Ithaca: Cornell University Press.
Risse, T., Ropp, S. C., & Sikkink, K. (1999). *The power of human rights: International norms and domestic change.* Cambridge: Cambridge University Press.
Risse, T., Ropp, S. C., & Sikkink, K. (2013). *The persistent power of human rights.* Cambridge: Cambridge University Press.
Risse-Kappen, T. (1994). Ideas do not float freely: Transnational coalitions, domestic structures, and the end of the Cold War. *International Organization, 48*(2), 185–214.
Risse-Kappen, T. (1996). Collective identity in a democratic community: The case of NATO. In P. J. Katzenstein (Ed.), *The culture of national security* (pp. 357–399). New York: Columbia University Press.
Rosenfeld, M. (1998). *Just interpretations: Law between ethics and politics.* Berkeley: University of California Press.
Rosert, E., & Schirmbeck, S. (2007). Zur Erosion internationaler Normen: Folterverbot und nukleares Tabu in der Diskussion'. *Zeitschrift für Internationale Beziehungen, 14*(2), 253–288.
Rothschild, J., & Wingfield, N. M. (2000). *Return to diversity: A political history of East Central Europe since World War II.* Oxford: Oxford University Press.
Rublee, M. R. (2008). Taking stock of the nuclear proliferation regime: Using social psychology to understand regime effectiveness. *International Studies Review, 10*(3), 420–450.
Ruggie, J. G. (1983). International regimes, transactions and change: Embedded liberalism in the postwar economic order. In S. D. Krasner (Ed.), *International regimes* (pp. 195–232). Ithaca: Cornell University Press.
Ruggie, J. G. (1993). Territoriality and beyond: Problematizing modernity in international relations. *International Organization, 47*(1), 139–174.
Russett, B. M. (1998). A neo-Kantian perspective: Democracy, interdependence, and international organizations in building security communities. In E. Adler & M. Barnett (Eds.), *Security communities* (pp. 368–394). Cambridge: Cambridge University Press.
Sandholtz, W., & Stiles, K. W. (2009). *International norms and cycles of change.* Oxford: Oxford University Press.
Schmitz, H. P., & Sikkink, K. (2002). Human rights. In W. Carlsnaes, T. Risse, & B. A. Simmons (Eds.), *Handbook of international relations* (pp. 517–537). London: Sage.
Shamir, S. (1992). From conflict to peace. Stages along the road. *United States Institute of Peace Journal, 5*(6), 7–9.

Sikkink, K. (2013). The United States and torture: Does the spiral model work? In T. Risse, S. C. Ropp, & K. Sikkink (Eds.), *The persistent power of human rights* (pp. 145–163). Cambridge: Cambridge University Press.

Simmons, B. A. (2013). From ratification to compliance: Quantitative evidence on the spiral model. In T. Risse, S. C. Ropp, & K. Sikkink (Eds.), *The persistent power of human rights* (pp. 43–60). Cambridge: Cambridge University Press.

Sjöström, E. (2010). Shareholders as norm entrepreneurs for corporate social responsibility. *Journal of Business Ethics, 94*(2), 177–191.

Solingen, E. (2012). Of dominoes and firewalls: The domestic, regional, and global politics of international diffusion. *International Studies Quarterly, 56*(4), 631–644.

Stipe, M. (2004). *The demise of Yugoslavia: A political memoir*. Budapest: Central European University Press.

Sunstein, C. R. (1996). Social norms and social roles. *Columbia Law Review, 96*(4), 903–968.

Tannenwald, N. (1999). The nuclear taboo: The United States and the normative basis of nuclear non-use. *International Organization, 53*(3), 433–468.

Taylor, C. (1971). Interpretation and the sciences of man. *Review of Metaphysics, 25*(1), 3–51.

Tilly, C. (1995). *Popular contention in Great Britain, 1758–1834*. Cambridge, MA: Harvard University Press.

Väyrynen, R. (2000). Stable peace through security communities: Steps towards theory-building. In A. Kacowicz, Y. Bar-Siman-Tov, O. Elgström, & M. Jerneck (Eds.), *Stable peace among nations* (pp. 108–129). Lanham: Rowman and Littlefield.

Wæver, O. (1995). Securitization and desecuritization. In R. D. Lipschutz (Ed.), *On security* (pp. 46–86). New York: Columbia University Press.

Wendt, A. (1992). Anarchy is what states make of it: The social construction of power politics. *International Organization, 46*(2), 391–426.

Wendt, A. (1999). *Social theory of international politics*. Cambridge: Cambridge University Press.

Wendt, A. (2003). Why a world state is inevitable. *European Journal of International Relations, 9*(4), 491–542.

Wiener, A. (2008). *The invisible constitution of politics. Contested norms and international encounters*. Cambridge: Cambridge University Press.

Wiener, A., & Puetter, U. (2009). The quality of norms is what actors make of it. *Journal of International Law and International Relations, 5*(1), 1–16.

CHAPTER 3

'Successful' Disintegration: The German Security Community

The reason for selecting the German Confederation as a case study of security community disintegration is based directly on Deutsch's seminal study on security communities, in which Karl Deutsch and his associates singled out the German Confederation as the only case under investigation in which a mature pluralistic security community failed:

> We have found only one case of a pluralistic security-community which failed in the sense that it was followed by actual warfare between the participants (…): this was the relationship of Austria and Prussia within the framework of the German Confederation since 1815. (Deutsch et al. 1957, p. 11)

The fact that Deutsch and his associates explicitly cite the German Confederation as an example of pluralistic security community disintegration makes it an obvious candidate for a case study in a book that deals with the disintegration of pluralistic security communities.

IR scholars have recently studied the German Confederation as a distinct regional order in world politics (see, e.g., Haldén 2011). The Confederation was formally established at the Congress of Vienna in 1815 with the task to preserve peace among the sovereign German states, in particular Prussia and Austria, and dissolved in 1866. As I show below, it can be argued that the German Confederation constituted a pluralistic security community in the sense that it established a political entity with common norms and institutions to resolve conflict peacefully accompanied by mutual trust and a collective identity.

The end of the Napoleonic Wars in 1815 left 'a strong and authentic desire for peace and order' (Albrecht-Carré 1968, p. 5). To be sure, peaceful change among the German states involved, by today's Western standards, extremely low levels of domestic political participation and societal integration. Still, strong elements of pluralism can be found in its founding treaties,[1] for example, the freedom of religion among the various Christian and Jewish denominations, the right to establish constitutional monarchies in the German states (in particular the Southern German states), as well as the relatively free movement of capital, labor, and goods. Also, the security community enjoyed high levels of intergovernmental exchange and personal contacts as well as, more broadly speaking, a sense of social belonging, historical attachment, and 'we-feeling', particularly among the various aristocratic elites in the German states that ensured peaceful interstate conduct.

In legal terms, the German Confederation was founded as 'a community of independent states' (Art. 2, Vienna Final Act). Hence, it can be argued that it also formally resembled what Karl Deutsch defined as a pluralistic security community (as opposed to an amalgamated security community). All member states enjoyed 'equal rights' even though smaller states and city-states shared their votes in the Confederal Assembly (Art. 3, German Federal Act). The institutional structure of the German Confederation was based on a formalized system of regular meetings among the member states to discuss issues of common concern and to resolve potential or actual disputes peacefully. The main institutional body was the Confederal Assembly presided by Austria. In the Confederal Assembly, 39 members shared 17 votes, which meant that the 11 largest member states were each granted one vote while the smaller member states combined their votes into six in a so-called curiat vote. For example, the free cities of Bremen, Hamburg, Lübeck, and Frankfurt together shared one single vote. The Confederal Assembly formed the principle decision-making body of the Confederation.

On decisions regarding the founding treaties of the German Confederation or related resolutions, the Confederal Assembly could be extended to the German Assembly. In this plenary meeting, each member state possessed at least one vote distributed according to the size of their territory. Prussia and Austria, for example, were each granted four votes. While decisions in the German Assembly could be made by two-third majority vote, the Confederal Assembly rested on the principle of consensus. In either case, the distribution of votes in the German Assembly and the consensus principle in the Confederal Assembly made it impossible even with the combined votes of the two largest member states to exercise veto power on any decisions. The institutional structure of the German Confederation reflected the social hierarchy among the German states with Prussia and Austria emerging as the dual core states of the security community.

THE NORMATIVE ORDER OF THE GERMAN SECURITY COMMUNITY

It can be argued that the German Confederation constituted a pluralistic security community in the sense that it established a political entity with common norms and institutions to resolve conflict peacefully as well as mutual trust and a collective identity. The members of the German Confederation conceived and imagined themselves as a security community based on the social and political interdependence of its rulers and elites, a shared Germanic history, language, and culture as well as a common Christian culture based on the medieval legacy of the 'Holy Roman Empire of the German Nation'. Its normative order explained below was linked to this collective identity and its associated common beliefs and meanings.

In particular, there was a strong antiliberal consensus among the members of the German Confederation. As Austrian foreign minister Metternich underlined, 'the only form of government which is suited to the concentration of peoples which makes up the Empire as a whole, is the monarchical form, because the cohesion of the parties would be absolutely impossible under a republican form of government' (cited in: Cronin 1999, p. 48). It can be said that the monarchs, governments, bureaucracy, and aristocratic elites of the member states of the German Confederation made up the norm regime that represented the aristocratic values, norms, and political ideology (the 'way of life') of the security community while simultaneously promoting and enforcing the normative order domestically as well as externally. In sum, the member states of the Confederation formed an intergovernmental ruling class of norm leaders eager to counter any perceived external, transnational, or domestic threat to that order. I will now explain the normative order of the German security community in more detail using the conceptual framework introduced in the previous chapter.

Norm of Common Values

The German security community was based on a consensus of mutual values. The primary values of the security community can be found in the German Federal Act of 1815 as well as the Final Act of the Viennese Ministerial Conferences of 1820 (Vienna Final Act) and were based on a shared belief in a monarchical political order and aristocratic rule. To be sure, there were significant differences between the free city-states of Bremen, Hamburg, Lübeck, and Frankfurt as well as the constitutional monarchies, which had formed in Southern Germany between 1818 and 1820, on the one hand, and the absolutist monarchies of Prussia, Austria, as well as in most of the rest of the German states, on the other hand. However, these variations have been frequently overestimated (see, e.g., Albrecht-Carré 1968, p. 6) because they represent norm conforming domestic derivatives of the same primary value: the monarchic principle. In fact, the Vienna Final Act guaranteed this diversity by explicitly stating that 'it remains up to the sovereign princes of the Confederal states to arrange this domestic matter of their states respecting both previously existing legal rights of the estates as well as current conditions' (Art. 55, Vienna Final Act). Among norm leaders, no one seriously questioned the legitimacy of monarchical rule and the principle of aristocratic solidarity as the primary value of the German security community enshrined in the Vienna Final Act: 'the entire authority of the state must, according to the basic concepts provided thereby, remain united within the head of state' (Art. 57, Vienna Final Act). Its members, thus, formed a common monarchic identity (Self) in opposition to liberalism and nationalism (Other) introduced by the revolutions in France and in USA. In sum, the primary value of the German security community included the conservative principles of monarchical legitimacy, monarchical authority, and monarchical solidarity.

Another primary value was based on a polycentric understanding of national sovereignty (Haldén 2011, p. 290). As I will show below, collective identification among the German states as members of the German Confederation must not be confused with German nationalism, which was championed by the norm challengers and developed only after 1830. Conversely, the norm leaders defined the 'German nation' not in terms of a unified territorial state but a diverse set of politically independent areas inhabiting a shared lingual and cultural space. In this sense, the German normative concept of 'polycentric sovereignty' differed sharply from the concept of the unitary nation-state associated with the French Revolution (Srbik 1925, p. 412; Haldén 2011, p. 290). The German 'federal national consciousness' (Langewiesche 1999) described a differentiated and multilevel phenomenon based on a parochial and decentralized German territory. A German collective identity thus coexisted with a set of diverse regional and local identities, for example, the Bavarians, the Rhinelanders, the Saxons, the Prussians, or the citizens of Hamburg. To this end, the German Confederation, a legal successor to the Holy Roman Empire of the German Nation, provided the political structure to integrate this particularistic national consciousness.

The secondary values of the German security community included religious beliefs, traditions, and different political and economic models. For example, in addition to Southern German constitutionalism mentioned above there were significant differences between Protestant and Catholic denominations, in particular among the two core states, the Protestant Prussia and the Catholic Austria. To incorporate these secondary values, the German security community included strong elements of pluralism in its founding documents. For example, the German Federal Act granted religious freedom to all Christian denominations and even the Jewish faith living within its boundaries (Art. 16, German Federal Act). Thus, historically and culturally constructed secondary values remained in conformity within the norm of common values. The concept of polycentric sovereignty further accommodated these differences. In this sense, the German security community served as a normative 'ribbon for the German states' (Deutsche Bundesversammlung 1823, 93) that combined unity of primary values with diversity of secondary values, which, as pointed out earlier, is a key component of the normative order of a security community.

Norm of Multilateral Practice

With the founding of the German Confederation, the peaceful resolution of conflicts of interest through institutionalized diplomacy and negotiation became the norm whereas war among its members became unthinkable and placed under a taboo. Article 11 of the German Federal Act as well as Article 19 of the Vienna Final Act define peaceful change as the core purpose and goal of the German Confederation, which echoes the Deutschian concept of security community (Deutsch et al. 1957, p. 124). According to the German Federal Act, the members of the German Confederation pledged 'not to make war among themselves upon any pre-tense or to follow up their contentions with force'. Any conflict between individual members was to be submitted to the Confederal Assembly to negotiate a peaceful settlement. If such a settlement failed, the matter was to be turned over to a court of arbitration at the confederate level. The judicial decision of the court was binding and had to be accepted immediately by all parties involved (Art. 11, German Federal Act). The Final Act of the Viennese Ministerial Conferences equally emphasizes the norm of peaceful conflict resolution by ensuring 'to obviate the necessity for self-defense' against individual member states, or in other words, to build trust among its participants. As a result, war as a means of interstate politics was ruled out within the territorial boundaries of the German Confederation, which, according to Karl W. Deutsch, is a key operational test to determine the existence of a pluralistic security community (Deutsch 1954, p. 41).

It should be noted that the Vienna Final Act did grant the Confederal Assembly the right to intervene in the internal affairs of its members 'whenever the domestic tranquility and security of the Confederation is threatened' (Art. 28). The formal threshold for such an intervention, however, was high and extremely limited in scope. First, it required a formal request by a member as well as a majority vote in the Confederal Assembly. Second, only in cases when the government of a member state was found to be 'notoriously unable' to restore domestic peace and was 'simultaneously prevented by circumstances from seeking the assistance of the Confederation' could the German Confederation act without the consent of a member state but, even in that case, the intervention 'should not be longer in duration than the government served by Confederate assistance deems necessary'. At first glance, this may seem to contradict the norm of peaceful conflict resolution. On the contrary, however, the right to intervene actually reinforced the normative order of the German Confederation because it was intended solely to prevent outside domination of the smaller German states by France or Britain. Internally, the political sovereignty of the member states of the German Confederation was guarded by Article 25 of the Vienna Final Act against any form of intervention, which clearly stated that 'maintaining domestic law and order in the Confederate states is up to the governments alone'.

In external matters, the Confederation spoke with a single voice. Even though members were allowed to form alliances with nonmembers those alliances were not to be directed against the Confederation or any individual member state. If the Confederation decided to collectively declare war against an outsider, members could not individually negotiate with the enemy nor could they conclude a separate armistice or peace settlement (Art. 11, German Federal Act). Conversely, any military attack on one member would be considered an attack on all. In such an event, defensive measures were to be taken immediately by the Confederal Assembly (Art. 36, Vienna Final Act). For this purpose, the member states agreed to form a permanent confederate military organization to guarantee the security and defense of the German Confederation (Art. 10, German Federal Act). This included the allocation of troops and money as well as the construction of fortresses under the direct control of the Confederal Assembly, which were subsequently built in Luxemburg, Mainz, Landau, Ulm, and Rastatt. During times of war, the Confederal Assembly was entitled to determine the supreme commander of the Confederate armed forces. All members were legally obliged to participate in acts of collective self-defense (Art. 45, Vienna Final Act). Thus, an attack on one member state was regarded as an attack against all since 'no single Confederal state can be injured from abroad without the injury affecting the whole of the Confederation simultaneously and in the same measure'. At the same time, it is important to underline that the Vienna Final Act emphasizes the defensive nature of the German Confederation and called on its members to practice self-restraint in their dealing with nonmembers (Art. 36, see also: Schroeder 1994, p. 604).[2]

Norm of Communication

The norm of communication involves not simply informing other members about imminent actions or policies but includes the permanent exchange of beliefs, interests, and perceptions. In Article 13, the Vienna Final Act requires its members to listen to and openly discuss opposing arguments in the Confederal Assembly. Moreover, Article 14 of the Vienna Final Act advises member states 'to settle the different opinions and motions with the greatest possible care and consideration for the circumstances and wishes of the individual members'. In line with the assumptions raised in the previous chapter, collective actions in the German security community thus clearly aimed not at coercion and instrumental calculations and incentives but at consensus building.

In practice, this meant that permanent consultation would need to take place in order to 'prevent (…) reciprocal complaints and unpleasant arguments of any kind'. Thus, the Vienna Final Act directed its members to inform and consult each other prior to domestic decision-making

(Art. 27 and Art. 28). The Carlsbad Decrees, issued at a later stage of security community development, further specified this norm of communication as the 'mutual responsibility' to preserve the values and the way of life of the German security community (Art. 5). Finally, the martial law (*Bundeskriegsverfassung*) of the German Confederation explicitly states that, in times of war, individual members should always take the interests of other members into account (Art. 7). In sum, the German norm of communication involved responsiveness in the sense of 'friendly consultation or diplomatic correspondence' and mutual 'care and consideration' among its members as well as required its members to 'inform the Confederal Assembly of the decrees and rules' taken within their jurisdiction (Art 6, Carlsbad Decrees).

Dysfunction

The period between 1815 and 1820 were the formative years of the German security community. The Vienna Final Treaty of 1820, the German Federal Act of 1815 as well as the Carlsbad Resolutions of 1819 built a permanent institutional order to promote and enforce the norms outlined above. The formation of a German security community was not uncontested. In 1817, for example, student fraternities in Thuringia burnt copies of the German Federal Act at the Wartburg festival protesting against the policies of Austria and Prussia. In 1819, the Carlsbad Resolutions firmly established a Central Investigation Agency to prosecute these 'demagogues'. As a result, political fraternities were outlawed, and the press as well as universities were closely monitored.

Despite these acts of domestic resistance and repression, they did not prevent the consolidation of the normative order of the German security community. At the same time, the Southern German states of Baden, Württemberg, and Bavaria as well as a few Northern states such as the Grand Duchy of Hesse, Saxe Weimar, and Nassau, became constitutional monarchies between 1815 and 1820. Their newly elected state parliaments were partially involved in political decision-making and even secured fiscal legislative powers. The Carlsbad Resolutions did not threaten this so-called Southern German liberalism (and its Northern variation) because the latter left the monarchical principle unquestioned. Moreover, constitutional systems were explicitly guaranteed and encouraged by Article 13 of the German Federal Act, which states that 'all Confederal states will be given a state-based constitution'. Of course, this was to be understood as constitutionalism controlled by the monarch.

To sum up, during the following decade from 1820 to 1830 the German Confederation manifested itself as a mature and stable pluralistic security community resting on the normative order outlined above. The security community did not experience any serious crises nor were there any noteworthy (let alone successful) attempts to challenge the established normative order. Instead, the so-called *Biedermeier* period introduced an era of political stability and peace among and within the German member states. Up to about 1830, a majority of German societies including the aristocracy, conservative public officials, as well as large parts of the emerging middle class supported or at least did not openly challenge the normative order of the German Confederation.

External Change: The July Revolution and the Introduction of New Ideas

In July 1830, however, a French coup overthrew the Bourbon monarchy and provoked mass uprisings in Belgium and in Poland against Dutch rule and Russian domination, respectively. In particular, the demand for Belgian independence significantly challenged the political and territorial settlement of 1815, which is why the British Prime Minister, the Duke of Wellington, referred to it as 'the most serious affair for Europe that could have arisen'. The supporters of this so-called July Revolution demanded liberal reforms and the end of monarchic rule. The July Revolution thus openly challenged the leading norms of aristocratic rule and monarchic regimes.

Events in France and Europe had significant repercussions in the German states. Here, the July revolution opened a window of opportunity for a group of norm challengers to enter center stage. These norm challengers—the so-called *Vormärz* (Pre-March)[3]—formed a social movement, which originally consisted predominantly of student fraternities, journalists, professors, lawyers, and politicians but would eventually include people from all ranks of German society. It basically picked up on the ideas of the French revolution and applied them to the German states. Their main political ideas thus included the formation of a political order built on the rule of the people, the ideas of individual freedom and equality, and, at a later stage, the idea of German nationalism.

The norm challengers of the *Vormärz*, however, differed on the concrete objectives and forms within which these ideas should take shape. On the one hand, there were factions, which consisted of predominantly merchants, bankers, factory owners, academia, and wealthy craftsmen, which will be summarized here as 'the Liberals'. These materially well-situated social groups benefitted from the normative status quo but were unsatisfied with their political exclusion and lack of participation. They were, thus, not interested in revolutionary change of the normative order but sought 'agreement' with the ruling aristocratic norm leaders that would ensure them equal political representation. On the other hand, there was a diffuse spectrum of radical liberals as well as the moderate and radical Left, which will be summarized here as 'the Democrats'. Democrats included small- and medium-sized craft producers and manufacturers, parts of the intelligentsia, junior craftsmen, day laborers, and factory workers. These groups became united behind the goal of a German nation-state based on the rule of the people and, in contrast to their Liberal companions, wanted to abolish the monarchy (Clark 2006, pp. 436–509).

The deep impact of the July revolution within the German Confederation was facilitated by the transnational migration of thousands of Polish revolutionaries, who became active in Liberal and Democratic social movements in various German states (Kolb 1975). Although less radical in scope and appearance than in neighboring France, the fall of 1830 witnessed a series of revolts and rebellions in the absolutist monarchies of the Electorate of Hesse, Brunswick, the Grand Duchy of Hesse, Saxony, Hannover, and parts of the Prussian Rhineland. In Brunswick and Saxony, the ruling elites were sacked. The Electorate of Hesse and Hannover adopted liberal constitutions. The most profound and lasting political change occurred in Baden where Liberals were now in control of both the state parliament and the government. In many German states, the newly established parliaments passed laws that introduced constitutional armies, parliamentary control of government ministers, legislative powers, unconditional freedom of the press, and the reduction of the fiscal period from six to two years.

These new ideas and their implementation obviously challenged the legitimacy of the Confederal Assembly and the treaties of the German Confederation. For example, in 1831 the parliament in Baden passed a law that abolished pre-censorship, which led to the publication of numerous opposition newspapers in Southern Baden, and a prominent member of the opposition, Karl Theodor Welcker held a motion in parliament arguing in favor of a German national parliament 'to promote German national unity as well as German free citizenship' (cited in: Winkler 2000, p. 81). The core states, represented by the Prussian foreign minister Ancillon and the Austrian chancellor Metternich, led the 'counterrevolution' in the Confederal Assembly and formed a confederate commission to settle the matter. Driven chiefly by Prussia and Austria, the commission ruled that the press law of Baden had violated confederate law and demanded its withdrawal. Yet, citing their political independence under the confederate treaties of 1815 and 1820, Baden and other German constitutional monarchies simply refused to follow the order.

This violation of community norms by the core states undermined symbolic interaction among member states. At the same time, the norm challengers of the *Vormärz* gained momentum at the Hambach festival in 1832. The Hambach festival gathered between 20,000 and 30,000 Liberals and Democrats to proclaim a free and united Germany. Even though there were still significant divisions within the movement itself—for example, Liberals wanted a class-based system of voting whereas Democrats wanted universal franchise—the Hambach festival presented a powerful event of symbolic interaction among norm challengers. Moreover, it directly challenged the norm leaders of the German aristocracy by demanding further political participation and the formation of a democratic German nation-state within a Europe of democratically elected states.

At the Hambach festival, one of the key organizers, the radical Democratic journalist Johann Georg Wirth, gave an enthusiastic speech in which he accused the norm leaders of the German security community of 'suppressing the liberty' of the German people whose 'blood (was being) sucked by 34 kings' as well as of curtailing the freedom and self-determination of many European nations such as Poland, Italy, Spain, and Hungary who had been 'robbed by traitorous families of aristocrats' (Wirth 1832, p. 42). Specifically, he singled out the unresponsive behavior of the two core states of the German security community, Prussia and Austria, as being responsible for this development:

> The cause of the unspeakable suffering of the European nations lies entirely in the fact that the dukes of Austria and the electors of Brandenburg (Prussia) have seized the greater part of Germany for themselves and (...) use their powers to suppress the freedom and the popular sovereignty of European nations, but also use their predominance over the smaller countries of Germany to make the powers of those countries serve the system of princely autocracy and despotic force.

According to Wirth, this 'dark alliance' of absolutist monarchies was holding back popular sovereignty, free trade, and equal distribution of wealth in Germany. On a broader scale, Wirth also linked the fate of Germany to freedom and prosperity in Europe:

> When, therefore, German money and German blood no longer submits to orders from the dukes of Austria and the electors of Brandenburg (Prussia), but rather to the decree of the people, then Poland, Hungary, and Italy will be free, because Russia will then have lapsed into powerlessness, and no other power will be around that could be used for crusades against the liberty of the peoples.

In sum, Wirth, in what turned out to become one of the most remembered speeches at the Hambach festival, called for the overthrow of monarchic rule in Germany as well as the democratization of Europe ending with the words: 'Hurrah! Three hurrahs to the united free states of Germany! Hurrah! Three hurrahs to the confederate republican Europe!' (cited in: Gruner 2012, p. 56).

There are, however, at least two reasons why the social movement at the Hambach festival did not turn into a revolutionary movement to immediately overthrow the normative order of the German Confederation. First of all, the Hambach festival did not produce any concrete resolutions to formulate the demands of the *Vormärz*. In other words, the movement, at this point, lacked the political will and the means to start a German revolution. Second, and already mentioned above, the division between Democrats and Liberals prevented the still heterogeneous movement from turning into a united opposition that was able to bring down the existing normative order of the security community. While Democrats at the Hambach festival viewed German national unity and individual political freedoms as inextricably linked, Liberals, like Karl von Rotteck of Baden, saw national unity as compromising demands for liberal rights as he claimed at a Liberal rally in Badenweiler: 'I want no other unity than together with freedom, and I rather want freedom without unity than unity without freedom' (cited in: Huber 1988, p. 133). Liberals feared that national unity could only be had under Prussian and/or Austrian dominance and given the core states' adherence to absolute monarchy that possibly meant to sacrifice liberal achievements in many German states at the altar of German nationalism. Liberals also feared the consequences of revolution, in general, pointing to the mass violence and anarchy that had taken place during the French revolution. The lasting impact of the Hambach festival remained, thus, largely symbolic, but no less forceful. For example, at Hambach, the black, red, and gold banner became the colors of the *Vormärz*, which would later become the primary symbol of the German revolution. The festival also produced a collective awareness among norm challengers and a reaffirmation of a shared political goal: normative change.

The core states, Prussia and Austria, as well as other key norm leaders, on the other hand, remained unresponsive. In 1832, they pushed through the Confederal Assembly the infamous Six Articles that would increase the repressive measures of the Carlsbad resolutions of 1819. The Six Articles as well as their extension (the so-called Ten Articles) included enhanced restrictions on the parliamentary right to petition, constraining the right of law schools to interpret constitutional law, further restrictions on free speech, on the right to assemble as well as on the formation of political associations, and the prosecution of so-called 'demagogues' of the *Vormärz* movement.

Specifically, the Six Articles called for the prohibition to distribute foreign-printed newspapers, writings, and pamphlets with political content and introduced general press censorships. It also outlawed the formation of any political association as well as the organization of popular assemblies and festivals 'whose time and place were previously neither customary nor permitted' (Art. 3, Ten Articles). This latter provision was intended to prevent another Hambach festival, which had been officially organized as a 'cultural event'. But even approved events and festivals were not allowed to include political speeches. In addition, the symbols of the *Vormärz* were declared illegal such as 'insignias on ribbons, rosettes (…) the unauthorized putting up of banners and flags, the erection of liberty trees and similar rebellious symbols' in order to erect firewalls against symbolic interaction and the introduction of new ideas by the norm challengers. Any violations of these rules were to be 'strictly (and) forcefully punished' (Art. 4, Ten Articles). Police surveillance of citizens as well as 'suspicious foreign arrivals' (this referred to Polish revolutionary migrants) was also increased. Importantly, all of these repressive measures were based on the norm of common values from which the norm leaders German security community claimed both the urgency as well as the legitimacy of their actions:

> Since, according to Article 57 of the Vienna Final Act, the whole authority of the state must remain united in the head of state, and (since) the sovereign can be required to permit the constitutionally guaranteed assembly of

the estates of the land to participate only in the exercise of certain rights, a German sovereign is also, as a member of the Confederation, not only justified in dismissing a petition of the estates contradictory hereunto, but the obligation toward such a dismissal results from the (very) purpose of the Confederation (Art 1, Six Articles).

In addition, the norm leaders engaged in ritualized symbolic interaction. For this purpose, they reaffirmed the norms of multilateral behavior and communication by assuring each other 'prompt military assistance on demand', to defend 'the *true meaning* of the German Federal Act (...) and the Vienna Final Act' (emphasis added, Art. 9, Ten Articles) against the norm challengers, and to notify and consult with each other about any policy measures taken or implemented in the member states. To sum up, at first glance the rise of the norm challengers appeared to further consolidate the normative order of the security community with its members rallying behind Prussia and Austria against a common Other that threatened to undermine the normative order of the security community.

However, these repressive measures simultaneously undermined symbolic interaction among norm leaders. Member states that had previously introduced constitutional monarchy, particularly in Southern Germany, were irritated as these measures clearly violated their political sovereignty in domestic affairs. For example, Article 3 of the Six Articles (which was intended to prevent the undermining of the Confederate normative order by liberal domestic lawmakers) specifically stated that the norms and laws of the German security community, represented by the Confederal Assembly, superseded the norms and laws of the individual member states: 'Domestic legislation of the German Confederal States may neither place any kind of obstacle before the aims of the Confederation' (Art. 3, Six Articles). This involved, for example, the sole right of the monarch to impose taxes.

From this perspective, the Six Articles represented a confederate intervention led by the absolutist member states (especially Austria and Prussia) into the domestic affairs of constitutional member states that was not in line with the norm of multilateral practice (which protects member-state sovereignty) revealing a further divide among norm leaders. In this sense, the Six Articles did not merely erect firewalls to prevent the spread of new ideas but, in fact, partially redefined the meaning of community norms. In particular, the Southern member states of Baden and Württemberg, which had already implemented liberal laws at this point, regarded the Six Articles as a direct threat to their political independence protected under the normative order of the German security community. Furthermore, the Six Articles even triggered an outside diplomatic intervention by Great Britain (whose king was a member of the German Confederation due to a personal union with Hannover) and France. In the end, these outside diplomatic interventions eventually persuaded Prussia and Austria to seek a compromise with the German constitutional states by insisting only on partial implementation of the Six Articles.

From this perspective, the Six Articles both strengthened and weakened the normative order of the German security community. On the one hand, by emphasizing the norms of common values, multilateral practice, and communication, the norm leaders were able to reassure each other of their shared norms and collective identity through ritualized symbolic interaction, which contributed to trust building. On the other hand, by disregarding the sovereignty of smaller member states, the core states, openly violated the norm of multilateral practice and thus disrupted symbolic interaction among norm leaders. Facilitated by an external 'shock' (the July Revolution in France) that spilled over into the German states, a dysfunctional security community struggled over the meaning of the norm of multilateral practice and over the meaning of the norm common values. On the one hand, the absolutist core states and their supporters viewed liberal reforms in the constitutional member states as a violation of community norms because such reforms now seriously undermined the political order in their own respective domestic spheres. On the other hand, the constitutional monarchies, in turn, interpreted the ensuing repressive measures by the absolutist monarchies as undermining their right to independently determine their own domestic affairs. In the end, the constitutional monarchies carried the day because they proved capable to check the norm violation against member-state sovereignty by the core states. As a result, the normative order of the security community was sustained.

It can be argued that the crisis following the July Revolution of 1830 suggests a case of the first stage of security community disintegration. During this stage of dysfunction, we expect to witness major changes in the external environment that increase the integration load on community members. In this case, there was an outside event (July revolution in France), which, in turn, triggered a domestic social movement seeking liberal–democratic reform and national unity. This introduction of new ideas or of alternative 'norm emergence' (Finnemore and Sikkink 1998) peaked in a crisis over the norms of common values and multilateral practices and a disruption of symbolic interaction among norm leaders. In contrast to their constitutional members, the absolutist monarchies viewed the liberal–nationalist reform movement as an outside threat to the security community (inspired by France and Poland). This perception, however, was not shared by the constitutional German monarchies most of which had already established constitutional rule in their respective domestic territories before 1830 and thus did not feel threatened by more liberal reform in the same way as the absolutist monarchies of Prussia, Austria, and elsewhere. Despite its collective awareness and symbolic interaction, the social movement of the *Vormärz*, at this point, remained too divided and regionally dispersed to turn into the 'general transformational force' that Austrian foreign minister Metternich and other norm leaders feared. At that point, the norm challengers of the *Vormärz* still stood as a marginalized political minority.

In sum, diverging interpretations of the meaning of common values (the preservation of the monarchic principle) and practices (confederate intervention into the domestic affairs of member states) led to different perceptions, a disruption of symbolic interaction and, to diverging understandings of the meaning of security community: for Prussia, Austria, and a few other absolutist member states the German Confederation served as a bulwark against liberal–democratic infiltrations and thus stabilized the existing normative order and collective identity. For Baden and other smaller constitutional member states the German Confederation guarded their political independence and was essentially open to various forms of domestic governance (albeit under monarchic rule). To be sure, this contestation and divergence of the normative meaning of the German security community, in general, and of the norm of common values and multilateral practice, in particular, appeared only in one isolated case that was quickly resolved because the norm violations were met by immediate and resolute resistance. However, as I will illustrate with the example of the Hannover crisis below, normative conflict over the norms of common values and multilateral practice soon broke out again which suggests that the members of the German Confederation remained locked in a state of dysfunctional security community at least until 1840.

Social and Internal Change I: The Hannover Crisis

Political upheavals and calls for liberal reform in 1830 had taken place in many absolutist monarchies of the German Confederation. In 1833, Hannover adopted a new constitution, which severely limited the powers of King Wilhelm IV (who was simultaneously the King of England) and transformed the absolutist monarchy into a constitutional monarchy. This development had been forced onto Hannover after the crushing of the so-called Göttingen Revolution, which had become the center of the liberal–democratic reform movement. What is more, peasants demanded land reform and the middle class wanted more political participation. In the heated atmosphere of the July revolution, the Hannover Constitution of 1833 thus served as a compromise that introduced political participation and fiscal powers for the state parliament.

The new constitution, however, lasted only a few years. In 1837, the personal union between the kingdom of Hannover and England was dissolved after the death of Wilhelm IV who had been unable to produce a successor. In England, the niece of Wilhelm IV, Victoria, ascended the throne while in Hannover the Duke of Cumberland succeeded Wilhelm IV, now calling himself Ernst August I. Ernst August had earlier voiced sharp protest against the Hannover Constitution when it was in passed in 1833 and, upon his accession to the throne, he made it immediately clear that he would not recognize any limits to his monarchical powers and quickly abolished the Hannover Constitution.

Unsurprisingly, this act sparked lively protest among members of the opposition. The city of Göttingen, once again, became the center of gravity for the norm challengers. A group of renowned and well-known university professors, one of whom had drafted the Constitution of 1833, issued a note of protest. This group of academics known as the 'Göttingen Seven' (although certainly no revolutionaries) turned into a symbol of the liberal–democratic opposition movement in Hannover. Thus, when Ernst August I removed the Göttingen professors from university and sent two of them into exile, a wave of solidarity surged across the kingdom and soon also spilled over into other German states.

The state parliament of Hannover, assisted by the city of Osnabrück and other German constitutional monarchies filed an appeal to the Confederal Assembly on the grounds that the unilateral abolition of the Hannover Constitution by Ernst August I had violated member-state sovereignty under the Vienna Final Treaty. The Treaty holds that any existing state constitution can only be changed or abolished through a 'constitutional process'. In the case of Hannover, the abolition of the constitutional monarchy should thus have involved, at the very least, the consent by the (elected) state legislature.

Given the formal request by the state parliament of Hannover to intervene, most member states expected the Confederal Assembly to sanction the rather obvious norm violation by Ernst August. However, Prussia and Austria were sympathetic to the reestablishment of an absolutist monarchy and fearful of setting a precedent. When the core states thus attempted to stall the ensuing consultation in the Confederal Assembly—an open violation of the norm of communication—most member states rejected to postpone the matter on the grounds that such inaction would ultimately undermine and potentially '*destroy the level of trust* in handling the legal situation within the Confederation' (emphasis added, cited in: Gruner 2012, p. 61).

A majority of member states did not share Prussia's and Austria's concerns but argued instead that inaction on behalf of the Confederal Assembly would invite more 'radical forces' to violently overturn existing constitutions in the other German states. It was only due to the clever tactical maneuvering by Metternich that the Prussian–Austrian coalition managed to organize a majority in the Confederal Assembly in 1840 that ruled the abolition of the 1833 Hannover Constitution to be consistent with the treaties of the German Confederation. For example, Metternich exploited fears among the smaller German states of an alleged French invasion. These fears were not ungrounded. After France had been humiliated during the Near East crisis of 1839/40, nationalist sentiment in Paris diverted toward regaining the German territories left of the Rhine River, which had been previously occupied by Napoleon Bonaparte. As a result, Metternich was able to bring a majority of member states behind his position.

In the end, the crisis over the Hannover Constitution was resolved at high political costs. The unwillingness of the Confederal Assembly to intervene in what most members viewed as a clear violation of the German Federal Act as well as the disregard for the norm of communication by the core states bolstered the perception, especially among smaller member states, that the Confederation had turned into a power tool that seemed to primarily serve the interests of the core states. Consequently, this led to a weakening of symbolic interaction and institutional failure since the Confederal Assembly had acted against the normative order of the German security community. Moreover, the crisis signaled to the *Vormärz* movement that the German Confederation in its current shape would never accommodate or address their demands for liberal–national reform within the existing normative framework. As a result, the disaggregated liberal–nationalist opposition began to transform into a pan-German progressive social movement seeking normative change.

The case of institutional failure during the Hannover constitutional crisis arguably represented a tipping point in the gradual degeneration of community norms. In the eyes of many member states, the obvious norm violation by Ernst August I had gone through unpunished. Moreover, the core states had placed their individual interest in preventing the spread of domestic liberal–democratic reform above the collective normative order of the security community. Instead of reiterating the norm of 'thick' communication within the German Confederation and thus showing self-restraint and responsiveness, Prussia and Austria had actively undermined the process of norm enforcement. Underlying this development were again contested meanings of common values within the context of security community. While the core states viewed the Confederation as a safeguard against liberal–nationalist reform, many smaller states expected the German Confederation to protect their political independence and self-determination. Such diverging meanings had already led to the crisis over the Baden press law and firmly kept the security community in a dysfunctional state. However, the outcome of the crisis over the Hannover Constitution was different from the previous one in a number of ways.

While in the previous case the norm violation was punished and the community norms eventually enforced by norm leaders, the latter case marks a situation in which the norm violators (Ernst August I aided by Austria and Prussia) were able to get away with it. This development can thus be said to have undermined the level of trust among community members as it left many German states questioning the meaning of the security community as an institution based on a shared normative order. A normative precedent had occurred that could be exploited by other norm violators in the subsequent years.

What is more, the inaction and unresponsiveness of norm leaders (in particular the core states) arguably contributed to the mobilization and organization of norm challengers within the member states. Up to this point, the *Vormärz* movement had been a rather loose and sparse collection of different factions with diverging goals. Since their demands and protests were not nearly as radical as in neighboring France and Poland, their needs and requests could have been easily accommodated by the norm regime within the framework of the German Confederation. Yet, most norm leaders remained unresponsive to these needs. Instead, the unwillingness of the Confederal Assembly to punish a norm violation (that was also directed against the *Vormärz* movement) on perfectly legal grounds send a clear signal to the norm challengers that their cause could not be achieved within the established normative order of the security community but only by overcoming it.

In sum, the Hannover constitutional crisis arguably marks the transition from the dysfunctional stage of the security community to a period of decline. Given the increased cohesion and mobilization of the norm challengers of the *Vormärz*, a cascade of norm violations now set in motion, which the norm leaders of the security community were unable to contain.

Decline

The political upheavals of the early 1830s, especially the Hambach festival of 1832, had motivated norm leaders to increase political repression in the German security community in order to protect the established normative order. As Metternich put it bluntly: 'We will come to strike in Germany!' (cited in: Siemann 1995, p. 349). The Confederal Assembly became the institutional locus for co-ordinating and erecting these firewalls against the spread of liberal ideas. In particular, the core states and other member states co-operated closely in intergovernmental policing and intelligence sharing. The result was a series of Confederal resolutions that introduced even stricter press censorship in the member states, the complete outlawing of any political parties and associations (including their symbols) as well as repressive measures directed against individual members of parliament at the domestic level.

Building Up Firewalls: The Sixty Articles

Specifically, university students were no longer allowed to form student unions and fraternities that were involved in political activities of any kind. If a student was found guilty, he usually faced expulsion from university as well as an occupational ban in all German member states. The universities were further obliged to inform universities in other member states about any misdemeanors (Verordnung des Kultusministeriums des Königreichs Sachsen 1834). Journeymen could no longer move freely from member state to member state and were barred from traveling to Switzerland where many political activists of the *Vormärz* had fled in order to avoid repressive measures (Verordnung des Königs von Sachsen 1835). Journeymen who participated in political associations or meetings had their travel documents taken away and equally faced an occupational ban if not imprisonment (Verordnung des Königs von Sachsen 1840).

These already harsh political measures were further intensified by a secret protocol (the so-called Sixty Articles) at the Vienna Ministerial Conferences of 1834. These measures were clearly directed to prevent the further spread of liberal ideas since students and journeymen (because of their high level of mobility) had been the primary distributor of these ideas in the German states.

To implement and execute these measures, the Central Investigation Agency (*Zentraluntersuchungsbehörde*) in Frankfurt examined 'the circumstances and extent of the conspiracy directed against the existence of the Confederation and against the (monarchical) order in Germany' (cited in: Siemann 1995, p. 351). The norm leaders legally justified these acts by citing Article 28 of the Final Act of the Viennese Ministerial Conferences, which allowed for collective intervention in the internal affairs of member states under certain conditions and were thus officially declared in line with the norm of multilateral practice even though there had been no formal request by member states.[4]

The newly founded *Zentraluntersuchungsbehörde* was not a supranational institution but served primarily the purpose of gathering information about the *Vormärz* movement and of distributing this information to local governmental agencies in the member states, who could then arrest and prosecute alleged norm challengers. In addition, the Agency collected data about any ongoing and related prosecution or court trials in the member states, which established a central directory of the *Vormärz* norm challengers administered by the Confederal Assembly. Hence, the Central Investigation Agency became an important structural barrier to the spread of liberal ideas. At the same time, the Agency's modus operandi strengthened the norm of communication by increasing and intensifying the level of consultation and information among security community members.

Yet, the Conference of 1834 also revealed norm divergence among members of the German Confederation, in general, and the core states, in particular. Prussia and Austria had agreed in principle that the Sixty Articles were necessary to protect the normative order of the German security community. However, given their experience with the Six Articles, Prussia and all other member states, except for Hessia-Darmstadt, only reluctantly gave in to the proposal introduced by the Austrian Prime Minister Metternich. In particular, the constitutional monarchies in Southern Germany were alarmed citing Article 13 of the German Federal Act as well as Article 54 of the Final Act, which not only guaranteed the formation of state assemblies but, in fact, even committed its members to implement constitutions in all of the German states:

> There shall be in all Confederal states a constitutionally guaranteed assembly of the estates of the land, the Confederal Assembly has to see to it that this regulation shall not remain unfulfilled in any Confederal state.

By contrast, at the Vienna Ministerial Conferences of 1834, Austria effectively redefined the meaning of the monarchic principle enshrined in Article 54 of the Final Act of 1820 to be limited to an absolutist monarchy in the German states (outlawing any form of constitutional rule) and even threatened to roll back constitutional developments that had already occurred:

> Each same contradictory claim aimed at a separation of powers is incompatible with the constitutional law of the united States (sic) in the German Confederation and cannot be used in any German constitution (cited in: J. Müller 2006, p. 20).

The Sixty articles thus redefined the norm of common values, which explicitly prescribed the inclusion of absolutist *as well as* constitutional adaptations of the monarchic principle in the German states.

Social and Internal Change II: Prussian Reform

The Prussian norm leaders, although sharing Austria's concerns in principle, gradually appeared more open to domestic liberalization and political reform. Prussian responsiveness toward the ideas of the norm challengers, in part, resulted from economic factors.

In contrast to Austrian feudalism and protectionism, the Prussian economic system had become more industrialized after 1830 and thus opened to the idea of trading with the other German states. The territorial division of the Prussian state, however, hindered its drive toward further economic integration. Internal trade had to pass through foreign territory, thus, facing trade barriers and tariffs. The Prussian norm leaders thus held a keen interest in lowering if not erasing these trade barriers between its Eastern mainland (with its industrial centers in Berlin and Silesia), on the one hand, and its Western territories in the industrialized Rhineland, on the other hand. Prussia eventually achieved this objective with the establishment of the German Customs Union (*Zollverein*) in 1834. The German Customs Union consisted of 18 German states, including Prussia, Bavaria, Wurttemberg, Saxony, Hessia-Darmstadt, and Thuringia. Austria did not join the Union mostly for economic reasons. Its mix of low economic development and highly protectionist markets was simply incompatible with the free trade policies of the German Customs Union.

However, one should be careful not to misread the establishment of a trade union as a sign of separation or even a precursor to a German nation-state (see, e.g., Tilly 1990). The German Customs Union was fully embedded into the normative order of the German Confederation. It was not directed against or sought to exclude any member state. In principle, any German state was free to join the agreement (as explained above, Austria did not join for purely economic reasons). In fact, the Customs Union promoted one of the central goals of the German Federal Act, namely to create a single German market to buttress German producers against British trade. In Article 19, the members of the German Confederation had committed each other to hold negotiations regarding the harmonization of trade, commerce, and river navigation. Early trade agreements had been subsequently concluded in 1828 between Bavaria and Württemberg as well as Prussia and Hessia-Darmstadt, respectively. A third customs union was later established by Hannover. Thus, the establishment of the German Customs Union did not represent an undermining of the existing normative order but, instead, constituted the logical next step toward further economic integration among the German states *within* the normative order of the Confederation. However, as we shall see below, the norm challengers of the *Vormärz*, including liberal entrepreneurs and traders in the Rhineland and elsewhere, accused the norm leaders of the German security community of stalling trade liberalization and thus favored a transformation of the Customs Union into a political union *outside* the normative order of the German Confederation. As one of the Union's most vivid proponents, the economist Friedrich List (1841, p. 8), argued:

> The Customs Union shall connect the Germans economically and materially as one nation; it is to forcefully represent the nation as a whole abroad by maintaining its external overall interests as well as by safekeeping its internal total productive forces and strengthen the material force of the nation; it shall arouse and raise the national consciousness by merging the individual provincial interests to form a national interest; *it shall have not only the present but also the future of the nation in mind* (emphasis added).

By 1840, these arguments by the norm challengers appeared to be confirmed by the unprecedented shift in Prussia's policies. The accession of Frederic Wilhelm IV to the Prussian throne inspired many hopes and expectations among the members of the *Vormärz*. For example, the Prussian king reinstated Ernst Moritz Arndt, who had lost his position due to the Carlsbad decrees, as professor in Bonn and appointed three members of the 'Göttingen Seven' as members of the Prussian Academy of Sciences. In 1847, Frederic Wilhelm convened a Prussian National Assembly consisting of the nobility, great landowners, and urban industrials.

Yet, while Frederic Wilhelm IV put an end to the overly repressive policies of his predecessor, he was certainly not a champion of liberal–democratic reform. In a letter to Theodor von Schön, the district chief of West and East Prussia, he dismissed any hopes for the establishment of a constitutional monarchy in Prussia: 'I feel totally by grace of God and, with His help, will feel that way until the end' (cited in: Winkler 2000, p. 86). The Prussian king's commitment to preserve the absolute monarchy in Prussia was reemphasized in his opening speech in front of the members of the newly convened National Assembly in Berlin:

> It urges me to state a solemn declaration: that no power on earth is ever to succeed to move me to change the natural relationship between prince and people (…) into a conventional, constitutional relationship; and that I will not admit now nor ever that a written document will intrude between our Lord in heaven and this country as a second providence to rule us with its paragraphs and to replace the old, sacred loyalty (Friedrich Wilhelm IV 1848a).

In this speech, he went even further by denying any political debates to take place in the Prussian parliament, which implied that he would not let opposing viewpoints from this institution interfere with his policies:

> But this is not your job: to represent (…) opinions. This is totally un-German and, on top of that, completely impractical (…) because it leads necessarily to unsolvable conflicts with the crown, which is to rule according to the law of God and of the country and according to its own definition, but (…) must not govern according to the will of majorities (…).

Critically, it can be seen how, by declaring parliamentary debates 'un-German', he discursively separates the ideas of the German *Vormärz* from the collective identity of the German security community.

Even though Frederic Wilhelm IV dashed any hopes for substantial liberal–democratic reform in Prussia, he did embrace German national sentiment. The Prussian king was not only a conservative but also admired Romanticism and its glorification of the former Holy Roman Empire. His policies thus emphasized the national prose and symbolism of the Holy Roman Empire of the German Nation, which materialized, for example, in the completion of the medieval Cologne cathedral. The rise of national symbols was not confined to Prussia alone. In many German member states, the liberal bourgeoisie initiated (and often paid for) the erection of national monuments to visualize and materialize hopes and expectations of German national unity. This involved statues of 'German heroes' such as Johannes Gutenberg in Mainz, Friedrich Schiller in Stuttgart, Albrecht Dürer in Nuremberg, and Johann Wolfgang von Goethe in Frankfurt. These national symbols, placed prominently in the public sphere, constituted a constant public reminder for the need and inevitability of German unification, which undermined the normative concept of polycentric sovereignty. From this perspective, the Prussian core state introduced a new kind of symbolism that interrupted symbolic interaction within the German security community by attaching new meaning (nationalism) to the norm of common values.

Prussian liberalism was top-down and served entirely the interest of the Prussian norm leaders. It mainly focused on economic liberalization and the transformation of society to adapt to the processes of industrialization while exploiting national symbolism for its own purposes. In this sense, Prussian reform had little to do with the introduction of individual rights and popular suffrage as partially implemented, for example, in Baden and elsewhere.

Prussia's rhetoric and symbolism of national sentiment, however, produced unintended consequences. To be sure, Frederic Wilhelm IV romanticized national sentiment that glorified German history was not a liberal one based on a community of the German people but a conservative one based on a community of aristocratic rulers. While Prussia's understanding of national unity were thus clearly not intended to abolish the existing normative order of the German Confederation, it nevertheless ran contrary to Austrian views that emphasized the discouragement of any form of nationalism because the latter could easily destabilize the multiethnic Habsburg Empire.

In sum, Prussia's reforms had significant implications for the German Confederation, in general, and the relationship between the two core states, in particular. The Prussian core state appeared increasingly unwilling to support Austria's uncompromisingly repressive course and instead opted for reforming the Confederal Assembly in order to do 'something positive, resolute and decisive, which will raise and calm the national feeling' (cited in: J. Müller 2006, p. 28). In 1842, Prussia finally had its way. Due to a lack of consensus between the core states, the Confederal Assembly decided to suspend the Central Investigation Agency indefinitely. This institutional failure subsequently undermined and weakened structural barriers and firewalls erected by norm leaders. Clearly, Prussia had no intention to join the camp of the *Vormärz* but, in contrast to Austria, Prussian norm leaders increasingly realized the need to show more responsiveness and potentially adapt the normative order to the changing political times. In short, both core states appeared determined to preserve the conservative normative order. Yet, while Austria insisted on the normative status quo, Prussia was open to cautious reform.

The Rise of Norm Challengers

As a result of institutional paralysis and increasing norm divergence between the core states, a vicious circle unfolded that the norm leaders of the German Confederation found hard to escape. Norm divergence among the core states increasingly paralyzed decision-making in the Confederal Assembly because the smaller German states, who had previously followed the united Austrian–Prussian lead were now undecided with which core state they should align themselves with on a given issue. The resulting institutional failure and lack of symbolic interaction led to a further degeneration of the normative order because, with the Confederal Assembly incapable of acting, the norm regime of the German security community proved equally incapable to enforce and promote its normative order. The suspension of the Central Investigation Agency is just one case in point.

With the structural barriers and firewalls down, the spread of liberal ideas could no longer be contained. The *Vormärz*, in turn, expanded its associations and attracted more followers and resources. The growth and expansion of the norm challengers made it even more difficult for norm leaders to punish norm violations through repressive measures because that would have required an apparatus and resources that one of the core states no longer provided (J. Müller 2006, p. 27). The rise of the norm challengers subsequently reinforced norm divergence among the core states leading to more institutional failure and disruption of symbolic interaction.

After 1840, the inability of the norm regime to enforce the normative order of the German Confederation became visible in a series of unpunished norm violations. In the absence of operational structural barriers and firewalls, the *Vormärz* began to openly challenge norm leaders by publishing politicalpamphlets, newspaper articles, and other writings that had been previously declared illegal under the Six Articles. For example, in September 1843, the *Düsseldorfer Zeitung* published an article calling for a unification of Germany while directly criticizing the norm leaders of the German security community. It is worth citing this article at length because it demonstrates that the norm challengers did not argue in favor of a liberal and unified Germany solely on political grounds but, as pointed out above, also invoked economic arguments to persuade the wider public.

> (M)uch worse than the current waste of expenditure is the way that, among 38 different states, just as many special interests are at work disadvantaging and quashing daily commerce down to the last detail. (...) what help is it if the German Federal Act grants the freedom to move from one German state into another if this other state sternly turns away the poor emigrant. (...) No, Germany's unity is no utopian dream; it must be achieved just as surely as it is impossible, over the long run, to omit something felt to be necessary, and the idea itself will come all the closer to realization, the more unbearable it becomes to compare the condition in which one [actually] lives with that magnificent (condition) in which one could live. (...) (I)f we ask why German unity did not come about a long time ago, we unfortunately keep coming back to the Congress of Vienna; (...) to the weak German statesmen and, (...) to a mass of special interests who would rather aggrandize themselves on a small scale than subordinate themselves and assume their natural place in a larger whole. (Düsseldorfer Zeitung 1843)

A similar article was published in the *Deutsche Zeitung* in October 1847:

> Of the Confederal Assembly, as it exists at present, nothing fruitful is expected for the promotion of the national concern. She has left her task—as outlined in the German Federal Act: to introduce constitutions in the German states, to promote free trade and commerce, and to allow the free use of the press—unsolved. By contrast, the press is placed under censorship, the negotiations of the Confederal Assembly are befogged (...) which lays obstacle in the way of any free development. (Deutsche Zeitung 1847)

The cascade of norm violations continued in 1842 when the German Confederation departed its military presence from the free city of Frankfurt, thus removing yet another structural barrier against the norm challengers. Earlier in 1833, a student rebellion, mainly fraternities from nearby Heidelberg and Würzburg, had led an attack on two police stations in Frankfurt with the aim to capture the treasury of the German Confederation as well as to take members of the Confederal Assembly as prisoners. The rebellion had been intended to set off a national uprising across the German states. The coup was uncovered, however, and the Confederal Assembly agreed to send troops to Frankfurt (the capital of the German Confederation) in order to prevent another attack against the Confederation. This military force in the Confederal capital consisted of 2500 Austrian and Prussian troops. Following the accession of Frederic Wilhelm IV to the Prussian throne, however, Prussia withdrew its troops and the occupation of Frankfurt ended abruptly. The removal of the Confederate army from the capital of the German Confederation not only eliminated a structural barrier but also carried enormous symbolic weight. The Frankfurt student rebellion had been a key event that had united the norm challengers of the *Vormärz*. Moreover, it constituted a threat to the norm leaders of the security community because the rebellion had directly challenged the norms and institutions of the German Confederation, not just a member-state government. Hence, the retreat of the Confederate armed forces from Frankfurt, the seat of the Confederal Assembly, significantly boosted the symbolic standing and legitimacy of the *Vormärz*.

Another case unfolded in Southern Germany. In 1844 the state parliament in Baden declared parts of the Final Act of the Viennese Ministerial Conferences unconstitutional. The declaration had been provoked by a long-standing divide between a liberal–democratic majority in the elected Second Assembly of the Baden parliament and the conservative–reactionary dominance within the appointed Baden government. The main reason for triggering this norm violation, however, was the unveiling of the secret protocols of the Carlsbad conference of 1819 as well as the secret Sixty Articles of 1834 by Carl Theodor Welcker, a member of the Second Assembly. The secret protocols revealed to the general public the entire fierceness of the repressive measures, which, as pointed out above, included a redefinition of community norms. As Welcker put it, it resembled 'the boldest attack on the German constitution, which the absolutist pork-barrel politics has ever dared' (Treitschke 1911, pp. 381–2). While the decision by the state parliament in Baden to declare parts of the Final

Act of the Viennese Ministerial Conferences unconstitutional was no less daring, the Confederal Assembly, however, did nothing to sanction the Baden provocation. As in the two previous cases, Prussian opposition prevented punitive measures by the Confederal Assembly against this norm violation (J. Müller 2006, p. 27).

These are just a few episodes in a cascade of norm violations that occurred within a very short period of time during the first half of the 1840s. Arguably, it injected the security community with a new dynamic. The increasing thrust and scope of norm violations by norm challengers combined with the institutional failure of the Confederal Assembly and norm leaders to punish these norm violations had started to seriously undermine the normative order of the security community (especially the norm of communication). This, in turn, served as a catalyst to strengthen the persuasiveness and legitimacy of the norm challengers of the *Vormärz* movement. The ensuing process of norm degeneration eventually culminated in the German revolution of 1848–1849, which marked the closest thing to a 'showdown' between norm challengers and norm leaders of the German security community. As will be argued below, it can be said that the security community now moved from a stage of decline to a stage of denial.

Denial

By the late 1840s, the norm challengers underwent a significant transformation in structure and scope. The *Vormärz* had previously remained, by and large, an urban phenomenon. Yet by the mid-nineteenth century, the German states (despite the growing influence of the industrialization) still consisted of predominantly agrarian societies with more than 55% of the population remaining employed in agriculture. Thus, a majority of the German people continued to live and work in rural areas and could thus hardly identify with the predominantly urban norm challengers (Hein 2007, p. 26). However, within almost two decades (between 1830 and 1848) the *Vormärz* recruited followers from all levels of society including peasants, day laborers, servants, craftsmen, industrial workers, and railroaders in what amounted to a 'fundamental politicization of society' (Siemann 1995) and the spread of liberal ideas.

This strengthening of the norm challengers was facilitated due to the spread of nonpolitical associations, which promoted the emergence of a nascent pan-German civic society, predominantly in the cultural and social sphere but also in areas of economic innovation. The most successful of these pan-German associations, the Central March Association (*Zentralmärzverein*), counted 500,000 members and over 900 local branch offices. These associations, though predominantly founded and run by the political groups of the *Vormärz*, were not strictly political in nature (which would have raised suspicion among norm leaders). Throughout the 1830s and thereafter, they nevertheless led to a camouflaged diffusion of liberal–democratic ideas under the banner of sociocultural exchange. For example, political slogans and flyers would be distributed in gymnastic associations and its members would subsequently practice joint military exercises and the art of self-defense in order to form militias. Cultural associations would organize banquets and invite political activists of the *Vormärz* to help them get in touch with ordinary people. Even the opening ceremony of a new factory or railway track turned into a political event symbolizing the achievements and strengthening of the liberal–democratic social movement (Hein 2007, p. 55). In academia, the annual conventions of the German philologists turned into quasi-parliaments where the future of the German nation-state was debated. In this environment, the members of the *Vormärz*, despite all their differences, began to define themselves not as a particular political party but as a cross-class social movement that sought to represent German society as a whole. In this sense, its cultural, academic, economic, and social associations served as important community-building institutions and symbolic interaction among the norm challengers of the *Vormärz*.

To be fair, not everyone who participated in this kind of symbolic interaction and institution-building really understood the political goals of the norm challengers. For example, many peasants protesting in front of town halls and royal mansions thought that 'freedom of the press' meant the freedom to 'press' their manorial lords for more money (J. Müller 2006, p. 29). The increasing number of grassroots followers nevertheless created a window of opportunity for the norm challengers to strategically construct a counter-narrative to the established normative order outside plenary halls. As one of the leaders of the moderate liberal opposition in the state parliament of Baden, Karl Mathy, pointed out: '(It is) time to try some fierceness but this fierceness must not be confined to plenary hall alone' (cited in: Hein 2007, p. 12). In other words, reformist Liberal groups now challenged the norm leaders on the streets siding with revolutionary Democratic factions, the peasants, industrial workers, and day laborers, that would soon mount the street barricades as the foot soldiers of the German revolution.

Given these transformations in scope and structure, most norm leaders reacted by retreating into denial as the established normative order came under increasing pressure by the norm challengers. Initially, many norm leaders, including the core states, completely ignored the signs of the time and reacted with the same unresponsiveness and repressive tools of the past. For example, Prussian norm leaders established conservative–aristocratic associations such as the Association for King and Fatherland (*Verein für König und Vaterland*) to (unsuccessfully) counter the growing societal influence of the liberal–democratic associations of the *Vormärz*. Caught in defensive denial, norm leaders simply refused to acknowledge the degenerated state of security community norms. By now, however, the norm challengers were able to dominate large parts of the public sphere integrating and mobilizing an increasing number of various social groups and carving out local areas of autonomy from the authority and legitimacy of norm leaders.

Attempting Normative Change: The German Revolution

In 1848, domestic economic hardship and crop failures triggered social upheavals in France. This external 'shock' sent shockwaves across Europe. The economic crisis of 1847/1848 had led to higher living costs and famine as well as accelerated demands for political reform in most European states while mobilizing large crowds of protestors. In France, the February revolution of 1848 ended the Orléans monarchy and established the Second French Republic. The French revolution of 1848 triggered social riots and uprisings in almost every European state except for Russia and Britain. Of course, the concrete objectives and developments differed from country to country. While in France, the protestors sought to break the dominance of the liberal bourgeoisie, revolts in the Eastern European states were predominantly directed against foreign rule.

In the German states, demands for liberal reform were coupled with calls for national unity. In the Habsburg Empire, the revolutions of 1848–1849 led to many domestic uprisings such as in Hungary, Slovakia, and Romania culminating in bloody street fights in Vienna. As a result, Prime Minister Metternich, the chief architect of the German Confederation, was forced into exile in Britain. The new Austrian government promised a constitutional process and allowed the formation of an elected national assembly. In Berlin, bloody street fights erupted in March of 1848 leading to the establishment of a constitutional monarchy in Prussia

(Hagan 2000, p. 46). Baden, Saxony, Hamburg, Mecklenburg-Schwerin, and the Bavarian Palatinate also experienced revolutionary uprisings during the same months and so did most of the other German states.

The main objectives of the German revolutions in March of 1848 became known as the 'March demands' (*Märzforderungen*): freedom of the press, jury courts, armed forces controlled by the parliament, national unity, and state constitutions. These demands effectively meant a replacement of the existing normative order not only in the individual German states but eventually the dissolution of the German Confederation, which, in the eyes of the norm challengers, represented this order.

The concerted nature of the political upheavals demonstrated that the *Vormärz* movement had finally transformed into an integrated and co-ordinated transnational political force that was able to mobilize large numbers of protestors. As such, it posed an existential threat to the normative order of the German security community. As the Prussian king, Frederic Wilhelm (1848b), stated:

> The understanding I have of the things teaches me incontrovertibly that this is the last hour to save the throne of Prussia, Germany, even the concept of divine authority in Europe. Now or never!

Instead of defending the normative order of the security community, most German constitutional monarchies, however, somewhat overwhelmed by the pressure from the streets, implemented the demands of the *Vormärz* for liberal reform and democratization almost immediately and entirely. As Prussian King Frederic Wilhelm IV conceded: 'We were lying on our bellies' (cited in: Lindner 1920, p. 321). In most German states, liberal–democratic reformers took key positions in government and parliaments, known as the so-called March governments (*Märzregierungen*). The German monarchies, including Prussia and Austria, attempted to accommodate political pressure from below by establishing national commissions for constitutional reform. Within two weeks, the norm challengers had seemingly achieved what the Prussian envoy in Bavaria called 'a revolution accomplished with ease' (cited in: Hein 2007, p. 15).

These individual political transformations at the member-state level inevitably affected the German Confederation as a whole. In the eyes of the *Vormärz* movement, the German security community had become the embodiment of the repressive political order of the absolutist monarchies and a structural barrier to the establishment of a liberal normative order. Despite having made significant concessions to the norm challengers, the aristocratic norm leaders of the German Confederation still sought to preserve the German security community. In March 1848, for example, the Prussian King Frederic Wilhelm called on the members of the Confederation to save its normative order:

> We have invited, together with the imperial Austrian government, our German confederates to unite immediately to a joint consultation on those measures which demand the welfare of the German fatherland under the present difficult and dangerous conditions, and are determined to go with all our power to act, that these discussions lead to a real regeneration of the German Confederation, so that the German people are truly united in it, strengthened by free institutions, no less but also protected against the dangers of revolution and anarchy, to regain its former greatness again so that Germany can take its proper place in Europe (Friedrich Wilhelm IV 1848c).

Again, however, norm leaders did exactly the opposite. The norm leaders decided to pursue a strategy of accommodating the revolutionary movement. Consequently, the Confederal Assembly repealed the Carlsbad Decrees by lifting sanctions against the press and the political opposition thereby formally erasing previous firewalls and structural barriers: 'Every German confederal state is free to lift censorship and to introduce freedom of the press' (Verordnung des Königs von Sachsen 1848). To symbolically accommodate popular demands for a German nation-state, the norm leaders converted the coat of arms of the German Confederation into the double-headed Imperial Eagle of the former Holy Roman Empire of the German Nation and even replaced its flag colors with the previously outlawed revolutionary colors of the *Vormärz* movement—black, red, and gold. Finally, the Confederal Assembly established a committee to draft a new constitution to replace the German Federal Act of 1815. In this sense, the norm leaders now moved from defensive to offensive denial by making tactical concessions and proposing new organizational structures.

However, the norm challengers shied away from co-operating with the norm leaders. Instead, the norm challengers sought to build a new institutional structure to subsequently implement a new normative order. The liberal–nationalist German movement, now in key positions in most member-state governments and parliaments, expected any constitutional committee to draft a new constitution that would implement liberal demands while simultaneously establishing a German nation-state.

In order to ensure the legitimacy of the new constitution and to marginalize the influence of norm leaders, the document was to be approved by 'the governments and peoples' of all member states. Eventually, this led to the formation of a German national parliament independent from the commission proposed by the norm leaders. Consequently, at a convention of leading Democrats and Liberals in Heidelberg in early March, its members appointed the so-called 'Committee of Seven' to prepare the election of a National Constitutional Assembly. The Committee of Seven formed the first permanent political institution of the *Vormärz*. By the end of March, a National Assembly, the so-called Pre-parliament (*Vorparlament*) of a future German nation-state, consisted of democratically elected representatives from all member states (except for Bohemia) and was predominantly made up of professors, pastors, lawyers, medical doctors, journalists, and intellectuals for which it was often ridiculed as the 'parliament of professors'. In this Assembly, the various Liberal factions secured a firm majority in the National Assembly followed by the Democratic factions and a few Conservatives.

The National Assembly convened for its inaugural session on 18 May 1848 at St Paul's Church in Frankfurt. Demonstrating the self-confidence of the newly established body, the so-called Frankfurt Assembly declared itself to be the 'sole sovereign of the German people'. This confidence was not unwarranted. The members of the first German national parliament had been elected by a majority of the German electorate (in some areas by 75% of the electorate). The electorate itself formed an equally solid base of legitimacy with roughly 80% of (male) Germans of legal age being allegeable to vote.

Naturally, political and socioeconomic expectations were high. As a public official from Württemberg put it in his report in June 1848: 'Nearly every peasant woman talks about the National Assembly in Frankfurt and the money she expects from it' (cited in: Winkler 2000, p. 114). The high level of political legitimacy, which the National Assembly in Frankfurt enjoyed, can be further illustrated by the immense number of petitions, which amounted to roughly 25,000 between 1848 and 1849 (Hein 2007, p. 70). The high number of petitions addressed to the Assembly was all the more significant since petitions had been traditionally addressed to the ruling monarch. Thus, the amount of petitions sent to the National Assembly symbolized the shift of political legitimacy within the security community. It can thus be reasonably argued that the National Assembly was in a position to successfully introduce a new normative order to rival if not replace the old normative order of the German Confederation.

The most immediate concern of the members of the National Assembly was the drafting of a new constitution entitled 'Fundamental Rights and Demands of the German People' in December 1848. Specifically, this constitution sought to abolish the existing conservative norm of common values, which emphasized the monarchic principle, and to replace it with the liberal norm of individual rights and popular sovereignty. For example, the new constitution stated in Article 1 that '(t)he German people consists of nationals of the states which form the German Empire' and declared that '(n)o distinction of classes before the law applies. The nobility as a class is abolished' (Fundamental Rights 1848). The new constitution further introduced the rule of law, freedom of the press, the freedom to assembly and to form associations, religious freedom, separation of church and state, academic freedoms, free movement of people and goods, free choice of employment, inviolability of the home and property, privacy of correspondence, the right for every citizen to hold public office, and the abolition of the death penalty. In this sense, the emerging normative order of the *Vormärz* mirrored the ideas and norms of the French and American revolutions and, in some cases, went even beyond them.

Perhaps the most significant development during the emerging normative order became the process of ratifying the national constitution to formally replace the existing legal framework of the normative order of the German Confederation. The timing of this process was far from ideal. The National Assembly had taken months to agree on the 'Fundamental Rights and Demands of the German People' to get rid of repression and aristocratic rule. As the new constitution stated:

> We now want to come out of what has been brought to us by the police state of the last centuries. We want to establish the rule of law in Germany (…). The paternalism that weighs from above on Germany shall be removed. (Fundamental Rights 1848)

The utmost priority of the members of the National Assembly was thus to protect the individual citizen from the state. Only once this prerogative had been established were the delegates willing to debate the future political system and its institutions. This approach reflected the liberal–democratic ideas, which the norm challengers had emulated earlier.

However, when the constitutional process finally commenced in October 1848, political tensions in the German states were rising again and many assemblies and ministries that had been created in the spring of 1848 now faced pressures from conservative 'counterrevolutions'. Nevertheless, the National Assembly managed to ratify a constitutional draft in March 1849 that nearly every member of the Assembly could agree on. According to this draft, the future German political community would be a federal state with a two-chamber system in which one chamber would include elected representatives from the 39 individual German states while the other chamber would consist of elected representatives. The new constitution also established a separation of powers in which the executive powers of the ministers of the federal government were controlled by the German parliament as well as by an independent constitutional court.

Critically, the Liberal majority in the National Assembly managed to accomplish that a heritable monarch, who was to represent the new German state in foreign matters, would head the federal government. Thus, the National Assembly established a constitutional monarchy and not a federal republic. While Democrats in the National Assembly failed to implement the latter, they still managed to accomplish the introduction of universal franchise. Moreover, a future German monarch was only allowed suspending veto powers. Thus, aside from a fundamental break with the norm of common values by establishing a democratically elected parliament and by strengthening the rights of the individual, the shape and content of this constitution sharply differed from the previous normative order of the German Confederation in another important way: it sought to turn a pluralistic security community (German Confederation) into an amalgamated security community (German nation-state). Both innovations clearly broke with the existing conservative normative order.

In line with this break with the old norms, the National Assembly excluded the former norm regime of the German Confederation from the constitutional process. Instead, the National Assembly installed a Provisional Central Authority that was formally invested with the executive powers of the Confederal Assembly. As the Introduction of a Provisional Central Government for Germany Act of 1848 (*Reichsgesetz über die Einführung einer provisorischen Zentralgewalt für Deutschland*) explicitly states: 'With the admission of the validity of the Provisional Central Government the existence of the Confederal Assembly ceases' (Reichsgesetz 1848). The Austrian Archduke Johann, who was a member of the nobility yet open to liberal reform, headed the Provisional Central Authority. This represented a compromise that all factions in the National Assembly, from right to left, could agree on. Johann's executive authority included all matters concerning 'the security and prosperity of the German federal state' including the military and foreign policy. His executive powers were checked, however, by the consent of the national parliament, especially in matters of 'peace and war' (Reichsgesetz 1848). On 12 July 1848, the member states of the former German Confederation formally accepted the new government as the legitimate successor to the Confederal Assembly.

Even though the norm challengers had by now successfully established new institutions and norms, they failed to consolidate the new normative order. This can be attributed to a number of reasons, two of which appear central here. First, the fact that, of all people, a member of the Habsburg dynasty (the presiding state of the German Confederation) now headed the process of implementing the decisions of the National Assembly created a problem of legitimacy for the new norm regime in the long run. Many radical Democrats outside the National Assembly quickly dismissed this decision as a betrayal of the German revolution because the Habsburg dynasty had also presided over the Confederal Assembly. Their extra-parliamentary opposition, however, would only turn into a problem at a later stage.

Second, and more importantly at this point, was the fact that the new Provisional Central Authority started with high normative expectations yet lacked the general means to enforce its norms. For example, on the inauguration of Archduke Johann on 6 August 1848, both core states—Prussia and Austria—as well as many other aristocratic rulers simply refused to let their troops pay homage to the new government, a symbolic move to signal that the new norm regime essentially lacked control over the military. Furthermore, the new ministries and offices of the Provisional Central Authority were highly dependent on the former norm leaders for recruiting staff and administrative knowledge and resources. In sum, lacking the material power tools such as an independent military, police, and administrative body, the Provisional Central Authority had to ultimately rely on others to enforce its decisions. In other words, it resembled only a quasi-government: 'a head without a body' (Winkler 2000, p. 116). Given this handicap, the normative promise by Archduke Johann to deliver 'freedom fully and unabridged (…) after years of oppression' quickly turned hollow. This became apparent when the new normative order met its first foreign policy challenge.

A Setback: The First Holstein Crisis

The Holstein crisis in August 1848 turned into a test case for the National Assembly and the Provisional Central Authority to defend the new normative order against an external threat. The European revolutions of 1849 had also taken hold in the Kingdom of Denmark. When the Danish King Frederic VII granted the drafting of a constitution, the Holstein question became a central issue. The duchies of Schleswig and Holstein were, by that time, both ruled by the Danish king. However, while Schleswig was legally part of Denmark, Holstein belonged to the German Confederation. Adding to that problem was the demographic heterogeneity in both territories, which both consisted of large German and Danish populations. When the Danish factions proposed to unite Schleswig and Holstein under Danish rule, German ethnic groups rebelled by suggesting to merge both duchies in the new German nation-state. When a group of German rebels formed a provisional national government of Schleswig-Holstein, war broke out between the newly established German government in Kiel and the Danish Kingdom.

In the ensuing war, Prussia assisted the German rebels by militarily intervening on behalf of (and approved by) the (by that time still existing) Confederate Assembly. The Holstein crisis thus quickly turned into a matter of prestige for the National Assembly in Frankfurt. Due to growing international pressure from Russia and Britain, Prussia unilaterally negotiated an armistice with Denmark and both sides signed a separate peace treaty at Malmo. Following the abolition of the Confederate Assembly, Prussia still claimed to (and legally did) represent the Provisional Central Authority as the legal successor to the Confederate Assembly. Yet, parts of Prussia's peace settlement with Denmark violated the provisions of the mandate granted by the Provisional Central Authority, namely the retreat of Prussian troops from Schleswig and Holstein, the dissolution of the provisional German government in Kiel, and the repeal of its orders and laws. The Provisional Central Authority, however, lacking the means to force Prussia into compliance, gave in by accepting the Peace of Malmo.

In light of this blatant violation of the new normative order and its institutions, the members of the National Assembly in Frankfurt were furious and voted against the peace treaty, albeit by a narrow margin of 17 votes (238 vs. 221). As the head of the parliamentary commission for international issues and the central authority, Frederic Christoph Dahlmann, exclaimed in an emotional appeal to his colleagues in the

National Assembly on 5 September 1848, the Holstein crisis was regarded as a key power struggle with the old norm leaders:

> The new German power (...) is trimmed from the beginning of its emergence; it should, if possible, be torn to pieces on all sides and finally broken! If we submit ourselves in the first test brought upon us by the forces of foreign countries (...), then, gentlemen, you are *never* going to raise your proud head again! Think about these words of mine: *Never!* (emphasis in the original, Frankfurt am Main: Bundespräsidialbuchdruckerei 1848a).

Radical Democrats in the National Assembly, such as Jacob Venedy, went even further by stating 'that we need to create a new empire, bring the whole world into war, to be a unified Germany' (cited in: Winkler 2000, p. 109). Such bold statements, however, masked the fact that the National Assembly had hardly any troops to fight such a war. Given its impotence to enforce its decision vis-à-vis Prussia or to continue the war against Denmark, the members of the National Assembly quickly realized their mistake and tried to save face. Two weeks later, the Assembly abolished its previous decision and approved the Malmo treaty by an equally narrow margin of 21 votes (258 vs. 237).

This controversial decision to side with a former norm leader in an important foreign policy matter naturally sparked wide protests. Some norm challengers of the *Vormärz*, particularly radical Democrats, even broke with the National Assembly by calling for its dissolution. In Frankfurt, protests turned violent culminating in the killing of two representatives of the National Assembly who had voted in favor of the Malmo Peace Treaty. In September 1848, Gustav von Struve, a radical Democrat, returned from exile and attempted a coup d'état in Baden. Yet, the main addressee of these protests in Southern Germany was not the former aristocratic norm regime but the new Frankfurt Assembly as leaflets by Struve reveal: 'Triumph! The Frankfurt Parliament is unmasked! There is no German Parliament anymore—only one enraged people, against him a handful of villains' (cited in: Hein 2007, p. 117). Adding insult to injury, the National Assembly was now forced to ask the aristocratic norm leaders, mainly Prussia and Austria, for military assistance in order to put down rebellions by radical Democrats, thereby further entangling themselves with the forces of the old normative order.

In addition, the Provisional Central Authority subsequently introduced harsh measures to prevent social unrest. As a result, the only recently introduced liberal rights of free assembly as well as the freedom of the press were significantly curtailed. Furthermore, the Provisional Central Authority called on the individual German governments to name any suspicious association or club within its jurisdiction capable of undermining or abolishing the National Assembly. Of course, such repressive measures were more representative of the previous normative order of the German Confederation and, in fact, had little to do with the ideas and norms of the *Vormärz*. Explaining his dissenting vote in the National Assembly, Jodocus Temme even compared these measures to the infamous Carlsbad Decrees and spoke out what many norm challengers of the *Vormärz* believed: 'We have not battled for our freedom to throw it away to a parliament in Frankfurt' (cited in: Winkler 2000, p. 113).

To sum up, the Holstein crisis demonstrates the predicament of the National Assembly. Prussia had negotiated a separate peace with a non-member without informing, let alone consulting with, the newly established National Assembly. When the Assembly rejected the Prussian norm violation, it could not enforce its decision let alone continue the war on its own. Leaving the Prussian norm violation unpunished, however, seriously undermined the new normative order by demonstrating institutional failure.

Adding to this predicament was the fact that in 1848, the norms of the German security community were blurred and vaguely defined. On the one hand, the National Assembly had introduced a new normative order based on common institutions, a written constitution as well as a Charter of Basic Civil Rights. On the other hand, the remnants of the old normative order had not been completely abolished since many former norm leaders of the aristocratic order still controlled the military, police, and most of the administrative bodies. To make matters worse, the Provisional Central Authority, an institution representing the new liberal–democratic normative order, introduced repressive measures that, in the eyes of many of its followers, simply resembled the old conservative–aristocratic normative order.

In this state of vaguely defined and sometimes overlapping normative orders, there was wide room for interpretation of collective norms and meanings. The election of an aristocratic norm leader to head the Provisional Central Authority of the liberal–democratic normative order put into place by the norm challengers nicely symbolizes this predicament. The implications of the Holstein crisis were, thus, a general erosion of the normative order, both old and new, because Prussia had not only defied the authority of the National Assembly but also violated the norms of multilateralism and consultation of the conservative–aristocratic normative order by negotiating a separate peace treaty and by failing to consult with let alone inform the other members about this unilateral move.

Defending the Old Normative Order: The 'Counterrevolution'

Another challenge to the new normative order originated from within and concerned the territorial question of the future German nation-state. The Provisional Central Authority was provisional in the sense that it was supposed to serve as an interim solution until the members of the National Assembly had agreed on the question of who should be chosen as the new German Emperor. This question eventually came down to either the Austrian Habsburgs or the Prussian Hohenzollers. It was clear to the members of the National Assembly—and the Holstein crisis had only magnified this problem—that the survival of a future German nation-state had to rely on the superior military capabilities of Prussia, Austria, or both in order to be protected from foreign invasion. To achieve this and to integrate Prussia and/or Austria into a future German nation-state, the new political order had to be a constitutional monarchy instead of a republic since, by the end of 1848 it was evident that neither Austria nor Prussia would turn into republics any time soon.

The debate over the future normative order was thus inherently tied to the territorial question of where to draw the borders of a future German nation-state. While many delegates from Northern Germany favored a smaller Germany under Prussian leadership, other delegates, predominantly Catholics from the Southern German states, rejected the exclusion of Austria and opted instead for a greater Germany including both core states. The idea of a greater Germany initially appealed to many delegates and thus formed a solid majority in the National Assembly. By the end of October, the National Assembly ratified a proposal that would have included German-speaking Austria, Bohemia, Moravia, and present-day South Tyrol in a future German nation-state. With this proposal, the National Assembly made it clear that it could only envision a nation-state along linguistic borders. This meant that the Habsburg Empire was to be effectively partitioned into its German-speaking part, integrated in a German nation-state alongside Prussia, and its non-German-speaking parts, linked to Austria only dynastically through a personal union but not constitutionally.

Unsurprisingly, the Habsburg dynasty would not compromise its territorial integrity. The successor to Metternich (who had fled into exile during the 1848 revolts in Vienna), Prince von Schwarzenberg, left no room for doubts: 'Austria's continued existence as a unified state is a German as well as a European need' (Regierungserklärung 1848, p. 370). The rejection by Austria, in turn, strengthened the position of supporters of a small solution to the German question and led to the election of Heinrich von Gagern as the new prime minister under Archduke Johann who clearly favored 'Prussia as the natural refuge of Germany' (cited in: Hein 2007, p. 112). Yet, von Gagern was careful enough not to completely alienate Austria. He thus proposed a dual structure of a tightly integrated German nation-state (an amalgamated security community) including Prussia but excluding Austria, on the one hand, and a loosely coupled pluralistic security community including Prussia and the Habsburg Empire, on the other hand.

Again, however, von Schwarzenberg would not settle for a secondary status of Austria: 'Austria is still a German power today. This position (…) it does not intend to give up' (Schwarzenberg 1848, p. 362). Instead, von Schwarzenberg formulated Austria's vision of the territorial order of the future German Confederation, which clearly departed from the idea of a unified German nation-state. Von Schwarzenberg proposed a 70 million multinational confederation, dominated by Austria, spanning from Holstein in the North to Triest in the South. Von Schwarzenberg's proposal ultimately buried any hopes for a greater German nation-state and set the tracks for a small German solution instead. As Georg Beseler explained in the National Assembly: 'This Middle Kingdom (*Reich der Mitte*) would be a political monstrosity: This Middle Kingdom we do not accept; Europe would not admit it; and it would not satisfy Germany' (Frankfurt am Main: Bundespräsidialbuchdruckerei 1848b). Thus, when the German Constitution was finally ratified in March 1849, a majority of 290 delegates in the National Assembly voted in favor of the Prussian King Frederic Wilhelm to become the new German Emperor.

Hopes for a quick inauguration of the German Emperor were not unjustified. The Prussian King Frederic Wilhelm had already publicly indicated that he was open to the idea of a German nation-state led by Prussia:

> Germany is in ferment within, and exposed from without to danger from more than one side. Deliverance from this danger can come only from the most intimate union of the German princes and people under a single leadership (…) I have taken this leadership upon me for the hour of peril

(…) I have today assumed the old German colors, and placed Myself and My people under the venerable banner of the German Empire. Prussia henceforth is merged into Germany. (Friedrich Wilhelm IV 1848d)

Yet, the Prussian position was also highly ambivalent. On the one hand, the Prussian government had shown much sympathy for the idea of a dual German structure with a tightly integrated as well as a loosely coupled security community. Moreover, the Prussian king had made numerous remarks indicating his preference for a German nation-state under Prussian leadership. On the other hand, however, King Frederic Wilhelm had warned Heinrich von Gagern in the summer of 1848 about the limits of the new liberal–democratic normative order: 'Do not forget that there are still princes in Germany, and that I am one of them' (cited in: Hein 2007, p. 121).

Making good on his warning to von Gagern, when a delegation of the National Assembly arrived in Berlin in April 1849, the Prussian King rejected their offer to become the emperor of a united Germany with a liberal–democratic constitution. Moreover, most of the major German member states including Prussia, Austria, Bavaria, Saxony, and Hannover rejected what they called a 'revolutionary constitution', mainly on the grounds that the National Assembly had excluded them in the process of drafting the document (Gruner 2012, p. 66). Making matters worse, constitutional European states such as France and Britain, whom the National Assembly had emulated, refused to even recognize the proclaimed German nation-state. Only a handful of minor European states as well as USA officially recognized the provisional government in Frankfurt.

Given a weakened liberal norm regime, the conservative 'counterrevolution' initiated by the aristocratic norm leaders quickly gained momentum in most German states. In Berlin, Frederic Wilhelm disbanded the Prussian National Assembly and installed a new constitution that granted him an absolute veto over parliamentary decisions. With this revolution from the top, the Prussian norm leaders had effectively regained control. In Vienna, royal troops recaptured the Austrian capital by the end of October and the revolutionary assembly in Vienna was immediately dissolved. The Schwarzenberg government reinstated the absolute monarchy and thus pursued a policy that openly rebuffed the norms of the National Assembly in Frankfurt. The assassination of Robert Blum, a member of the National Assembly, by Austrian troops in November 1848 demonstrated this behavior in drastic terms.

Blum, the leader of the moderate Democrats in the National Assembly in Frankfurt, had traveled to Vienna during the Austrian civil war when revolutionary forces had taken over the city. When the Austrian army eventually recaptured Vienna, Blum was court-martialed and shot for siding with the revolutionaries despite his immunity as a member of the German National Assembly. With this blunt and symbolic act of rejecting the new liberal–democratic normative order, the Schwarzenberg government sent a clear message that it was not willing to accommodate, let alone recognize, the authority of the National Assembly in Frankfurt. To be sure, Blum was not a neutral visitor. His presence in Vienna had served the main purpose of showing solidarity with the rebellion. Still, his assassination, accompanied by only muted protest from the National Assembly, further destabilized the new liberal–democratic normative order. One of its fiercest critics was Friedrich Engels who analyzed the situation from his London exile:

> The fact that the decision on the fate of the revolution was made in Vienna and Berlin, the fact that in these two major cities the most important questions of life were done without even taking the slightest notice of the existence of the Frankfurt Assembly—this fact alone is sufficient to determine that this body was a mere debating club, consisting of a set of dupes that could be misused by governments as parliamentary puppets to give a show to amuse the shopkeepers and artisans of small states and cities, as long as you consider it appropriate to distract the attention of these gentlemen. (Marx and Engels 1960, p. 79)

By 1849, the attempt to establish a new normative order by forming a German nation-state with a republican constitution and a national parliament had failed. This can be attributed in part to the limited scope of the liberal–democratic revolution in many member states and the simultaneous persistence of aristocratic norm leaders. In Prussia, for example, democratically elected politicians headed a bureaucracy that was still loyal to the Prussian king. As one member of the Prussian parliament eloquently noted: '(It was like) producing a new texture with the same old wheelwork, the same machines that had existed before' (Hein 2007, p. 30). Through the old bureaucratic apparatus the former norm leaders continued to exercise political influence and successfully resisted the overwriting of previous institutional knowledge. In other words, the liberal normative order was simply put on top of the existing conservative normative order without replacing it.

Another reason for the failure of the liberal normative order was the fact that once in power, many norm challengers began to enforce the new order with many of the same military and political repressive measures that they had previously accused the aristocratic norm leaders of. Moreover, to do so they had to rely on the military and policing powers of the former norm regime to enforce their decisions. Finally, these decisions and measures taken by the norm challengers reopened internal divisions that reflected the earlier basic dividing line of the 1830s between moderate Liberals, willing to accommodate the aristocracy, and the more radical Democrats, keen on establishing a German republic. The latter turned into an extra-parliamentary opposition with some even calling for the dissolution of the National Assembly.

Because the norm challengers had failed to consolidate the new normative order in the shape of a German nation-state, the former norm leaders were able to formally restore the conservative normative order of the German Confederation. In a last effort to save the German revolution, many norm challengers took their cause to the streets again. In May 1849, Julius Fröbel, leader of the Democratic faction in the National Assembly, called on his followers and the general public at the Joint Congress of the associations of the *Vormärz*:

> The hour has come when it will be decided whether Germany should be free and strong or enslaved and despised. The representatives of the German nation, elected by all citizens and also of you, have decided on the Constitution for all of Germany and proclaimed it as inviolable law. The whole nation is determined to carry out the Constitution (…). The larger princes and their governments refuse to obey the Constitution. They are rebels against the will and the law of the nation (Congreß 1849).

In Dresden, the radical Saxon Fatherland Association (*Sächsischer Vaterlandsverein*) proclaimed: 'Hasten quickly with weapons and ammunition! It depends on us!' In Offenburg, the elected members of the second parliamentary chamber, speaking in front of about 35,000 people, accused the reconvened German Confederal Assembly of 'high treason' and declared that 'the Baden people will support the popular movement (…) with all resources available to it'. (cited in: Becker 1849, p. 127)

As a result, violent riots broke out in many German states. In Baden and Saxony, the violent riots stopped just short of a civil war but were eventually crushed by the Confederal armed forces, predominantly made up of

Prussian soldiers. The National Assembly, in turn, voted in favor of even more radical resistance against the counterrevolution. Many representatives, especially from the Liberal factions, however, were appalled by the violence and radicalism now gaining ground. As representative Gustav Mevissen, a factory owner from Cologne, explained: '(Violent protests) will drive all property owners to the side of the government. The absolute monarchy will be preferred to the red republic' (cited in: Hein 2007, p. 132). Mevissen's statement was, of course, highly exaggerated. The liberal norm challengers certainly did not want to return to absolute monarchy but had always favored a constitutional framework that accommodated the monarchs and nobilities. Neither had anyone, except for a very small minority most of which lived in exile, proposed a proletarian revolution in Germany. However, his general argument that the Liberal factions of the *Vormärz* preferred 'stability' and 'order' (even if that order had to be enforced by the aristocracy) over 'chaos' and 'anarchy' is certainly accurate. In this situation, the liberal–democratic normative order and its institutions quickly eroded before they had taken hold. By now, the National Assembly had lost two-thirds of its members and was forced to move to Stuttgart because Frankfurt was located in too close proximity of the Confederation's military bases and thus exposed to military intervention. However, this move did no longer make any difference. In June 1849, the rump of the National Assembly was eventually dissolved by Confederal troops from Württemberg. In 1851, the Confederal Assembly formally revoked the constitution of the norm challengers.

In the end, the norm challengers failed to consolidate 'their' normative order. These circumstances provided the aristocratic norm leaders with a window of opportunity to repair and reestablish 'their' normative order. Yet, as the following section will show, the security community continued on a path toward disintegration. What explains this puzzle? An important part of the answer lies in the state of denial that most norm leaders had retreated into at this point. In order to accommodate increasing norm violations and political pressure for liberal–democratic reform such as freedom of the press and political participation as well as the popular cry for national unity, many norm leaders had agreed to make tactical concessions to relieve the pressure from the streets and adapted to these growing integration loads. This included, for example, the introduction and display of symbols, which represented metaphors of German unity and nationalism such as the coat of arms of the Holy Roman Empire of the German Nation or the flag colors of the norm challengers. Also, some norm leaders engaged in the public display of responsiveness toward the needs of the norm challengers by agreeing on constitutional reform contrary to their aristocratic self-perception.

The tactical nature of this symbolic deepening of integration was apparent. In many ways, norm leaders simply pretended to sign up to liberal reform without ascribing any meaning to their actions. In Prussia, for example, norm challengers mounted the barricades in Berlin and forced King Frederic Wilhelm IV to withdraw his troops from the Prussian capital. Both sides suffered heavy losses. The next day, King Frederic Wilhelm IV bowed in front of the dead bodies of the insurgents wearing a brassard with the colors of the revolution (black, red, and gold). What appeared to be a sincere display of recognizing changing political realities, however, turned out to be no more than lip service as Frederic Wilhelm IV wrote in a letter to his brother, Prince Wilhelm: 'The national colors (of the revolution), I had to put on yesterday voluntarily to save everything. If the pitch is successful (…) so I put it off again!' The King of Württemberg made a similar statement in his letter to the Russian envoy Gorcakow: 'With the appointment of the new ministry I gain time and avoid bloody scenes' (both cited in: Hein 2007, p. 31).

This state of cognitive dissonance (acting contrary to one's own beliefs) arguably produced a 'crowding-out effect' by undermining social mechanisms of norm compliance in the German security community through overjustification. For example, the Prussian king privately justified his public behavior of giving in to demands of the norm challengers on the grounds that outside external pressure from the streets had 'forced' him to act. In light of these external pressures, the king also verbally reinforced his identity as a monarch in contrast to the revolution thus tying his identity not to voluntary participation in the German security community but to the outside pressures from the norm challengers. The outside pressure from norm challengers decreased norm leaders' intrinsic motivation to promote the aristocratic normative order relying on an extrinsic motivator instead. This meant that norm leaders began to unlearn that norm-abiding behavior was considered an extension of their identity as part of the community and instead attributed norm compliance to the external circumstances of the German revolution. This arguably introduced a new behavioral logic with normative change promoted by the norm challengers acting as an external incentive to maintain the conservative normative order and aristocratic identity among norm leaders. In other words, norm leaders started to believe that they were only defending the norms of the security community against the external circumstances of the German revolution. When the German revolution failed, this also eliminated the external incentive and, hence, the motivation for norm compliance among norm leaders of the security community.

To sum up, norm leaders found themselves trapped in a state of denial. Even though there had been successful liberal revolutions in virtually all member states (including Austria), some aristocratic norm leaders pursued an ostrich-like policy of trying to preserve what could no longer be saved. Other norm leaders expected that a mere symbolic deepening of integration and other tactical concessions would halt or reverse the process of norm degeneration. These acts formed a psychological defense mechanism because admitting defeat or failure would have been too uncomfortable to accept by the norm leaders. As a leaflet of the *Vormärz* declared: 'Now that one of the most powerful thrones (Louis Philippe of France) has drowned and the roaring wave of peoples' freedom threatens to strike the rest of thrones, now comes this appeal, now suddenly trust and freedom of the press' (Das deutsche Volk 1848). This state of cognitive dissonance (acting contrary to one's own beliefs) unintentionally produced a 'crowding-out effect' that induced norm leaders of the German security community to depart from the logic of appropriateness and to increasingly follow the logic of consequence. This transformation in social behavior became apparent during the following years.

DISINTEGRATION

Following the retreat of the norm challengers after the failed revolution of 1848/49, all norm leaders, including Prussia and Austria, agreed in principle to restore the normative order of the German Confederation. As the Prussian Prime Minister, Otto von Manteuffel, stated in the Prussian National Assembly: 'Yes, it is a turning point in our policy. We shall decisively break with the revolution!' (cited in: Poschinger 1901, p. 384). As a result, for example, the 'Fundamental Rights and Demands of the German People', which had been passed by the National Assembly, was abolished. Moreover, in September 1849, an interim organization, the Confederal Central Commission (*Bundeszentralkommission*), was established to replace the Provisional Central Authority. The main purpose of the Confederal Central Commission was 'the preservation of the German Confederation as an international association of the German princes and free cities to preserve the independence and inviolability of its member states' (Bundesreaktionsbeschluss 1851, p. 95).

Another key aspect of the restoration of conservative norms after the revolution of 1848/49 was the decision to roll back domestic liberal reforms in the member states. For this purpose, the resolution of 1851 (*Bundesreaktionsbeschluss*) effectively turned the German Confederation into an instrument of the so-called 'counterrevolution'. The resolution demanded to undo any 'revolutionary' institutions and practices, namely 'to carefully investigate the measures taken in the states, particularly the state institutions and provisions adopted since the 1848, and if they do not comply with the basic principles of the State (German Confederation) to reestablish this necessary compliance again without delay'. Such 'revolutionary' institutions and practices included, for example, a constitutional oath by the armed forces, any form of democratic elections, fiscal rights for parliaments, the establishment of political parties, freedom of the press, and the right to form associations. These measures were far more invasive and far-reaching and intrusive than the repressive measures of the Carlsbad Decrees and the Sixty Articles. In Hesse, for example, the Confederal Assembly even drafted the new state constitution.

Initially, the process of restoring the normative order of the German Confederation took place with impressive speed. In principle, all members shared the conviction that the restored normative order of the Confederation would have to be modified and adapted in order to prevent another revolution. However, this forceful demonstration of norm leader unity could not hide the fact that the German states, and in particular its core states, by now differed greatly about the concrete meaning and scope of how to reform the conservative normative order. Despite the urgency of the matter, the member states were incapable to agree on reforming or adapting the normative order of the security community after 1848.

This was, in large part, due to the crowding-out effect explained above. As a result, rivalry between the two core states, Prussia and Austria, now came to dominate the scene. As a result, a multitude of reform plans and concepts proposed by various member states emerged leaving the security community incapable of reinventing itself. Among the multitude of reform plans, Bavaria took the initiative by suggesting a triple directorate consisting of Prussia, Austria as permanent members and one additional German state on a rotating basis to lead the reformed Confederation. Other reform concepts revolved around the idea of establishing a dual Confederation with Prussia being responsible for Northern Germany and Austria overlooking the South. However, none of these reform plans came to fruition due to the increasing divide among the core states.

Austria basically wanted to return to the status quo ante while strengthening its position within the German Confederation. This was to be achieved by the accession of its non-German-speaking parts and the establishment of a unified customs union comprising all the German states. By integrating the entire Habsburg Empire politically and economically, Austria sought not only to preserve its elevated social status as the former presiding state of the Confederal Assembly but also to expand its material power within a future German Confederation with its sheer size, population, and territory.

The other core state strongly objected to such plans. Prussia rightly feared that it would be marginalized in a greater German Confederation and opted for a smaller solution instead that would strengthen its own position in a newly formed Confederation. Consequently, it dismissed attempts to simply reinvigorate the German Federal Act of 1815 and the Vienna Final Act of 1820. Prussia now favored the von Gagern model, a two-tier model with a tightly integrated German security community that excluded Austria, on the one hand, and a loosely integrated German union that included Austria, on the other hand.

Predictably, the Prussian proposal was quickly rejected by Austria but also by Hannover and Saxony. Seeking a compromise that could accommodate demands for national unity while also ensuring the sovereign rights of the German states, Bavaria, Hannover, Saxony, and Württemberg designed a constitution on their own that was to serve as a viable alternative to the Prussian model. While Austria halfheartedly signed up to the compromise in 1850, this time, Prussia rejected the compromise. Instead, Prussia continued to pursue its envisioned tightly coupled German security community and invited delegates to the city of Erfurt where it proclaimed the formation of a German national parliament. Somewhat surprisingly, the proposal for the so-called Erfurt Union, a united Germany under Prussian rule, was immediately endorsed by the newly founded main organization of the remaining Liberal factions of the *Vormärz*, the German National Association (*Deutscher Nationalverein*). In its founding document in August 1859, the members of the German National Association called for the dissolution of the German Confederation and declared their solidarity with the Prussian position of forming a German nation-state:

> We perceive great perils for the independence of our German fatherland, (…). These perils are ultimately caused by Germany's flawed overall constitution, and they can only be eliminated by a prompt alteration in this

constitution. (...) To this end it is necessary for the German Confederal Assembly to be replaced by a solid, strong, and lasting central government for Germany, and for a German national assembly to be convened. (...) Under the current circumstances, the most effective steps toward achieving this end can only emanate from Prussia; it is essential, therefore, to work toward getting Prussia to assume the initiative. (Eisenach Declaration 1859)

Fearing the replacement of the German Confederation, Austria, aided by Bavaria, Hannover, Saxony, Württemberg, the Electorate of Hesse, and the Grand Duchy of Hesse, in turn, convened in the Confederal Assembly in Frankfurt threatening to use force against Prussia. Prussia objected to this decision on the grounds that given ongoing consultations about reforming the German Confederation, the Confederal Assembly was not entitled to act in this particular way (Gruner 2003, p. 26). To underscore its point, Prussia refused to acknowledge the bodies of the reinstated German Confederation in Frankfurt and ceased to participate in them.

The threat to use force against a security community member and the subsequent secession of Prussia from the German Confederation were both clear violations of the norm of multilateral practice. The former one stood in stark contrast to the norm of peaceful conflict resolution. All members of the German Confederation had 'pledge(d) themselves (...) not to make war among themselves under any pretense, or to follow up their contentions with force' (Art. 11, Vienna Final Act). The latter one violated Article 5, which prohibited any act of secession: 'The Confederation has been founded as an indissoluble union, and therefore no member of the same is at liberty to secede from this union' (German Federal Act). Hence, the crisis over the Erfurt Union demonstrated that, even though the norm leaders had reintroduced the normative order of the German Confederation, they were unable to consolidate it. Instead, based on crowding-effects, relations among the core states became dominated by zero-sum thinking and a general lack of self-restraint and responsiveness. The German Customs Union crisis further illustrates this point.

Othering: The Crisis over the German Customs Union

As pointed out above, the German Customs Union was founded in 1834 to serve mainly Prussian economic interests. Given its divided and dispersed territory, Prussia had been keen on establishing a free trade zone in

Northern Germany to facilitate internal trade as well as external trade with the German states. It also further consolidated Prussian economic dominance in Northern Germany even though this dominance would have probably existed regardless of the customs union. Until the 1830, virtually all German states north of the Maine river, except for Hannover (who formed the Central German Commercial Union), had joined the customs union while Austria, whose economy was highly protectionist and by far less developed than Prussia, had no economic incentive to join. Bavaria and Württemberg formed their own custom union as well.

As pointed out before, the various economic communities within the political community of the German Confederation had not caused any problems for the normative order. In fact, the custom unions strengthened the normative order by furthering economic integration, a stated objective of the German Confederation. However, the situation changed significantly when, in 1851, Prussia merged the German Customs Union with the Central German Commercial Union of Hannover without prior consultation with its fellow member states. Austria as well as Wurttemberg and Bavaria strongly objected to this unilateral move and demanded at a joint conference to discuss the matter. In Darmstadt in 1852, the Southern German states demanded that Austria be allowed to join the *Zollverein* as well. Prussia, however, simply disregarded the plea by the other norm leaders and went ahead with the accession of Hannover. Its only concession was to offer Austria a bilateral trade agreement that was concluded in February 1853.

Prussia's behavior during the German Customs Union crisis undermined the norm of multilateral practice by excluding another member state from joining an organization that formally belonged to the German Confederation. In addition, it clearly violated the norm of communication by refusing to consult with let alone take into account the concerns of other members of the security community. Most importantly, Prussia operated outside of the institutional framework of the German Confederation, which was remarkable given the fact that Confederal peace commissions were also responsible for dealing with economic conflicts among its members. Prussia's behavior thus not only violated security community norms but also disrupted symbolic interaction as well as invited institutional failure. During the German Customs Union crisis, Prussia treated the Southern German states not as members of the same community (Self) but as outsiders (Other).

The Breakdown of the Normative Order: The Hessian Crisis

The constitutional crisis in the Electorate of Hesse involved a similar pattern. In 1831, Hesse had introduced liberal reforms and established a constitutional monarchy. In 1850, however, the Elector Frederic Wilhelm I suspended the constitution and established martial law to implement his measure by force. The Hessian armed forces, however, refused to execute the order because they had sworn their oath to defend the Elector *as well as* the constitution. As a result, Frederic Wilhelm I called on the Confederal Assembly to send the Confederate armed forces in order to put down any opposition. As in the Hannover case cited earlier, this request for a Confederate intervention was expected to be rejected by the Confederal Assembly since the treaties of the German Confederation clearly stated that an established member-state constitution could only be changed through 'a constitutional process' and not by armed force.

When the Confederal Assembly decided on the matter, the only member to object was Prussia. However, since Prussia was boycotting the Confederal Assembly at this point, the remaining members agreed to send the Confederate intervention force (predominantly made up of Bavarian and Austrian soldiers) into Hesse to 'reestablish order' on the request of a member state. The Confederate armed forces arrived in Hanau in Southern Hesse in November 1850. Prussia reacted by marching two of its divisions into Northern Hesse. The subsequent confrontation was of little military relevance because it ended in a minor skirmish near Bronnzell leaving four Austrian soldiers wounded and one Prussian horse dead. However, its normative implications were fundamental. For the first time since the formation of the German security community, two members had used force against each other, and not just any two members but the two core states.

In the end, the Prussians backed down. Fearing a major war against Austria, the Prussian king decided to retreat. But the fatal damage to the security community had already been done. The subsequent peace treaty at Olmütz was a humiliating defeat for Prussia (Clark 2006, pp. 496–7). The German core state was forced to dissolve the Erfurt Union, to return to the institutional bodies of the Confederation, and to take part in the Confederate intervention in Hesse and Holstein. By signing the Olmütz Agreement, Prussia effectively (though not voluntarily) submitted to the revival of the German Confederation under Austrian leadership (Taylor 2001, p. 101).

The split between the two core states was now obvious and permanent. At this point, Prussia and Austria viewed each other as enemies, constructing their reciprocal images not in terms of a plural Self but in terms of Self and Other. Attempts to reinvigorate the Confederation at the Dresden Conference in May 1851 were thus doomed to fail mainly due to the Prussian–Austrian antagonism. Prussia and Austria could hardly find consensus on anything at the Dresden Conference except to enlarge the German Confederation by acceding their Eastern territories that had previously not been part of the Confederation, which, at that point, of course carried hardly any relevance. The open split between the core states of the German security community meant that the most important norm leaders could no longer find a common ground to maintain or reform the pre-1848 normative order despite the fact that both sides continued to share common values such as monarchic legitimacy and antiliberal sentiment.

The core states still shared norms of common values and were determined to defend the monarchic principle domestically against liberal norm challengers. For example, Austria and Prussia formed a military alliance to erase 'the parties of the revolution' and to wage a 'war of obliteration' against the 'liberal press' (Schutz- und Trutzbündnis 1854). This can be further illustrated, for example, by the appointment of a 'reactionary committee' that was supposed to investigate and outlaw or disband any liberal association, institutions, and constitutional amendments in the German states. Furthermore, the German states decided on a series of measures—the Confederal Reactionary Resolution (*Bundesreaktionsbeschluss*) of 1851 that greatly affected the press, which now faced repressions similar to the Carlsbad decrees.

However, the core states no longer viewed each other as members of a security community. Prussia, for example, made sure to marginalize the norm-(re)building role of the Confederation during the negotiations over the Confederal Reactionary Resolution by insisting on 'as few and simple principles as possible whose detailed definition and implementation shall be left to the individual German states' (cited in: J. Müller 2006, p. 40). As a result, few states actually enforced these measures at the domestic level. For example, Prussia, Austria, and Bavaria never even formally ratified them. Moreover, in most member states, domestic laws and regulations were implemented that either ran contrary to the measures decided upon by the Confederation collectively or introduced even harsher repression. For example, Saxony–Coburg and Gotha guaranteed the freedom to assembly while Austria prohibited virtually any kind of association.

It can thus be concluded that even though the normative order had been formally reinstated after the failed German revolution of 1848–1849, its norms had become blurred and hence differed greatly in their interpretation by the individual member states. As a result, the shared meaning of the normative order broke down. This can be illustrated by another example. In 1859, the German National Association (*Deutscher Nationalverein*), a pan-German political association, had been formed with the aim to revive the ideas of the norm challengers of 1848–1849 and to establish a liberal–democratic German nation-state under Prussian leadership. The German National Association obviously posed a direct threat to the German Confederation and should have been outlawed immediately by the Reactionary Committee based on the Confederal Reactionary Resolution of 1851. However, the German National Association was not disbanded by the norm leaders but continued to exist even after the formal dissolution of the German Confederation in 1866. The main reason for this lack of enforcement of community norms lay in the fact that most member states had simply refused to implement the Confederal Reactionary Resolution. To make matters worse for the norm regime, some member states even demanded a repeal of the repressive policies and the dissolution of the reactionary committee. When institutional failure prevented a consensus in the Confederal Assembly, Baden, Wurttemberg, and Saxony eventually went ahead and unilaterally repealed the measures.

Based on these accounts, it can be argued that a learning process developed among many norm leaders. To be sure, the norm leaders had by no means internalized the ideas and norms of the *Vormärz*. However, they must have certainly realized that, given the experience of the German revolution of 1849, the persuasiveness of the new ideas introduced by the norm challengers could not be contained by repressive measures. Instead, many norm leaders including politicians and public officials in Baden, Saxony, Saxony-Weimar, Hessen-Darmstadt, and Saxony–Coburg and Gotha appeared convinced that the German Confederation could only be preserved by adapting a constitutional reform that reflected political realities.

Prussia basically shared this conviction to seek an adaptation of the normative order to preserve the security community against the norm challengers. In fact, Prussian leaders now argued that a united Germany needed a strong Prussian core state to guarantee peace and prosperity. As Otto von Bismarck explained in the Prussian parliament:

Germany is not looking to Prussia's liberalism, but to its power; Bavaria, Wurttemberg, Baden may indulge liberalism, and yet no one will assign them Prussia's role; Prussia has to coalesce and concentrate its power for the opportune moment, which has already been missed several times (cited in: Schüßler 1924, pp. 139–40).

Prussian norm leaders generally realized that the normative order of the German security community would have to be reformed in some way. Following the failed German revolution, Prussia had thus begun to think seriously about reforming the German Confederation by establishing the Erfurt Union.

No such learning process developed in Austria whose leaders almost desperately held on to the fading pre-1848 normative order. While the norm leaders of the Habsburg Empire acknowledged the fact that 'modern political events' like the revolutions of 1830 and 1848–1849 had undermined the normative order of the German security community and 'devalued the Confederation in the general opinion', they worried that any attempt to reform the normative order of the security community would ultimately lead to further division among norm leaders and thus would, in the end, only aid the liberal–democratic norm challengers:

> In Germany there has been an unstoppable and progressive process of turning away from the existing Confederation; but until now a new Confederation has not been concluded, and thus the most recent period in German history is nothing but *a condition of complete fracture and general disintegration.* One does not, in fact, think too unfavorably about this condition when one admits that German governments now are basically no longer standing together in a solid, mutual contractual relationship, but rather are just lingering on alongside each other, foreboding impending catastrophe. But the German revolution, quietly stoking, awaits its hour. (emphasis added, Austrian Memorandum 1863)

The Disintegration of Security Community

External crises further demonstrate the disintegration process of the German security community. For example, the Crimean War (1854–1856), a military confrontation between Russia, on the one side, and an Anglo–French coalition, on the other side, ended almost 40 years of peace among the major European actors. This had significant implications for the overall European order. The so-called Holy Alliance between Prussia, Austria, and Russia had dissolved over the Crimean War leaving Austria isolated due to a gradual rapprochement between Russia and Prussia as well as Russia, France, and Britain.

In May 1854, the smaller member states of the German Confederation gathered in Bamberg to consult over their position in the Crimean War. They quickly agreed on the need to reform the German Confederation with Saxony taking the lead by proposing 'a federal system in Germany' (J. Müller 2006, p. 42). However, the Bamberg proposal received little support from the core states. Instead, Prussia had originally even considered forging an alliance with Britain and France against Austria in order to reinvigorate its Erfurt Union. Hence, the Crimean crisis further demonstrates that the relationship between the two core states had transformed into rivalry. During the Crimean war between Russia and the Ottoman Empire, Prussia and Austria had remained neutral at first. In the summer of 1854, however, Austria decided to join the Anglo–French coalition without consulting the members of the German states. This unilateral move, in turn, irritated Prussia as well as other major German states, and contributed to the decision by the Confederal Assembly not to assist Austria in the subsequent Italian crisis.

After the failed attempt by the Kingdom of Sardinia to unite the Italian states during the Crimean War, Sardinia aligned itself with France to challenge the Austrian Empire in Italy. At that point, the Habsburg Empire still controlled large parts of Italian territory, which prevented the Sardinian goal of Italian unification. The Franco–Sardinian coalition successfully provoked Austria to attack the Kingdom of Sardinia, which led to the outbreak of war in May 1859. In the German Confederation, the debate revolved around the question whether to support Austria or to remain neutral. Most member states opted for neutrality citing the defensive nature of the German Confederation as laid out in the German Federal Act of 1815. Since Austria had formally not been attacked but started the war (albeit provoked by France), the member states felt not legally obliged to assist Austria in the war.

The Prussian position was the key because most member states waited to see how the other core state would react. When the Prussian delegate in the Confederal Assembly, Otto von Bismarck, declared Prussian neutrality, Austria was left isolated. Only when an Austrian defeat by the Franco–Sardinian alliance became imminent did Prussia mobilize its troops in the Rhineland—not to aid Austria but to secure its own borders against a possible French invasion. Fearing a Prussian attack, the French agreed to sign a peace treaty with Austria, which led to a significant weakening of the Habsburg Empire including the loss of territory. To be sure, the members of the Confederation were not legally obliged to assist Austria. Still, the Habsburg Empire (perhaps rightfully) felt that the Confederation had been morally obliged to enact the norm of collective defense since France and Sardinia had provoked the war in the first place. After all, the German Confederation was to act 'externally as a whole power bound in political unity' (Art. 2, Vienna Final Act). It can thus be argued that the Italian crisis demonstrates the degenerated state of the norms of multilateral practice, namely collective self-defense, solidarity, and mutual assistance.

To sum up, both external events, the Crimean War and the Italian crisis, demonstrated that the German Confederation had turned into a geopolitical playing field of the core states. While Austria sought to strengthen the Confederation to contain Prussian power ambitions, Prussia tried to marginalize it in order to keep Austria at bay (Akten zur Geschichte des Krimkriegs 1990, p. 28). Such power games left little room for communicative action, let alone 'thick' multilateral practice. The liberal intellectual Ludwig August von Rochau described the zero-sum thinking in the Prussian–Austrian relationship of 1853 in the following terms: 'Prussia must grow in order to survive, Austria must not allow Prussia to grow to avoid its demise—that is the true character which defines the reciprocal relationship between the two states' (cited in: Winkler 2000, p. 137).

Yet, it was not simply power struggles that led to the disintegration of the normative order of the German Confederation. In the end, the members of the German Confederation, and the two core states in particular, can be said to have 'learnt to be different' because they ultimately constructed opposite meanings about the German security community. Prussia more openly embraced the ideas of the norm challengers in terms of a constitutional German nation-state (albeit top-down, not bottom-up) while Austria clung to the traditional ideas of absolute monarchic rule in a greater yet pluralistic Germany. As the pro-Austrian German Reform Association (*Deutscher Reformverein*) proclaimed in October 1862:

> (Any) reform must preserve for all German states the possibility of remaining entirely in the community (and) reform must be brought about only by agreement and on the basis of the current Confederal constitution. (Program of the German Reform Association 1862)

This statement demonstrates that the split, which had occurred between the two core states, transcended the intergovernmental level. Transnational associations also reinforced the split.

There were two main contenders at the level of civil society that acted largely independently from while ultimately backing the core states. The German National Association mentioned above, a pan-German political organization made up predominantly of Liberal Protestants but with strong ties to the worker's educational and local cultural and sports associations, favored small-scale German unification under Prussian leadership and significantly shaped public opinion with its weekly newspaper. In its Eisenach Declaration the German National Association concluded that 'in the current international political circumstances' German independence and national unity could only be achieved and maintained with the help of Prussia:

> It is the duty of every German man to support the Prussian government to the best of his ability, insofar as its efforts proceed from the assumption that the mission of the Prussian state essentially coincides with Germany's needs and mission, and insofar as its activity is directed toward the introduction of a strong and free overall constitution for Germany. (Eisenach Declaration 1859)

In contrast to the National Association, the German Reform Association, a heterogeneous pan-German political organization founded in 1862, rejected what its members regarded as Prussian hegemony and backed Austria instead. The Reform Association favored a greater Germany because 'in order to secure the necessary moral authority, it is essential to have a larger number of members'. (Program of the German Reform Association 1862)

In this state of disintegration, Austrian norm leaders made a last effort to save the Confederation. In 1863, the Austrian Emperor Franz Josef I invited all member states to Frankfurt to discuss plans for reforming the German Confederation. All member states except Prussia send delegates to the convention. In Frankfurt, Austria proposed a Reform Act that was quickly adopted by all participating German states to amend the German Federal Act of 1815 and the Vienna Final Act of 1820. The main innovations were the introduction of a five-member directorate as well as a legislative body consisting of appointed delegates to replace the Confederal Assembly. The main issues, however, were to be decided by an institutionalized council of princes and kings.

Prussia, however, had no intention to participate in any kind of revival of the German Confederation, which was by now regarded as an Austrian power tool to contain Prussia's interests in Germany. This viewpoint was articulated in Bismarck's Christmas Memorandum of 1862, in which he demanded to free Prussia from 'the net of the confederal acts' and seek closer integration with the members of the German Customs Union instead (cited in: Stern 1977, p. 25). Yet, Prussia needed a pretext to reject the Reform Act in order to avoid being seen as obstructionist. This led to a remarkable development. In a note written by Bismarck, the Prussian king formulated preconditions for reforming the German Confederation including a democratically elected national assembly. Given Prussia's dismissal of liberal–democratic reform, in general, and Bismarck's publicly stated antipathy toward any form of popular representation, in particular, it seems reasonable to assume that such preconditions were neither plausible nor credible. It did allow Prussia, however, to save its face while sabotaging any attempt to preserve the German Confederation under Austrian leadership. Prussia's behavior left Austria little choice but to go it alone. In October 1863, the Habsburg Empire proposed to implement the Reform Act without Prussia but only a minority of member states, fearing war between Prussia and Austria, followed his invitation to Nuremberg. In the end, the Reform Act was cast aside.

Tensions between Prussia and Austria mounted during the second crisis over the Northern duchies Schleswig, Holstein, and Lauenburg. At first, it appeared as if the core states had finally found common ground on an issue of great significance to the German Confederation which, at that point, still existed if only on paper. In March 1863, the Danish king declared his intention to unite Schleswig, Holstein, and Lauenburg with Denmark. This represented a legal violation of international agreements as well as conflicted with the German Federal Act of 1815, which prohibited any change to the territorial or constitutional status of the three duchies that were dynastically tied in personal union to Denmark but were simultaneously members of the German Confederation.

Consequently, the Confederal Assembly agreed to send in Prussian and Austrian troops to restore the territorial status quo. To further complicate matters, the German Prince Frederic VIII, claiming his hereditary title, announced his intention to rule over Schleswig and Holstein as well. German nationalists, both liberal and conservative, and resulted in an outpouring of popular support, greeted the latter development with much enthusiasm. Associations, town hall meetings, declarations, and fundraisers took place in virtually every part of the Confederation much to the discontent of Prussia and Austria. The core states, however, fearing a foreign intervention by Britain, France, and Russia, were determined to restore the status quo in line with the London Agreement of 1852. When the other member states refused to fall in line, Prussia and Austria agreed to continue to restore the status quo in Northern Germany by military force outside the institutional framework of the German Confederation.

The outcome of the second Holstein crisis thus placed the core states in open opposition to the smaller members of the German Confederation. After they had been outvoted by the smaller member states in the Confederal Assembly, Prussia and Austria declared in January 1864 that regarding the issue of Schleswig and Holstein, they would no longer feel bound by decisions made by the Assembly. The core states had effectively placed themselves outside the institutional and normative framework of the German Confederation, which rendered subsequent protests and sanctions on behalf of the Confederal Assembly meaningless.

Efforts on behalf of the Confederation, represented by the Foreign Minister of Saxony, Frederic Ferdinand von Beust, to mediate the crisis and demonstrate the capability of the Confederal states to act collectively against an external enemy (Denmark) subsequently failed. In February 1864, Prussia and Austria waged war against Denmark without prior consent by the Confederal Assembly. Prussia and Austria quickly defeated the Danish troops and, after a fierce dispute over the future territorial status, agreed in the Gastein Convention of 1865 to occupy both regions with Prussia controlling Schleswig and Austria controlling Holstein. The core states had settled their dispute outside the institutional framework of the Confederation. This act of confronting the members of the Confederation with a fait accompli can hardly be understood as being in line with the norm of communication.

Contrary to what one might be inclined to think, however, the crisis over Schleswig, Holstein, and Lauenburg did not lead to Prussian–Austrian realignment but instead created the momentum for the final showdown between the two core states. Having resolved the second Holstein crisis, Prussia now seemed determined to seek a military confrontation with Austria. In April 1866, the Prussian envoy in Frankfurt repeated Bismarck's earlier proposal to set up a democratically elected German National Assembly. Knowing that Austria would reject such a proposal, Prussia declared the German Federal Act of 1815 and the Final Act of 1820 to be 'broken' and 'no longer binding' (cited in: J. Müller 2006, p. 48). With this act, Prussia had formally seceded from the German Confederation. Prussia's secession subsequently escalated into a military confrontation between the two core states. Anticipating a military confrontation, Prussia and Austria but also Saxony, Wurttemberg, and Bavaria had been mobilizing their armed forces since April 1866. In June, Prussian troops invaded Holstein and the Electorate of Hesse leading to war between Prussia and the Habsburg Empire. In this war, each of the remaining German states picked their sides. While 13 member states supported Austria, 18 member states followed Prussia. After three weeks, the Prussian coalition had defeated Austria and its allies. The German Confederation was officially dissolved in the Peace treaties of Nikolsburg and Prague on 26 July 1866.

In the end, the crowding-out effect during the stage of denial had introduced a new behavioral logic among the members of the German security community. As a result, the logic of appropriateness was replaced by the logic of consequence leading to open rivalry between Austria and Prussia who, as the external crises above illustrate, appeared no longer willing to settle their disputes by peaceful means within the security community framework.

The Normative Order of the German Security Community Revisited

In this section, I revisit the normative order outlined at the beginning of this chapter to evaluate the presence and scope of normative change in the German security community. As argued in the previous chapter, a security community reaches a stage of disintegration when new norms take hold and collective meanings and identities are replaced. Even though norm leaders attempted to repair the conservative normative order after the failed German revolution of 1848–1849, its symbols and institutions were by now a mere shadow of the past: a false piety that members no longer sincerely believed in and to which members attached diverging meanings. Normative change can thus be said to have affected all three dimensions of the normative order of the German security community.

Norm of Common Values

As explained in the beginning of this chapter, the established norm of common values of the German Confederation originally rested on the monarchic principle and the concept of polycentric sovereignty. At first glance, we find little dispute about the first principle among norm leaders. Despite their differences, the core states as well as the smaller member states signed up to the Metternich credo that a community of aristocratic rulers and monarchical systems was the only way to achieve stable peace among the German states. Thus, even though the norm leaders differed on many accounts, they firmly held on to the conviction that, even in war, the principle of monarchical solidarity—understood as defending the monarchy against liberal–democratic norm challengers—was to be left untouched.

At closer look, however, we find considerable divergence over the exact meaning of the monarchic principle. This can be illustrated by the Prussian–Austrian dualism within the German Confederation. While both Austria and Prussia had turned into a constitutional monarchy during the March revolts of 1848, it was only Prussia that left the new system in place with only minor changes. Austria, on the other hand, completely erased any constitutional elements once the norm challengers were defeated and quickly reinstated an absolute monarchy in the Habsburg Empire. In the subsequent years, Austria even attempted to redefine the norm of common values to mean *exclusively* absolutist monarchical systems ruling out any domestic variations. Prussia, on the other hand, refused to accept such a redefinition of the normative order by insisting on the original meaning of the Confederal treaties that explicitly protected and promoted the right of member states to introduce constitutional monarchies. Prussia, on the other hand, openly challenged the concept of polycentric sovereignty by flirting with the idea of a German nation-state, an idea strongly resisted by Austria.

In a security community, it is typically the core states that act as norm setters and define normative meanings. However, following the 1850s, a clear definition of the norm of common values remained void with Prussia and Austria undergoing different learning processes. This norm divergence, in turn, facilitated confusion, different interpretations, and a general lack of norm enforcement among other members of the German Confederation. In sum, while the monarchic principle as such did not disappear, its meaning was no longer tied to the German Confederation thereby reducing its validity and binding character among members of the security community. The norm of polycentric sovereignty, on the other hand, was eventually replaced by the German nation-state.

Norm of Multilateral Practice

The norm of multilateral practice originally involved a normative understanding of security multilateralism that allowed for the use of force against outsiders but committed the members of the German security community to resolve their internal conflicts peacefully and to practice self-restraint. Following the German revolution of 1848–49, this norm was replaced.

The redefinition of peaceful conflict resolution can be based on the fact that after 1849 member states threatened to use force against each other. On at least two occasions—the Holstein crisis and the Constitutional crisis in the Electorate of Hesse—Prussia and Austria threatened each other with war and, in the latter case, even waged a military skirmish. The fact that this involved the core states of the security community makes this redefinition of peaceful conflict resolution even more significant. By the 1860s, the meaning of peaceful conflict resolution had been firmly replaced by an understanding that violent conflict resolution no longer marked a taboo in inter-member politics. The reintroduction of war as a possibility as well as a means of politics among members of the security community—culminating in the War of 1866 with the German states picking sides between Prussia and Austria—can thus be seen as a key indicator of normative change and, subsequently, the disintegration of the pluralistic security community.

Moreover, the norm of mutual self-restraint and collective defense against outsiders was redefined. A case in point is Prussia's and Austria's military intervention in Holstein. According to Article 11 of the German Federal Act, members had agreed to speak with one voice in its dealings with outside threats and to refrain from concluding a separate armistice or peace settlement. Yet, this is exactly what both core states did both during and after they ended their military confrontation against Denmark. Initially, the Holstein crisis seemed to confirm the norm of multilateral practice by demonstrating solidarity against a common Other. In the end, however, the crisis marginalized the norm of multilateral practice and eventually even led to war between Prussia and Austria.

Another example is the Italian crisis. Even though Austria formally started the war against France and the Kingdom of Sardinia, it should have been clear to the members of the German Confederation that Austria was not the aggressor but had been provoked into war by the clever French tactical maneuvering. Given the fact that Austria presided over the German Confederal Assembly and had not caused the war, the unwillingness of the security community members, in particular Prussia, to aid Austria rendered mutual self-restraint and collective defense meaningless. Instead, Prussia waited until Austria appeared close to defeat before eventually deciding not to assist Austria but to counterbalance France. This adds plausibility to the argument that by now, normative change had taken hold by transforming multilateral behavior from the logic of appropriateness to the logic of consequence. In the end, the norm of multilateral practice was replaced internally by reintroducing war as a means of politics as well as externally by a lack of mutual self-restraint and collective defense.

Norm of Communication

What can be said about the norm of multilateral practice is equally true for the security community norm of communication. The norm of communication was originally characterized by the willingness among its members to be convinced by the better argument and rested on the principles of genuine and timely consultation, information, and mutual responsiveness to the interests and needs of other members.

Initially, the reform debates of the 1850s and regular meetings among security community members to discuss numerous reform proposals seemed to demonstrate a collective willingness and determination to maintain high levels of responsiveness and thus appeared to confirm the norm of communication. However, 'thick' communication in the form of timely and transparent consultation and information, even though it occurred among selected member states such as during the reform summits in Frankfurt, Bamberg, and Nuremberg, more often than not it did not occur at all as the crisis over the German Customs Union or the Holstein crisis illustrate. By the early 1860s, 'thin' or strategic communication had become the norm with Prussia and Austria constantly exchanging diplomatic notes to threaten and coerce each other while only a few member states such as Saxony appeared continuously willing to follow the norm of 'thick' communication. In sum, the norm of communication was replaced after the revolution of 1848–1849 to mean instrumental calculation and coercion instead of communicative action and persuasion.

CONCLUSION

The link between normative change and the disintegration of the German security community can also be seen in the redefinition of identity politics. It becomes apparent from looking at the examples presented here that the member states, and most importantly the core states Prussia and Austria, no longer shared the sense of we-feeling and common Self that would have been necessary to maintain a pluralistic security community. The ideas of liberalism and nationalism advanced by the norm challengers presented a powerful alternative to the collective identification along purely dynastic lines undergirding the new liberal normative order. The German nation increasingly became the anchor for an emerging national identity in many German states. Even though Prussia was deeply skeptical of liberal–democratic reform, it signed on to these national sentiments. To some extent, national sentiments were even internalized and actively promoted by its norm leaders, such as King Frederic Wilhelm IV. In doing so, however, Prussian and Austrian norm leaders increasingly constructed their relationship in terms of Self and Other.

The unraveling of the collective identity resulting from the erosion of the normative order had significant implications. Prussia, for example, no longer viewed itself as part of the security community when it proposed to form the Erfurt Union and ceased to participate in the community's main bodies and institutions. Austria, on the other hand, did not see the need to practice self-restraint and responsiveness vis-à-vis Prussia and other member states when those norm leaders were openly pushing for secession. Finally, during the second Holstein crisis, both core states set themselves apart from the other members by identifying themselves as outsiders.

To sum up, the German security community disintegrated under the combined impact of the persuasiveness of new ideas, disrupted symbolic interaction, institutional failure and the social unlearning of its normative order. The norm challengers of the *Vormärz* played a significant role in this process of norm degeneration by acting as a catalyst and promoter of normative change. The norm challengers emerged as significant political force after the July revolution in 1830 and constantly challenged the normative order of the pluralistic security community thereafter. The increasing thrust and scope of norm violations by norm challengers and the erection of structural barriers and firewalls to prevent the diffusion of liberal ideas by norm leaders subsequently led to an undermining of symbolic interaction and institutional failure in the security community because the implementation of repressive measures by norm leaders, in turn, led to frequent violations of community norms, in particular violating the political independence of certain member states. This, moreover, sparked normative conflicts among norm leaders, in particular among the core states, which paralyzed collective decision-making in the institutional bodies of the security community. When the barriers and firewalls subsequently came down, the norm challengers were able to gain clout leading to the German revolution of 1848–1849. While the norm leaders were eventually able to repel the norm challengers after the failed revolution of 1849, the empirical narrative shows that norm leaders' prior denial of the degenerated normative order had the unintended consequence of introducing the logic of consequence. Due to this crowding-out effect, the norm leaders were less and less able to identify with the meanings and symbols of the German security community. Prussia is perhaps the most prominent example here. In the end, the old normative order of the German pluralistic security community was replaced by a new normative order among the German states: an amalgamated security community with a single Prussian core state. It seems plausible to suggest that the norm challengers not only facilitated this development but, in the end, actively shaped the process of normative change.

Notes

1. The main founding treaties of the German Confederation were the German Federal Act of 1815 and the Vienna Final Act of 1820.
2. '(T)he individual Confederal states are obliged on their part neither to cause such injuries nor to inflict such (harm) on foreign states' (Art. 36, Vienna Final Act).
3. The term 'Pre-March' describes a social movement as well as the period in German history between 1830 and 1848. Its name results from its role as a precursor to the March revolution in Germany in 1848.
4. Article 28 states that '(w)hen public peace and legal order are threatened in several Confederate states by dangerous associations and attacks, and the only way this can be countered is through co-operation of the whole (Confederation), then the Confederate Assembly is authorized and called upon, after previous consultation with the governments threatened in the first place, to discuss and conclude such disciplinary measures'.

References

Akten zur Geschichte des Krimkriegs. Serie II. Preußische Akten zur Geschichte des Krimkriegs. Bd. 2. 9. August 1854 bis April 1856. In W. v. Baumgart, W. Elz, & W. Zürrer (Eds.) (1990). München: Oldenbourg.
Albrecht-Carrié, R. (1968). *The concert of Europe*. New York: Harper and Row.
Austrian Memorandum. (1863). In E. R. Huber (Ed.) (1978). *Deutsche Verfassungsdokumente 1803–1850. Vol. 1: Dokumente zur deutschen Verfassungsgeschichte*, 3rd edn (pp. 135–139). Stuttgart: W. Kohlhammer.
Becker, J. P. (1849). *Geschichte der süddeutschen Mai-Revolution des Jahres 1849*. Genf: Becker.

Bundeskriegsverfassung von 1821. In W. Rüstow (Ed.) (1859). *Die Grenzboten. Militärische Tagesfragen.* Berlin: Deutscher Verlag.

Bundesreaktionsbeschluß über Maßregeln zur Wahrung der öffentlichen Sicherheit und Ordnung im Deutschen Bund vom 23. August 1851. In E. R. Huber (Ed.) (1986). *Dokumente zur deutschen Verfassungsgeschichte. Vol. 2: Deutsche Verfassungsdokumente 1851–1900* (pp. 1–2). Stuttgart: W. Kohlhammer.

Clark, C. M. (2006). *Iron kingdom: The rise and downfall of Prussia, 1600–1947.* London: Penguin.

Congreß sämtlicher März-Vereine Deutschlands (Congress of the Associations of the Vormärz in Germany). (1849). *Aufruf an das Deutsche Heer! Deutsche Krieger!* Berlin: Central and Regional Library. 6 May.

Cronin, B. (1999). *Community under anarchy. Transnational identity and the evolution of cooperation.* New York: Columbia University Press.

Das deutsche Volk an die sogenannte deutsche Bundesversammlung (1848/49:119/30 Nr.46; GOS-Nr. d0009991). Leipzig: Stadtgeschichtliches Museum.

Deutsch, K. W. (1954). *Political community at the international level. Problems of definition and measurement.* Garden City: Doubleday.

Deutsch, K. W., Burrell, S. A., Kann, R. A., Lee, M., Jr., Lichterman, M., Lindgren, R. E., Loewenheim, F. L., & van Wagenen, R. W. (1957). *Political community and the North Atlantic area. International organization in the light of historical experience.* Princeton: Princeton University Press.

Deutsche Bundesversammlung. (1823). Inaugural speech of the German confederal assembly by the Austrian envoy Count Karl Ferdinand von Buol-Schauenstein. In *Protokolle der Deutschen Bundesversammlung* (Band 15). Frankfurt am Main: Bundespräsidialbuchdruckerei.

Deutsche Zeitung. (1847). Heidelberg, 15. Oktober. In F. Salomon (Ed.) (1932) *Die deutschen Parteiprogramme,* 1 (pp. 69–72).

Düsseldorfer Zeitung. (1843). 3. and 5. September, no. 244, 246. In J. Hansen (Ed.) (1919). *Rheinische Briefe und Akten zur Geschichte der politischen Bewegung 1830–1850* (Vol. I, pp. 589–592). Düsseldorf: Droste.

Final act of the Viennese Ministerial Conferences (Vienna Final Act) of 15 May, 1820. In E. R. Huber (Ed.) (1978). *Deutsche Verfassungsdokumente 1803–1850, Vol. I, Dokumente zur deutschen Verfassungsgeschichte* (pp. 91–99). Stuttgart: W. Kohlhammer.

Finnemore, M., & Sikkink, K. (1998). International norm dynamics and political change. *International Organization,* 52(4), 887–917.

Frankfurt am Main: Bundespräsidialbuchdruckerei (1848a). *Stenographic report on the negotiations of the German Constituent Assembly at Frankfurt* (Vol. III, pp. 1881–1882). Frankfurt.

Frankfurt am Main: Bundespräsidialbuchdruckerei (1848b). *Stenographic report on the negotiations of the German Constituent Assembly at Frankfurt* (Band IX, p. 4626). Leipzig.

Friedrich Wilhelm IV. (1848a). Almighty opening speech at the Berlin National Assembly on 22 May. In J. Killisch (1861). *So sprach der König: Reden, Trinksprüche, Proclamationen, Botschaften, Kabinetts-Ordres, Erlässe u.s.w. Friedrich Wilhelms IV., Königs von Preussen. Denkwürdigkeiten aus und zu Allerhöchstdessen Lebens- und Regierungsgeschichte vom Jahre 1840 bis 1854 in systematisch geordneter Zusammenstellung* (pp. 86–87). Stuttgart: Verlag Karl Göpel.

Friedrich Wilhelm IV. (1848b). Memorandum to His Majesty, the King of Prussia Friedrich Wilhelm IV., on the Prussian State Constitution on 15 September. http://www.documentArchiv.de/nzjh/preussen/1848/preussische-verfassung_denkschrift.html. Accessed 30 Oct 2013.

Friedrich Wilhelm IV. (1848c). Patent by His Majesty the King of Prussia Friedrich Wilhelm IV. Due to the convening of the Prussian United Assembly on 14 March. http://www.documentArchiv.de/nzjh/preussen/1848/vereinigter-landtag-einberuf_patent.html. Accessed 30 Oct 2013.

Friedrich Wilhelm IV. (1848d). Proclamation of His Majesty the King of Prussia Friedrich Wilhelm IV, on 21 March. http://www.documentArchiv.de/nzjh/preussen/1848/friedrich-wilhelmIV-volk-dt-nation_prkla.html. Accessed 30 Oct 2013.

German Federal Act of 8 June 1815. In E. R. Huber (Ed.) (1978). *Deutsche Verfassungsdokumente 1803–1850, Vol. I, Dokumente zur deutschen Verfassungsgeschichte* (pp. 84–90). Stuttgart: W. Kohlhammer.

Gesetz betreffend die Grundrechte des deutschen Volks (Fundamental Rights and Demands of the German People) on 27 December 1848. http://www.documentArchiv.de/nzjh/1848/grundrechte1848_ges.html. Accessed 30 Oct 2013.

Gruner, W. D. (2003). Historical dimensions of German statehood: From the old Reich to the new Germany. In A. B. Gunlicks (Ed.), *German public policy and federalism: Current debates on political, legal, and social issues* (pp. 15–47). New York: Berghahn.

Gruner, W. D. (2012). *Der Deutsche Bund, 1815–1866.* München: C.H. Beck.

Hagan, J. D. (2000). Domestic political sources of stable peace. The great powers, 1815–1854. In A. Kacowicz, Y. Bar Siman-Tov, O. Elgström, & M. Jerneck (Eds.), *Stable peace among nations* (pp. 36–54). Lanham: Rowman and Littlefield.

Haldén, P. (2011). Republican continuities in the Vienna order and the German Confederation (1815–66). *European Journal of International Relations, 19*(2), 281–304.

Hein, D. (2007). *Die Revolution von 1848/49.* München: C.H. Beck.

Huber, E. R. (1988). *Deutsche Verfassungsgeschichte seit 1789. Vol. 2: Der Kampf um Einheit und Freiheit, 1830–1850.* Stuttgart: W. Kohlhammer.

Karlsbader Beschlüsse (Carlsbad Decrees) von 1819. In E. H. Huber (Ed.) (1978) *Deutsche Verfassungsdokumente 1803–1850, Vol. 1, Dokumente zur deutschen Verfassungsgeschichte* (pp. 102–104). Stuttgart: W. Kohlhammer.

Kolb, E. (1975). Polenbild und Polenfreundschaft der deutschen Frühliberalen. Zur Motivation und Funktion außenpolitischer Parteinahme im Vormärz'. *Saeculum*, 26, 111–127.

Langewiesche, D. (1999). Föderativer Nationalismus als Erbe der deutschen Reichsnation: Über Föderalismus und Zentralismus in der deutschen Nationalgeschichte'. In D. Langewiesche & G. Schmidt (Eds.), *Föderative Nation. Deutschlandkonzepte von der Reformation bis zum Ersten Weltkrieg* (pp. 215–242). München: Oldenbourg.

Lindner, T. (1920). *Weltgeschichte in zehn Bänden. Revolution und Reaktion. Der Übergang zu unserer Zeit, 1848–1859*. Stuttgart and Berlin: Cotta.

List, F. (1841). *Das deutsche Eisenbahnsystem als Mittel zur Vervollkommung der deutschen Industrie, des deutschen Zollvereins und des deutschen Nationalverbandes überhaupt*. Stuttgart and Tübingen: Cotta.

Marx, K., & Engels, F. (1960). *Werke, Vol. VIII: Revolution und Konterrevolution in Deutschland*. Berlin: Dietz.

Müller, J. (2006). *Der Deutsche Bund, 1815–1866*. München: Oldenbourg.

Poschinger, H. (1901). *Unter Friedrich Wilhelm IV. Denkwürdigkeiten des Ministers Otto Freiherrn von Manteuffel* (Vol. 1). Berlin: Mittler.

Program of the German Reform Association (1862). In E. R. Huber (Ed.) (1986). *Deutsche Verfassungsdokumente 1851–1900, Vol. II, Dokumente zur deutschen Verfassungsgeschichte* (pp. 109–110). Stuttgart: W. Kohlhammer.

Regierungserklärung vor dem österreichischen Reichstag am 27. November 1848 (Government Statement before the Austrian Reichstag on 27 November 1848). In H. Fenske (Ed.) (1976). *Vormärz und Revolution* (Vol. IV). Darmstadt: Wissenschaftliche Buchgesellschaft.

Reichsgesetz über die Einführung einer provisorischen Zentralgewalt für Deutschland beschlossen von der verfassungsgebenden deutschen Nationalversammlung am 28. Juni 1848 (Imperial Law on the Introduction of a Provisional Central Government of Germany Ratified by the Constituent German National Assembly on 28 June 1848). In E. R. Huber (Ed.) (1986). *Deutsche Verfassungsdokumente 1851–1900* (Vol. II, pp. 122–123). Stuttgart: W. Kohlhammer.

Schroeder, P. W. (1994). *The transformation of European politics, 1763–1848*. Oxford: Oxford University Press.

Schutz- und Trutzbündnis zwischen Österreich und Preussen vom 20. April 1854 (Offensive and Defensive Alliance between Austria and Prussia from 20 April 1854). *Reichsgesetzblatt für das Kaisertum Österreich*, 1854, 732.

Schüßler, W. (1924). *Bismarck: Die gesammelten Werke*. Berlin: Stolberg.

Schwarzenberg, F. v. (1848). Letter by von Schwarzenberg to the Austrian Representative in Frankfurt am Main, Baron von Menßhengen, on 28 December. In E. R. Huber (Ed.) (1978). *Deutsche Verfassungsdokumente 1803–1850. Vol. 1: Dokumente zur deutschen Verfassungsgeschichte*, 3rd edn. Stuttgart: W. Kohlhammer.

Siemann, W. (1995). *Vom Staatenbund zum Nationalstaat. Deutschland 1806–1871.* München: C.H. Beck.

Six Articles, 28 June 1832. In E. R. Huber (1978). *Deutsche Verfassungsdokumente 1803–1850. Vol. I: Dokumente zur deutschen Verfassungsgeschichte* (pp. 132–133). Stuttgart: W. Kohlhammer.

Srbik, H. (1925). *Metternich. Der Staatsmann und der Mensch.* München: F. Bruckmann.

Stern, F. (1977). *Gold and iron. Bismarck, Bleichröder and the building of the German empire.* New York: Random House.

Taylor, A.J.P. (2001). *The Course of German History: A Survey of the Development of German History Since 1815.* New York: Routledge.

The Eisenach Declaration of the German National Association (1859). In E. R. Huber (Ed.) (1986). *Deutsche Verfassungsdokumente 1851–1900, Vol. II, Dokumente zur deutschen Verfassungsgeschichte* (pp. 104–105). Stuttgart: W. Kohlhammer.

The Ten Articles from 5 July 1832. In E. R. Huber (Ed.) (1978) *Deutsche Verfassungsdokumente 1803–1850. Vol. I: Dokumente zur deutschen Verfassungsgeschichte* (pp. 134–135). Stuttgart: W. Kohlhammer.

Tilly, R. H. (1990). *Vom Zollverein zum Industriestaat. Die wirtschaftlich-soziale Entwicklung Deutschlands 1834 bis 1914.* München: Deutscher Taschenbuch-Verlag.

Treitschke, H. v. (1911). F.C. Dahlmann. In H. v. Treitschke (Ed.), *Historische und politische Aufsätze.* Leipzig: Hirzel.

Verordnung des Königs von Sachsen Anton die Publication der, wegen des Wanderns der Handwerksgesellen unter'm 15. Januar und 12. März 1835, gefaßten Bundesbeschlüsse betreffend, erlassen am 6. Juli 1835 (Provision of the King of Saxony Anton Concerning the Publication of the Combined Federal Decrees of 15 January and 12 March 1835 Because of Hiking Journeymen, Issued on 6 July 1835. http://www.documentArchiv.de/nzjh/sachsen/1835/handeswerksgesellen-wanderung-bschl_vo.html. Accessed 30 Oct 2013.

Verordnung des Königs von Sachsen Friedrich August II. die Publication eines, auf die Abstellung der Gesellenverbindungen und Gesellen-Handwerksmißbräuche abzweckenden, unterm 3. December 1840 gefaßten Bundesbeschlusses betreffend, erlassen am 2. Januar 1841 (Provision of the King of Saxony Friedrich August II Concerning the Publication of the Combined Federal Decree of 3 December 1840, on the Secondment of Journeymen Compounds and Journeymen Misuses, Issued on 2 January 1841. http://www.documentArchiv.de/nzjh/sachsen/1841/handwerksgesellen-verbindung-beschl_vo.html. Accessed 30 Oct 2013.

Verordnung des Kultusministeriums des Königreichs Sachsen den Bundesbeschluß vom 13. November 1834 über die Universitäten und andere Lehr- und Erziehungsanstalten betreffend, erlassen am 2. Januar 1835 (Provision of the

Ministry of Education of the Kingdom of Saxony Concerning the Federal Decree of 13 November 1834 on Universities and Other Teaching and Educational Institutions, Issued on 2 January 1835. http://www.document-Archiv.de/nzjh/sachsen/1835/universitaeten-bschl_vo.html. Accessed 30 Oct 2013.

Verordnung Sr. Majestät des Königs von Sachsen Friedrich August II. zu Bekanntmachung des wegen Aufhebung der Censur in den Staaten des Deutschen Bunds unterm 3ten März 1848 gefaßten Bundesbeschlusses, erlassen am 9. März 1848 (Provision of His Majesty the King of Saxony Friedrich August II to Notice of the Application for Annulment of Censorship in the States of the German Confederation Under the Combined Federal Decree of 3 March 1848, Issued on 9 March 1848. http://www.documentArchiv.de/nzjh/sachsen/1848/zensur-aufhebung-deutscher-bund_vo.html. Accessed 30 Oct 2013.

Winkler, H. A. (2000). *Der lange Weg nach Westen, Vol. 1: Deutsche Geschichte vom Ende des Alten Reiches bis zum Untergang der Weimarer Republik*. München: C.H. Beck.

Wirth, J. G. A. (1832). Das Nationalfest der Deutschen zu Hambach. http://www.deutschestextarchiv.de/wirth_nationalfest02_1832. Accessed 21 Sept 2015.

CHAPTER 4

'Unsuccessful' Disintegration: The Transatlantic Security Community

The NATO typically serves as a textbook example of a security community as Karl Deutsch and his associates made the North Atlantic area the primary empirical focus of their inquiry (Deutsch et al. 1957).[1] Few contemporary scholars would doubt that a transatlantic security community exists today. NATO even describes itself as a 'transatlantic security community' (Rasmussen 2010). Recently, the rift in the transatlantic security community over the war in Iraq in 2003 has sparked a lively academic debate about the nature of NATO as a security community implying that disintegrative processes may have been occurring (Cox 2005; Pouliot 2006; Bjola and Kornprobst 2007; Anderson et al. 2008; Kitchen 2009; Koschut 2010).

It is important to point out in this context that even though security communities frequently develop common organizational structures, the two need not be congruent. Thus, while NATO certainly forms the core organizational structure for the transatlantic security community, certain NATO members may not be recognized as members of the transatlantic security community. For example, there continue to be military stand-offs between Greece and Turkey over Cyprus making their membership in the security community at least questionable. On the other hand, there are a number of countries like Sweden or Austria that are not formal members of NATO but may still be counted as part of the transatlantic security community. Karl W. Deutsch et al. (1957, p. 10) defined the transatlantic security community as 'all countries bordering upon the North Atlantic

Ocean or the North Sea, along with their immediate land-neighbors in Europe (...) (t)he United States, Canada, and what is usually considered Western and Southern Europe'. To this area, we should add today the Central and Eastern European states that joined NATO after the end of the Cold War.[2] Even though the terms 'transatlantic security community' and 'NATO' are used almost interchangeably throughout this chapter, this important distinction should be kept in mind.

The transatlantic security community originally developed around a core area (USA and Great Britain) as a result of the World War II alliance against Germany. This war alliance transformed into a permanent regional institutionalized structure with the founding of NATO in 1949. All member states retain their sovereignty and multilateral decision-making is based on consensus. The main institutional body is the North Atlantic Council in which member states convene on a regular basis to discuss security issues of common concern. Today, it seems fair to claim that the USA forms the single core state of the transatlantic security community given its vast military and economic capabilities but also its historical image as Europe's pacifier after two major wars.

The Normative Order of the Transatlantic Security Community

The transatlantic democratic West as an imagined regional space forms the bedrock of the collective identity of the transatlantic security community. This transatlantic identity is defined as the totality of a collection of different languages, ethnic groups, and religious settings, united by a common history, traditions, and values.[3] This identity influences the way how people, as part of an imagined space, think about the surrounding world and their particular way of life (O'Hagan 2002, pp. 11–2). The identity of a 'transatlantic West' as well as its associated beliefs and meanings are closely linked to the normative order of the transatlantic security community outlined below. Norm leaders can be found at virtually any level of society including state leaders, government and public officials, as well as political elites, business people, pundits, academics, and interest groups. These norm leaders advocate a Western democratic 'way of life' thereby reinforcing its norms and meaning at the domestic level. I will now further elaborate on the normative order of the transatlantic security community.

Norm of Common Values

The transatlantic security community rests on a consensus of mutual values. The primary values of the transatlantic security community can be found in the North Atlantic Treaty of 1949. The preamble commits its members to the principles of democracy, individual freedom, and the rule of law as well as to the principles of the UN Charter. The principle of free market economies is added to that list in Article 2. In sum, the primary values of the transatlantic security community are the principles laid out in the UN Charter (collective security, national self-determination, human rights, and international law) along with the liberal principles of democracy, individual freedom, the rule of law, and free market economies. These primary values together define the distinctive way of life of the transatlantic security community as pointed out in the most recent Strategic Concept:

> NATO member states form a unique community of values, committed to the principles of individual liberty, democracy, human rights and the rule of law. The Alliance is firmly committed to the purposes and principles of the Charter of the United Nations, and to the Washington Treaty, which affirms the primary responsibility of the Security Council for the maintenance of international peace and security. (NATO 2010)

In addition to these primary values, there are secondary values based on individual choices or life styles including religious beliefs or consumer behavior such as the dispute over genetically modified food as well as societal achievements such as the welfare state, which are contested and represent either different approaches to cope with individual and societal risks and/or are historically and culturally constructed.

In sum, North Atlantic integration has never been limited to security and military defense against an outside threat but insists on the formation of a community of values and the preservation of a distinctive (liberal–democratic) way of life. As the former Canadian Prime Minister Louis Stephen St Laurent explained in the Canadian House of Commons in 1948: 'The purpose of a North Atlantic association would not be merely negative. It would create the dynamic counter-attraction to Communism—the dynamic attraction of a free, prosperous and progressive society, as opposed to the totalitarian and reactionary society of the Communist world' (Hansard 1948, p. 3449). In a similar way, Lord Ismay, the first Secretary General of NATO, points out: 'The fundamental goals of the Treaty (are) the attainment by the fourteen countries of "conditions of stability and well-being" and the "strengthening of their free institutions". The military effort, urgent as that is, represents one of the means, but not all, to achieve that end' (Ismay 1955, 192).

Norm of Multilateral Practice

The ability of members to predict the behavior and performance of other members characterizes the transatlantic security community as a community of multilateral practice. In this community, the peaceful resolution of conflicts of interest through diplomacy and negotiation becomes the norm while war among its members becomes unthinkable. This collective knowledge is rooted in a normative understanding of multilateralism, which involves a strong or 'thick' type of multilateralism. As pointed out before, 'thick' multilateralism transcends the instrumental logic of egoistic and utility-maximizing behavior (which would be weak or 'thin' multilateralism) but instead refers to the practice of self-restraint and the social construction of a collective identity (Adler 2001, p. 146; Adler and Greve 2009, p. 71). Most importantly, Article 1 binds its members to the peaceful resolution of international conflict in accordance with the Charter of the UN:

> The Parties undertake, as set forth in the Charter of the United Nations, to settle any international dispute in which they may be involved by peaceful means in such a manner that international peace and security and justice are not endangered, and to refrain in their international relations from the threat or use of force in any manner inconsistent with the purposes of the United Nations. (NATO 1949)

Article 1 thus defines peaceful change as the core purpose and goal of NATO, which obviously reflects the Deutschian concept of security community (Deutsch et al. 1957, p. 124).

Whereas peaceful resolution of conflicts is the general norm among members of the transatlantic security community, Article 5 of the NATO Treaty explicitly allows for the individual or collective use of force against outsiders. This mutual-defense clause essentially defines the meaning of the North Atlantic area and sets it apart from its pre–World War II Other. As Lord Ismay argues:

> There is a wealth of meaning behind those short, simple phrases. They make clear to any would-be aggressor that his attack would be met by the combined resistance of all the member states. They mean that the United

States has in set terms abandoned its traditional peacetime isolationism from the affairs of Europe and has linked its fate to that of the free countries of Europe for mutual self-defence. Article 5 also means that some of the European countries have abandoned the habit of mind which in the past led them to refrain up to the last moment from committing themselves in advance to joint defence policies. (NATO 2013)

In the transatlantic security community, the use of force is strictly limited to the right of self-defense in accordance with the UN Charter. Its sole purpose is 'to restore and maintain the security of the North Atlantic area' (North Atlantic Treaty). According to the preamble of the North Atlantic Treaty, its members 'are resolved to unite their efforts for collective defence and for the preservation of peace and security' (NATO 1949). This involves a consensus on acceptable and appropriate military means and capabilities as well as the ability to execute a collective response.

Norm of Communication

Even though the multilateral norm implies the primacy of collective action, Article 3 of the treaty explicitly allows for unilateral actions (including the use of force) by members states. This possibility adds significance to the norm of communication among members of the transatlantic security community.

As argued above, communication involves not simply informing other members about imminent actions or policies but includes the permanent exchange of values, beliefs, interests, and perceptions (Kitchen 2009, p. 101). The purpose of such 'thick' communication is to prevent unilateral actions or conflicts of interests from happening in the first place. This 'thick' understanding of communication leads to the norm of consultation as laid out in Article 4 of the North Atlantic Treaty. The NATO Committee on the North Atlantic Community further specified the meaning of the norm of communication in 1951 and defined consultation as a habit of interstate relations in the transatlantic area in order to create coherence and consensus in policy matters. The NATO Committee on Non-Military Cooperation was even more explicit, when it declared in 1956:

> Consultation (…) means more than exchange of information, though that is necessary. It means more than letting the NATO Council know about national decisions that have already been taken; or trying to enlist support for those decisions. It means the discussion of problems collectively, in the early stages of policy formation, and before national positions become fixed.

At best, this will result in collective decisions on matters of common interest affecting the Alliance. At the least, it will ensure that no action is taken by one member without a knowledge of the views of the others. (NATO 1956)

Collective action in the transatlantic security community hence aims not at coercion and instrumental calculations and incentives but at consensus building (Risse 2000, p. 7). This means that regional consultation needs to take place prior to domestic decision-making if members intend to take into account and respond to the interests and perceptions of other members because once a domestic decision on a foreign policy matter has been made, democratic leaders will act with resolve in order to avoid audience costs at home (Starr 1992; Bueno de Mequista et al. 1999). The transformed and intimate nature of thick communication among members of the transatlantic security community—an increase in mutual responsiveness—can be illustrated by a comment by Paul-Henri Spaak, the second Secretary General to NATO, during a NATO Council meeting: 'The discussions were (...) becoming more and more like cabinet discussions and less and less like formal international meetings' (cited in: Deutsch et al. 1957, p. 195). In sum, the transatlantic norm of communication involves timely and regular consultation, information, and responsiveness.

Dysfunction

The velocity of social upheavals within socialist states in 1989 took the members of the transatlantic security community by complete surprise. Of course, there had been warning signs like Gorbachov's reform policies in the late 1980s as well as domestic protests in the Eastern bloc. However, the thrust and speed with which political and social transformations took place in Eastern Europe and the Soviet Union redrew the security landscape almost overnight.

External Change: The End of the Cold War and the Introduction of New Ideas

Crucially, with the dissolution of the Warsaw Pact on 1 July 1991, the continued relevance of NATO seemed in question. Especially in Moscow, but also within the transatlantic security community itself, scattered voices called instead for the construction of a comprehensive collective security system including both NATO members and the former Warsaw Pact states. French president François Mitterand even suggested the forming of a pan-European confederation that would include Russia but not the USA (Lundestad 2003, p. 237).

Consequently, given the thrust of this external 'shock', it seemed at first uncertain whether and in what form the transatlantic security community would even continue to exist at all. In this period of uncertainty, three possible security architectures emerged: First, the option of a European security community combining the Western European Union (WEU) and the European Community (EC); second, a pan-European security community integrating all the countries of Europe and North America using an institutionalized and reformed Conference for Security and Cooperation in Europe (CSCE); finally, a transatlantic security community with a reformed and expanded NATO at center stage.

Given this level of uncertainty, it is plausible to suggest that the developments following the fall of the Berlin Wall and the dissolution of the Warsaw Pact ushered in a crisis of identity for the members of the transatlantic security community. Sudden and largely unanticipated major changes in its external environment argued forced NATO members to reflect on the meaning and purpose of transatlantic security, a re-evaluation of its community norms, and the potential search for new meanings and objectives. Many members raised fundamental and existential questions like 'Who are we?' and 'Where are we going from here?' These questions were partially answered in the London Declaration in June 1990, in which its members reaffirmed their collective identity and sense of community as a source of ideational reassurance pledging to extend the transatlantic peace to Eastern Europe:

> We need to keep standing together, to extend the long peace we have enjoyed these past four decades. Yet our Alliance must be even more an agent of change. It can help build the structures of a more united continent, supporting security and stability with the strength of our shared faith in democracy, the rights of the individual, and the peaceful resolution of disputes. We reaffirm that security and stability do not lie solely in the military dimension, and we intend to enhance the political component of our Alliance as provided for by Article 2 of our Treaty. (NATO 1990)

In other words, the members of the transatlantic security community interpreted the outcome of the end of the Cold War as being directly linked to and in part resulting from their common normative values. After all, had not protesters on the streets of Leipzig, Gdansk, Prague, and Budapest demanded liberal values like individual freedom and democracy?

From this perspective, norm leaders viewed the end of the Cold War not as weakening but as a reaffirmation and strengthening of NATO's collective identity and norms. Initially, this conviction ensured the continued relevance and legitimacy of the transatlantic security community as 'the underlying political compact that binds North America's fate to Europe's democracies' (NATO 1990). As the New Strategic Concept of 1991 explained:

> Based on common values of democracy, human rights and the rule of law, the Alliance has worked since its inception for the establishment of a just and lasting peaceful order in Europe. This Alliance objective remains *unchanged*. (emphasis added, NATO 1991)

Hence, according to this view, prevalent among most norm leaders, the continued presence of the transatlantic security community appeared to be still needed to ensure peaceful change in Europe.

This also meant that the transatlantic normative order would have to be adapted and extended to its former adversaries. Accordingly, former inside/outside configurations of amity/enmity were no longer relevant: 'The Atlantic Community must reach out to the countries of the East which were our adversaries in the Cold War, and extend to them the hand of friendship' (NATO 1990). This led to the formation of institutional frameworks to extend and share transatlantic norms with the new partners. These new institutional frameworks, such as the NATO Cooperation Council (NACC) and later the Partnership for Peace (PfP), can be viewed as 'schools of learning' where established members would teach the transatlantic community norms to former outsiders.

Another new idea that was introduced by the members of the transatlantic security community sought to extend NATO's military capabilities beyond the strictly defined territory in the North Atlantic Treaty in order to be able to assist the crisis management by the UN and the newly formed Organization for Security and Cooperation in Europe (OSCE) in the former Yugoslavia. This idea was not entirely new, as out-of-area missions had been debated within NATO before. However, whereas the idea of militarily operating beyond the North Atlantic area had been practically unfeasible during the Cold War, it became a viable option after the dissolution of the Soviet Union and the Warsaw Pact (Kitchen 2010).

In 1992, the Defense Planning Committee officially introduced the idea of NATO's participation in out-of-area peacekeeping operations:

> NATO possesses unique capabilities to contribute to peacekeeping operations. We, as Defence Ministers, have an important role to play in developing NATO's ability to support such operations in response to requests from the UN or CSCE. (...) We have concluded that support for UN and CSCE peacekeeping should be included among the missions of NATO forces and headquarters. (NATO 1992a)

The NATO Council adopted a statement later that year, which reaffirmed the norm common values of the transatlantic security community regarding the primacy of the UN:

> We duly agree on the preparedness of our Alliance to support, on a case-by-case basis and in accordance with our own procedures, peacekeeping operations under the authority of the UN Security Council, which has the *primary* responsibility for international peace and security. (emphasis added, NATO 1992b)

By declaring its willingness to militarily intervene outside NATO's territory, the norm leaders of the transatlantic security community thus effectively introduced a new 'out-of-area' norm that was to serve as an amendment to the norm of multilateral practice. NATO's 'efforts for collective defense and for the preservation of peace and security' were now geographically no longer confined to the Euro-Atlantic area nor limited to traditional military attacks by outsiders but could be, at least in principle, extended to the global level and included new and unconventional threats:

> Alliance security must also take account of the global context. Alliance security interests can be affected by other risks of a wider nature, including proliferation of weapons of mass destruction, disruption of the flow of vital resources and actions of terrorism and sabotage. (NATO 1991)

However, these norm innovations (enlargement/out-of-area operations) were unspecified and thus quickly invited skepticism and anxiety among norm leaders regarding their concrete meaning. For example, while most member states agreed in principle to reach out to Eastern European countries, a heated debate developed in the security community over its scope. In the USA, for example, there were quite substantial internal differences over the issue enlargement. While US Secretary of State Warren Christopher wanted to gradually pursue enlargement, his Assistant Secretary of State for European and Canadian Affairs, Steve Oxman, publicly opposed it (Atlantic Council 1993). Britain, on the other hand, feared that Eastern enlargement could reduce American commitment within NATO as well as undermine the goal of creating a democratic and peaceful Russia. Though in principle in favor of enlargement, British Foreign Minister Hurd warned against letting 'rhetoric run ahead of reality'. Specifically, British diplomats, citing the norm of multilateral practice (in particular collective defense), questioned whether the British public was ready to go to war for a country like Poland (cited in: Asmus 2002, p. 46). France equally opposed enlargement albeit for opposite reasons. French norm leaders worried that enlargement could increase American commitment in Europe and thus undermine a nascent European Security and Defense Identity (ESDI). As French Defense Minister François Leotard stated:

> To knock at NATO's door is to knock at America's door and ask for American guarantees. That is understandable, but it is not our conception. We want the request for security directed to the countries of Europe. (cited in: Yost 1998, pp. 112–3)

On this particular question, French policymakers even acted as norm challengers by implicitly introducing the idea of an independent European security community to replace NATO. The problem with France's position was that majorities of Eastern European leaders and citizens simply did not agree with that position (Fierke and Wiener 1999, p. 723).

Meanwhile, the idea of Eastern enlargement remained highly controversial among transatlantic norm leaders. In London, the German Defense Minister Volker Rühe gave a speech at the International Institute of Strategic Studies during which he enthusiastically advocated NATO enlargement. However, the reaction among British and other NATO diplomats in the audience was rather lukewarm. As a result, German Chancellor Helmut Kohl and the German Federal Foreign Office both quickly disassociated themselves from the speech. As the then US Ambassador to Germany, Richard Holbrooke, later recalled, Kohl had told him at a private dinner that

> NATO can exclude taking in countries of Eastern Europe. At the NATO summit in January, we must talk of restructuring and reorienting NATO. We must tell these East European countries that they can count on our support, but not our membership. (cited in: Asmus 2002, p. 47)

Hence, when NATO Secretary General Manfred Wörner raised the idea of placing enlargement on the agenda for the upcoming NATO Summit, other norm leaders told him that the topic remained too controversial (NATO 1993).

The debate arrived at a turning point when US President Clinton, disappointed by Russian reforms and wary over NATO's future, made the issue of enlargement a top priority for his administration as well as a litmus test for NATO's continued relevance and legitimacy. In a meeting with Central and Eastern European head of states, the US president told them bluntly that their request for membership presented to him 'the clearest example I know (…) that NATO is not dead' (Clinton 1993). Clinton later explained his point in more detail to his Italian counterpart:

> The US cannot signal a withdrawal from Europe. NATO looking eastward will help explain the need for NATO to our domestic electorates. I believe that the US must lead, but we must do so by reasoning with our allies and finding a common position. (White House 1993)

With NATO's core state now actively pushing for the idea of enlargement, the question soon shifted from 'if' and 'why' to 'how' and 'when' Eastern European states would join the transatlantic security community. Over the following years, the core state persuaded other key norm leaders in Britain and Germany as well as most of the smaller member states to go ahead with NATO enlargement. Finally, at the NATO Summit in Brussels in 1994, even France joined in the consensus to implement the idea of Eastern enlargement.

As to the out-of-area norm, controversy among norm leaders created a similar dispute. Some, like Republican US Senator Richard Lugar, forcefully argued that NATO would have to go 'out-of-area or out-of-business' (Lugar 1993). NATO Secretary General Manfred Wörner also openly favored the introduction of an out-of-area norm but had to acknowledge that a lack of consensus among NATO member states on this question prevented the establishment of such a norm at this stage:

> The discussions we had (…) show that member nations want to deal with out of area questions in a way that does not involve NATO as such. It will be handled more on a case by case basis I believe. (Time 1991)

French norm leaders remained most openly opposed to the introduction of an out-of-area norm fearing that this would marginalize Western

Europe within the transatlantic security community. As one French official was quoted: 'We don't want NATO to become a directorate for global security affairs, and we fear that US attempts to invent impossible missions for NATO will only fuel Soviet fears and pacifism in Europe' (cited in: Wyatt-Walter 1997, pp. 170–1).

Apparently, the transatlantic security community was split on this issue with France, supported by Spain and Italy, in opposition to out-of-area operations, on the one hand, and the USA, supported by Britain, Germany, the Netherlands, Denmark, and Norway willing to extend collective defense outside NATO territory, on the other hand. Germany, however, still faced domestic legal restrictions on sending troops abroad that were left unresolved until the German Federal Court ruled out-of-area missions constitutional in 1994.

What made the debate over the introduction of a new out-of-area norm so controversial was the prospect that the consolidation of such a norm could lead not only to a geographical expansion of NATO's activities to instable regions like Africa, Asia, and the Middle East. Critically, many norm leaders worried that such norm adaptation would inevitably result in a substantial redefinition of the norm of multilateral practice thereby changing the meaning of transatlantic security. According to this view, Article 5 would be extended to include threats that were not traditionally recognized by many as affecting transatlantic security such as the proliferation of weapons of mass destruction, disruption of the flow of vital resources, and actions of terrorism and sabotage which the New Strategic Concept of 1991 had already listed as potential threats to take into considerations as an issue of collective defense.

ESDI also stirred concerns, in particular on the side of US norm leaders. To be sure, the USA welcomed the fact that the Europeans would take on more responsibility for their own defense and security and that Europe seemed to be willing to handle its fair share of the transatlantic burden leaving the USA with more resources and capabilities to focus on domestic issues as well as the promotion of American security interests in Asia and the Middle East. The core state worried, however, that the transformation of the WEU into ESDI could potentially create an alternative to the transatlantic security community effectively excluding the USA from European security consultations and potentially stirring division within NATO thus undermining the transatlantic normative order.

To counter such fears, EC members set up a new institutional framework for mutual consultation. This framework included biannual consultations between the president of the European Council, the head of the European Commission as well as the president of the USA, biannual consultations between the EC foreign ministers and the US Secretary of State, ad hoc consultations between the foreign minister of the rotating EC Presidency and the US Secretary of State, biannual consultations between the EC Commission and the US government at the cabinet level, and briefings by the EC Presidency to US officials on European Political Cooperation (EPC) meetings at the ministerial level. In doing so, both sides not only reaffirmed and extended the transatlantic norm of communication but also specified its implementation and meaning in the so-called Transatlantic Declaration:

> To achieve their common goals, the European Community and its Member States and the United States of America will inform and consult each other on important matters of common interest, both political and economic, with a view to bringing their positions as close as possible, without prejudice to their respective independence. In appropriate international bodies, in particular, they will seek close cooperation. (EU 1990)

In addition to the norm of communication, the Transatlantic Declaration also contained a firm commitment to the norms of common values and the norm of multilateral practice. On common values, both sides reaffirmed their determination to 'support democracy, the rule of law and respect for human rights and individual liberty, and promote prosperity' as well as their shared commitment to 'reinforcing the role of the United Nations'. On multilateral practices, EC members and the USA agreed to act 'on the basis of a pattern of cooperation proven over many decades (…) strengthening and expanding this partnership on an equal footing'.

Despite this reaffirmation and strengthening of transatlantic community norms, the US position remained ambiguous. On the one hand, President George H.W. Bush declared that 'a strong, united Europe is very much in America's interest. A more united Europe offers the United States a more effective partner, prepared for larger responsibilities'. On the other hand, the President warned the European members of secretly undermining the transatlantic normative order by stating that 'if our premise (of American leadership in NATO) is wrong—if, my friends, your ultimate aim is to provide independently for your own defense, then the time to tell us is today' (New York Times 1991).

When President Bill Clinton entered into office, the US stance toward deepening European security and defense integration softened noticeably. From the outset, the Clinton administration reassured European norm leaders that they had 'not viewed with alarm (...) the prospect that there could be greater European security cooperation between the French and the Germans and between others as well' (cited in: Lundestad 2003, p. 257). Only British norm leaders stood somewhat aside by stressing the need for EU enlargement while opposing deeper European security integration. To be sure, Clinton's pledge for ESDI was meant as complementing NATO's attempt to pursue democratic and market-based reforms in Eastern Europe while preparing them for NATO accession. It was certainly not be mistaken as replacing NATO, a point which US Secretary of State Warren Christopher made clear: 'The first principle is that NATO is and will remain the anchor of America's engagement in Europe and the core of transatlantic security' (NATO 1994a). In that same meeting, however, French norm leaders remained strongly opposed to such statements, which they interpreted as an 'Americanization of European security'.

In the end, the introduction of the Combined Joint Task Forces (CJTF) in 1993 bridged this divide somewhat. These multinational and multiservice forces enabled the EC/WEU members to conduct military operations outside of NATO but only with the consent of and following consultations with NATO members (NATO 1999a). At the NATO Summit in Brussels in 1994, member states not only reaffirmed transatlantic norms as 'the expression of a shared destiny' but also endorsed the formation of ESDI as a 'European pillar' *within* the transatlantic security community:

> We therefore stand ready to make collective assets of the Alliance available, on the basis of consultations in the North Atlantic Council, for WEU operations undertaken by the European Allies in pursuit of their Common Foreign and Security Policy. We support the development of separable but not separate capabilities which could respond to European requirements and contribute to Alliance security. (NATO 1994b)

From Washington's perspective, this compromise prevented a 'decoupling' of ESDI from NATO and thus preserved the transatlantic normative order in the future. However, it left the question unanswered of how EC members could act independently when it still depended on US consent for using its military capabilities.

On the whole, it can be argued that developments in the early 1990s led to a dysfunctional state of the transatlantic security community. The end of the Cold War represented a major external 'shock' that forced members to pause and reflect on the future meaning and purpose of the transatlantic security community. In turn, these rapid shifts in the external environment offered a window of opportunity for the introduction of new ideas and beliefs that were previously unthinkable such as Eastern enlargement or out-of-area missions. This altered situation produced confusion and temporary ambiguity in which 'old' ideas of collective defense gradually gave way to or coexisted with 'new' ideas of collective security. The idea of a separate European security and defense identity as an alternative to the transatlantic normative order and the unresponsive way in which some members like the USA and France at times dealt with these issues revealed a set of discourse and behavior that resulted in some cases of interruption of symbolic interaction and NATO rituals. Hence, norm leaders sometimes deviated from the collective norm of multilateral practice and communication taking the security community 'off track'.

Of course, one should be careful not to overemphasize these dysfunctional effects. Norm leaders, for example, developed remarkable integrative capabilities to adapt the normative order by reaffirming its common values, finding a consensus on the introduction of a new out-of-area norm as well as by setting up new institutions and consultation frameworks like the CTJF or the PfP. Also, there were hardly any substantial norm violations by individual members except for the occasional unresponsiveness by France and the USA. Most importantly, norm challengers remained virtually absent (with the exception of France implicitly arguing in favor of a separate European security and defense identity to replace NATO). Instead, the norm leaders themselves introduced new ideas and norms. In sum, it would be thus premature to conclude that the transatlantic security community had already set on a course toward disintegration at this early stage.

Still, the re-evaluation and adaptation of community norms and meanings in light of an external 'shock' had created significant norm disputes and disruptions of symbolic interaction among norm leaders. Moreover, they had only occurred in meeting rooms and plenary sessions. The jury was still out on the actual implementation of these norm innovations into political practice. As the next section will show, it was the disrupted symbolic interaction and institutional failure coupled with frequent norm violations that occurred during this implementation phase that makes it plausible to suggest that the transatlantic security community subsequently entered a stage of decline.

Decline

NATO's stage of decline arguably lasted roughly from the mid-1990s to the turn of the millennium. A cascade of norm violations shaped this period, as conflict management in the former Yugoslavia significantly undermined the normative order of the transatlantic security community. The Balkan crisis and the following break-up of Yugoslavia led to the first war fought on European soil since World War II. Those who had expected peace and stability after the end of the Cold War (Fukuyama 1989) must have been disillusioned by the violence, killing, and human suffering, which reached its first tragic peak in the war in Bosnia. Thus, this external 'shock' can be seen as a major test for the reformed transatlantic normative order after the Cold War.

For the first time since World War II, American norm leaders initially turned a major security issue entirely over to the European NATO member states. In the words of former US Secretary of State James Baker, '(i)t was time to make the Europeans step up the plate and show that they could act as a unified power. Yugoslavia was as good a first test as any' (Baker 1995, p. 637). The European norm leaders gladly accepted this challenge but failed to recognize that American passivity in fact cut NATO entirely out of the picture. Lacking the military and institutional capabilities to deal with a regional crisis, however, European norm leaders soon realized that they could not end the war in Bosnia. The USA, on the other hand, equally failed to realize that by effectively excluding NATO from the conflict in the Balkans, the Clinton administration contributed to NATO's institutional failure (Gompert 1996, pp. 127–8).

Convinced that the conflict in the dissolving Yugoslavia in general, and the war in Bosnia in particular, constituted a major threat to European integration, the Western European states virtually competed over finding a strategy to end the fighting. Initially, diverging interests within the EU reinforced a European lack of military and institutional capabilities to resolve the crisis. It would take Western European policymakers over a year, until 1993, to realize the negative implications of this Babylonian approach. By 1993, the Europeans had overcome their initial differences and eventually embarked on a joint strategy of imposing a UN arms embargo, contributing to UN ground forces in Bosnia (United Nations Protection Force [UNPROFOR]), and by making diplomatic efforts to reach a cease-fire while getting the warring parties at the negotiation table to work out a lasting peace agreement.

By the summer of 1995, US norm leaders realized the harm that its 'hands-off' policy vis-à-vis Bosnia had already caused to American credibility within NATO. In a memorandum on 21 June 1995, US Ambassador to the UN Madeleine Albright warned the president that 'the disaster in Bosnia was now "destroying" the administration's credibility'. She further stated that

> (US) reluctance to lead an effort to resolve a military crisis in the heart of Europe has placed at risk our leadership of the post-Cold War world, (…) Chirac's statement that "the position of leader of the Free World is vacant" has been chilling my bones for weeks. (cited in: Dobbs 1999, p. 363)

While the threat to American credibility presented an incentive for US engagement, President Clinton, though welcoming Albright's position, remained hesitant to take the initiative and instead opted for a policy of containing the conflict in Bosnia in order to avoid having to get involved (Daalder 2000, p. 7). Having laid out these overall presumptions, I will now look at the course of events in order to show how frequent conflict over and violations of transatlantic norms of values, multilateralism, and communication surfaced during conflict management in Bosnia.

Social and Internal Change I: The Bosnian Crisis

In its early stages, the Clinton administration had formulated a foreign policy of 'assertive multilateralism' which sought to decrease the costs of US global leadership while, at the same time, ensuring that NATO's multilateral engagement would not be decoupled from the USA. In the long run, this policy aimed at further integrating the USA into the concept of collective security in order to form a 'principled international community' (US Policy Information and Texts 1993, p. 31). In doing so, Washington would set an example to the military engagement of other states (under the UN system) thereby decreasing the burden of US global military commitment (Washington Post 1993, p. 33). At least in theory, such a policy aimed at creating a standing UN army called 'UN rapid reaction force' (Rudolf 2000, p. 304).

However, the military escalation and public humiliation during the Somalia mission (United Nations Operation in Somalia [UNOSOM]) altered this American policy dramatically when, in October 1993 and in front of TV cameras, Somali militias dragged the body of a dead US soldier through the streets of Mogadishu. Simultaneously, the failure of the UNPROFOR mission to resolve the ongoing conflict in Bosnia added to a growing delegitimization of the UN in the USA. Members of Congress increasingly withheld annual US assessments and contributions to the UN hoping to impose reform on the world organization (Patrick and Forman 2002). In the White House, doubts about the effectiveness of the UN to manage peace operations as well as pressure from an increasingly unilateral-oriented Congress resulted in Presidential Decision Directive (PDD) 25.

PDD 25 rejected any permanent designation or 'earmarking' of US troops to the UN and set clear prerequisites for American involvement in multilateral peace operations. President Clinton later summarized these guidelines to mean that 'our mission will be limited, focused and under the command of an American general' (White House 1994). Here, the Bosnian conflict marks a turning point as the USA shied away from pursuing an 'assertive multilateralism' as well as genuine support for UN peace operations in favor of a stronger focus on and articulation of US interests. In an often-quoted speech, President Clinton reflected on America's role in the world after the war in Bosnia stating that

> at the end of the Cold War, America truly is the world's indispensable nation. There are times when only America can make the difference between war and peace (…) We cannot and should not try to be the world's policeman. But where our interests and values are clearly at stake, and where we can make a difference, we must act and lead. (Clinton 1996)

Hence, as a direct result of the Bosnian crisis, the American norm regarding multilateralism was summed up as 'together where we can, alone where we must' (International Herald Tribune 1993, p. 8).

Most European norm leaders, on the contrary, emphasized the normative values of the transatlantic security community by resorting to the UN as the primary authority to resolve regional conflicts. Specifically, European norm leaders focused on reducing the ability of the conflict parties in Bosnia to continue to fight by reducing the overall amount of weapons entering the war zone. Consequently, European norm leaders asked the UN to impose an arms embargo on Bosnia (UN Resolution 713), which was to be enforced by a UN peacekeeping force (UNPROFOR) consisting of European ground troops primarily contributed by Great Britain and France. As a second track, European peace initiatives began with the

Lisbon initiative in February 1992, which aimed at dividing Bosnia into three regions dominated by separate ethnic groups combined in a single confederation. Yet, following a conversation with US Ambassador to Yugoslavia Warren Zimmermann (who had allegedly advised the Bosnian Muslim leader Alija Izetbegovic that 'if he didn't like it, why sign it?'), Izetbegovic immediately renounced the Lisbon agreement (Petras and Vieux 1996, p. 16).

In early 1993, the European norm leaders teamed up again with the UN and formulated the Vance-Owen Peace Plan (VOPP), which recommended the division of Bosnia and Herzegovina into ten provinces with the Croats, Muslims, and Serbs each having the majority in the three provinces, respectively. Sarajevo was intended to be the seat of the confederate government and to remain an open province. Again, the driving force behind the VOPP, and later the Owen-Stoltenberg plan, was the EU. While the Bosnian Serbs as well as the Bosnian Croats signaled their willingness to accept the agreement, the Bosnian Muslims rejected it because they were apparently led to believe that the USA would soon offer a better deal. As David Owen, who represented the EU in the negotiation process, stated: 'We can't get the Muslims on board. That is largely the fault of the Americans because the Muslims (...) think Washington may come into it (war) on their side any day now' (cited in: Petras and Vieux 1996, p. 18). By that, Owen was referring to increasing American pressure to lift the arms embargo and launch air strikes (the so-called 'lift-and-strike' strategy) against Serbian targets in Bosnia.

In another round of negotiations, the Contact Group, which included the USA, Russia, and members of the EU, granted 51 % of Bosnian territory to a Muslim-Croat federation while the Bosnian Serbs would receive 49 %. This time, the Bosnian Muslims agreed but the Bosnian Serbs rejected the plan. Actions taken by the Bosnian Muslims, who had launched a major offensive in the fall of 1994, as well as actions on behalf of the USA, which exerted diplomatic pressure in favor of the Bosnian Muslims, isolated the Bosnian Serbs and thus buried the work of the Contact Group (Daalder 2000, p. 28).

Eventually, during the Dayton Peace negotiations, led by US Secretary of State Warren Christopher and the chief US negotiator Richard Holbrooke, the US administration seized control of the Bosnia crisis and successfully drafted a peace proposal leaving Britain, France, and Germany to perform a mere supporting role. As the head of the German delegation at Dayton, Wolfgang Ischinger, later recalled:

> Already the place was unusual. In September 1995, I had told the Deputy Secretary of State, Strobe Talbott, in Washington, that it was entirely unacceptable for Europe to hold the planned 'proximity talks' (peace negotiations) outside of Europe. At the urging of Richard Holbrooke, Washington eventually got its way by proposing Dayton. (…) Moreover, the procedure was unusual at Dayton: (…), the US delegation entirely monopolized the negotiations on the geographical distribution and some other key issue to the undisguised anger of one or other contact groups partner. What also contributed to allied annoyance was the American tactic to suppress press contacts of the various delegations de facto. At the same time, Richard Holbrooke conducted ongoing talks with selected US journalists—of course, with an emphasis on the particular US role. (Auswärtiges Amt 1998, p. 32)

A pattern emerges from these various negotiation rounds that centers on the core state's behavior during these peace initiatives. First of all, US norm leaders would declare its support for peace while refusing to endorse any particular plan on the table when presented by the European norm leaders. Hence, it became unmistakably clear to European norm leaders that 'there (would) be no peace agreement (…) unless NATO and (…), the United States took the lead' (cited in: Petras and Vieux 1996, p. 4). Second, American norm leaders would exclusively give military advice and technical support to Bosnian Croats and Muslims while isolating the Bosnian Serbs. This undermined UN and European-led peace efforts by letting the former two conflict parties believe that by resisting European initiatives, they could improve their own negotiating position vis-à-vis the Bosnian Serbs by relying on US backing.

As a result, European diplomacy in Bosnia accompanied by UN peacekeeping was doomed to fail. To be fair, this was not entirely due to the American unresponsiveness toward European norm leaders. The European concept for negotiation, which centered on the UN, was based on neutrality and, in an asymmetrical conflict such as Bosnia, a policy of neutrality, aided by the arms embargo, ultimately favors the stronger war fraction (Frankfurter Allgemeine Zeitung 1993, p. 7). Hence, UN and European diplomacy in Bosnia indeed had serious flaws. Still, it became obvious that the core state was attempting to unilaterally establish control over crisis management in Bosnia effectively sidelining both the UN and European institutions. As President Clinton outlined in 1994,

> As we work to resolve that tragedy (Bosnia) and ease the suffering of its victims we also need to change our security institutions so they can better

address such conflicts and advance Europe's integration. Many institutions will play a role, including the European Union, the Western European Union, the Council of Europe, the Conference for Security and Cooperation in Europe and the United Nations. But NATO, history's greatest military alliance, must be central to that process. (Clinton 1994)

NATO's institutional failure over Bosnia was echoed by the new NATO's Secretary General Willy Claes who, in January 1995, complained extensively and in rather blunt terms about European cooperation with the UN in Bosnia: 'NATO has made itself ridiculous as a military organization. (...) (I)f we cannot set the rules of our military operations, they (UN) will have to find other idiots to support peacekeeping' (Financial Times 1995). A few weeks later, Claes went even further by openly questioning the transatlantic norm of common values which includes the primary authority of the UN:

> NATO is more than a sub-contractor of the UN. (...) (I)t will keep its full independence of decision and action. There may even be circumstances which oblige NATO to act on its own initiative *in the absence of a UN mandate*. (emphasis added, NATO 1995)

Even though UNPROFOR had indeed failed to achieve any major progress to resolve the Bosnian crisis, its main European contributors, France and Great Britain, vigorously held on to the mission once their troops were stationed on the ground. They opposed any unilateral US actions (including a Congressional resolution to lift the UN arms embargo and carry out NATO air strikes against the Bosnian Serbs) that would have undermined the role of the UN in Bosnia and, subsequently, would have endangered European troops on the ground. Having placed thousands of soldiers in vulnerable positions, British and French norm leaders strongly opposed the US 'lift-and-strike' strategy. Instead, they held on to the UN arms embargo, which, on the other hand, was opposed by the USA as an allegedly ineffective measure said to be primarily aiding the Bosnian Serbs.

European norm leaders bounced back by accusing Washington of not having contributed ground troops to UNPROFOR and thereby having limited the effectiveness of the peace operation (Daalder 2000, pp. 32–3). The credibility of the UN was at stake, particularly after UNPROFOR was unable to secure its own safe areas against Serbian aggression accompanied by images of (European) UN soldiers taken hostage by Bosnian Serbs.

By that time, norm divergence over the authority of the UN in Bosnian crisis management had led to a transatlantic crisis that seriously undermined the security community. As Richard Holbrooke, the chief architect of the Dayton Peace Agreement, later observed: 'By the spring of 1995 it had become commonplace to say that Washington's relations with our European allies were worse than at any time since the 1956 Suez crisis' (Holbrooke 1999, p. 361). This had significant implications for the transatlantic norms of multilateral practice and communication.

By 1994, US President Bill Clinton appeared increasingly frustrated about not being in control of events and, during an internal briefing before a meeting with French President Jacques Chirac, demanded that '(w)e have to seize control of this (Bosnia)' (cited in: Woodward 1996, p. 260). US Vice President Al Gore supported the President: 'It's the issue from hell. The Europeans are self-delusional. (...) The need for us to protect and preserve the alliance is driving our policy' (cited in: Daalder 2000, p. 91). In an extraordinary diplomatic effort, the administration subsequently pressured its European allies into approving NATO air strikes to protect UN safe areas and managed to end the so-called 'dual-key principle' so that UN civilian officials no longer had to agree to NATO air strikes.

In August 1995, Clinton sent his National Security Advisor Anthony Lake on a trip to Europe to confront the European norm leaders with a fait accompli. Ivo H. Daalder, at that time responsible for coordinating US policy toward Bosnia in the National Security Council, recalls: 'Lake would tell the allies what the United States would do, not ask them what they wanted' (Daalder 2000, p. 110). This impression is validated by Lake's presentation to President Clinton en route to Europe during which Lake stated:

> The line I'm going to take in the meetings with the allies is that this is the U.S. policy (...) This is what we intend to do. We'll hope you'll come with us (...) but (...) this is a strategy we're wedded to and now's the time to move on. (cited in: Woodward 1996, p. 267)

Two things can be said about these statements. First, US norm leaders apparently saw no need to consult with other European member states. The purpose of Lake's mission was simply to 'inform' norm leaders in London, Paris, and elsewhere 'about the decision the president has taken' in order to 'tell them what to do' (cited in: Daalder 2000, p. 110).

Moreover, US norm leaders appeared uninterested in a cohesive norm regime but instead tended to undermine symbolic interaction during the peace negotiations over Bosnia. In doing so, the core state also violated the transatlantic norms of communication and multilateral practice on a major issue (Bosnia) that was of tremendous concern to European norm leaders. Second, by confronting European norm leaders with a fait accompli, the USA sent the message that Washington would no longer listen to the concerns of smaller member states but, instead, was willing to go it alone if necessary. This represented another violation of transatlantic norms of multilateral practice and communication.

In the end, European norm leaders eventually gave in to US pressure without sanctioning US behavior. In 1994, European norm leaders appeared overwhelmed by an American determination to lead at any cost—even if that meant violating the transatlantic normative order. The unresponsive behavior of the core state implied that US security interests were more important than the seemingly petty concerns of European norm leaders. The subsequent Dayton Peace Accords demonstrated the success of US diplomacy by effectively sidelining the European norm leaders and simultaneously establishing a US-constructed peace arrangement for Bosnia. As Richard Holbrooke (1999, p. 361) observed, '(a)fter Dayton, American foreign policy seemed more assertive, more muscular (…) De Charette had it right: "America was back"'. At that point, dependence on the core state became unmistakably clear to European norm leaders. As Dominique Moïse summarized, 'we (Europeans) realized sadly that, without the United States to kick us we don't move (…) (a)nd we don't feel at ease alone with ourselves' (cited in: Stafford 1996, p. 61).

To sum up, US unresponsiveness during the Bosnian crisis had violated and undermined the transatlantic normative order alienating many European norm leaders. Arguably, the Bosnian conflict represented a significant step for the transatlantic security community from a dysfunctional state to an early stage of decline. The degeneration of the normative order would become even more apparent during the Kosovo crisis a few years later.

Social and Internal Change II: The Kosovo Crisis

The Kosovo crisis constituted another test to the post-Cold War transatlantic normative order. Following the killing of 45 Kosovo Albanians at Raçak in January 1999, American as well as European norm leaders became increasingly engaged in the conflict management. Initially, the transatlantic norm regime demonstrated consensus over shared normative values, above all human rights. As a result, some have even referred to this phenomenon as the 'New Humanism' (Chomsky 1999, p. 1). In the USA, Secretary of State Madeleine Albright even insisted that

> we are not going to stand by and watch Serb authorities do in Kosovo what they can no longer get away with doing in Bosnia. (Albright 1998)

In Europe, British Prime Minister Tony Blair forcefully declared that 'a new generation draws the line' (Newsweek 1999, p. 37). Echoing Clinton and Blair, NATO Secretary General Javier Solana stated that '(t)his war is about values and the moral constitution of the kind of Europe in which we will live in the 21st century' (Spiegel 1999, p. 18).

This reiteration of transatlantic normative values was understandable given that the atrocities committed in Raçak and elsewhere seriously challenged the transatlantic normative order. After all, the New Strategic Concept of 1991 had strengthened the political wing of the alliance as a community of values. Thus, President Clinton concluded that 'NATO itself would … (be) discredited for failing to defend *the very values that give it meaning*' (emphasis added, New York Times 1999a). In the year of NATO's 50th anniversary and the acceptance of three new members from the former Warsaw Pact, the image of overcoming Cold War divisions stood in stark contrast to violence and disintegration in Yugoslavia.

In this situation, the USA, as the core state of the transatlantic security community, chiefly defined the Kosovo crisis as threatening the collective norms and identity of the transatlantic security community. From the US point of view, NATO needed to demonstrate that it still played a role as the guarantor of peace and security in Europe. This seemed even more important given decreasing domestic support among European norm leaders for NATO's continuing relevance and legitimacy in a post–Cold War world. Public approval of NATO's relevance in a post-Cold War security environment indicated a slight drop between 1996 and 1998 from 69 % to 60 % in Germany and from 60 % to just above 50 % in Italy. In France, barely over 50 % of respondents continued to view NATO as relevant. Even in Great Britain, support for NATO decreased during these two years by 4 % (Worldviews 2002, p. 28). While these numbers still show overall support for NATO, the general downward trend equally indicates a growing NATO fatigue.

In the Kosovo crisis, the most serious transatlantic norm dispute arose over the question of a UN mandate. While most norm leaders in Europe underlined the fact that NATO as a regional organization should only act under the premise of a UN mandate, this norm was openly questioned on the other side of the Atlantic. As US Assistant Secretary of State Princeton Lyman noted

> that is a sore point with many other countries, including America's European allies, who feel much more comfortable with the political cover of a UN mandate even when they agree that (military) force is merited. (Lymann 2000, p. 129)

Even though the UN Security Council had passed Resolution 1199 calling for an end to violence in Kosovo, it soon became clear that Russia and China would not back any UN-authorized use of force against Serbia. NATO, on the other hand, was under considerable pressure to sort out the Kosovo crisis before its 50th anniversary summit. That summit had been intended by the transatlantic norm regime as a powerful example of symbolic interaction of NATO's continued relevance in a post-Cold War world. As pointed out above, the confrontation with Slobodan Milosevic over Kosovo posed a crucial test to NATO's norms and identity conflicting with the summit's envisioned objectives (MccGwire 2000, p. 9).

There have been many arguments and explanations why NATO went to war against Serbia and it is debatable as to what exactly led to this 'humanitarian intervention'. However, this is not the place to discuss this matter further. What is of relevance to this study is the fact that the core state appeared determined to use force against Serbia even if that meant to defy the transatlantic norm of common values, which included the primary authority of the UN. As noted in the previous section, the Somalia experience had already soured US taste for participating in UN-led peace operations. In addition to that, the Bosnia crisis had convinced American norm leaders that NATO should be more capable to resolve regional conflicts and to provide for the implementation of a peace agreement than the seemingly slow and ineffective crisis management of the UN.

European norm leaders, however, felt deeply uncomfortably with the idea of going to war over Kosovo without a UN mandate. At last, the USA conceded to include the UN in post-conflict management in Kosovo but not during the bombing campaign. In the end, the deployment of a post-conflict international security and civilian presence in Kosovo

(Kosovo Force [KFOR]) would be put under UN auspices. This has led some to conclude that the position of the UN, in general, and the role of the UN Security Council, in particular, have been strengthened by the Kosovo case (see, e.g., Joetze 2000, p. 8). Yet, such argumentation is misleading. The decision to hand over responsibility to the UN after the bombing of Serbia had ceased must be viewed in the context of the air campaign. As the failure to conduct a limited set of air strikes and the prospect of having to use ground troops threatened NATO's cohesion became apparent, American norm leaders attempted to open another window for diplomacy by getting Russia on board. This proved to be of critical importance to the military intervention and would have been impossible without reverting to the UN (Daalder and O'Hanlon 2000, p. 205). Such a tactical move demonstrates a perfect example of 'thin' multilateralism (Luck 2003, p. 165). This interpretation is reinforced by President Clinton's statement on the announcement of the end of the air strikes on Serbia on 10 June 1999:

> We have made sure that the going into Kosovo will have NATO command and control and rules of engagement set by NATO. (...) In the meantime, the United Nations will organize a civilian administration while preparing the Kosovars to govern and police themselves. As local institutions take hold, NATO will be able to turn over increasing responsibility to them and draw down its forces. (Clinton 1999)

This statement implicitly reveals Clinton's priorities by not only mentioning NATO before he refers to the UN but, more importantly, by reducing the UN role in crisis management to a solely civilian one. In his statement, the US president further leaves out the fact that NATO's mandate for KFOR included Russian troops and was in fact formally placed under UN auspices. In this context, it was also characteristic for the mindset of US norm leaders that when US Deputy Secretary of State Strobe Talbott, a personal friend and advisor to President Clinton, reflected on the events in Kosovo, he did not mention the UN at all (Talbott 1999).

The European norm leaders, on the contrary, were much more ambivalent if not outright opposed to this downgrading of the UN. In fact, the absence of a UN authorization for NATO's air campaign posed a major problem to most European norm leaders who interpreted the norm of multilateral practice to mean that NATO could not use force for other purposes than self-defense unless the UN Security Council had approved an explicit mandate first. Thus, when NATO commenced the air campaign, many European norm leaders were desperately searching for an alternative source of legitimacy to mask this obvious violation of community norms, which led them to emphasize the urgency of the humanitarian situation. As French President Jacques Chirac had earlier explained in October 1998:

> Any military action must be requested (...) by the Security Council. (...) I would add, and repeat, that the humanitarian situation constitutes a ground that can justify an exception to a rule (...) And if it appeared that the situation required it, then France would not hesitate to join those who would like to intervene in order to assist those at are in danger. (cited in: Guicherd 1999, p. 28)

German Foreign Minister Joschka Fischer went even further by bluntly declaring that '(i)f people are massacred, you cannot mutter about having no mandate. You must act' (New York Times 1999b).

Given these statements by European norm leaders, it would be misleading to single out the USA as the sole norm violator in this case. Yet, the core state's role of actively pushing for a military intervention without a UN mandate appears crucial. Given the resoluteness and unresponsiveness of the US core state, European norm leaders realized that they had little choice but to follow the American lead. Key British norm leaders marked an exception by openly embraced the American position. Striking an Anglo-American chord, Prime Minister Tony Blair declared that '(o)n its 50th birthday NATO must prevail' (Newsweek 1999, p. 37).

However, there were also dissenting voices such as John Weston, the former Permanent Representative of the UK to the UN, who, in 1997, had cautioned that 'American exceptionalism cannot mean being the exception to the laws everyone else has to obey' (Diplomatic World Bulletin 1997, p. 1). The German General Heinz Loquai (2000), at that time a senior military advisor to the OSCE, openly criticized the USA for waging a war without a UN mandate. In Germany, despite Joschka Fischer's forceful remarks cited above, the ruling Social Democrats and the Green Party were both internally divided over the Kosovo issue culminating in the red 'color bomb' attack (symbolizing the blood of supposed NATO victims in Serbia) on German Foreign Minister Joschka Fischer at a special convention on Kosovo by the Green Party (a vivid example of the disruption of symbolic interaction within the transatlantic security community). Even in the USA, the Kosovo intervention was not popular among the general public. Until the beginning of the air campaign, only 43 % of the US public spoke out in support of going to war over Kosovo. At the domestic level, most transatlantic societies were deeply divided if not in outright opposition to the intervention. Great Britain and Greece represented the two extreme poles within the transatlantic security community. In Great Britain, a solid majority of the population supported going to war. Conversely, in Greece, the public strongly opposed a NATO intervention by a stunning 97 % (Program on International Policy Attitudes 1999).

In the end, given this domestic divide, most European norm leaders, with the exception of Great Britain, were far from united in defending one normative value of the transatlantic security community (human rights) by collectively violating another norm of the transatlantic security community, namely the authority of the UN. As a result, EU members, following the Cologne Summit in June and the Helsinki Summit in December 1999, seemed determined to increase their capability to act militarily, on occasion, independently from NATO. This step can be viewed as a way to avoid granting the USA a veto right within NATO over the decision of whether or not to seek UN authorization for resolving a conflict militarily. In addition, it also demonstrated the growing centrifugal forces within the transatlantic security community as the decision to militarily intervene in the Kosovo case without a UN mandate represented a clear violation of the transatlantic norm of common values. What is more, contestation and violations of transatlantic norms were not confined to common values but also undermined the norms of multilateral practice and communication as the military intervention against Serbia also illustrates.

From the beginning, transatlantic norm leaders disagreed not only over the nature, scope, and duration of already imposed sanctions against Serbia but, more significantly, on how to enforce them. In the absence of a clear military strategy and in the aftermath of the Raçak massacre, the American core state sought to craft a consensus among norm leaders to pursue so-called 'punitive' air strikes against Serbian territory. Some of NATO's senior officials like the chairman of NATO's Military Committee, General Klaus Naumann, had long argued for a credible demonstration to back diplomacy with force (Daalder and O'Hanlon 2000, p. 33). The main obstacle to conduct air strikes, however, proved to be the opposition by European norm leaders. With the exception of Great Britain and, to some extent, France, the European norm leaders argued that they were not willing to use force against Serbia, even after the Raçak massacre. German and Italian norm leaders, in particular, whose air bases were crucial to a successful bombing campaign, presented strong arguments for delaying the use of force to stop the war in Kosovo citing unforeseeable consequences of a military attack and lack of domestic support.

In response to these concerns, US norm leaders refined their strategy to win over European support. For example, by incorporating the political objectives of the Contact Group (which included Russia) for conducting air strikes against Serbia and by warning the Kosovo Liberation Army (KLA) not to exploit the situation to advance its cause under NATO cover, Washington initially settled differences among norm leaders. However, what appears to be a textbook example of 'thick' communication and responsiveness (and thus in conformity with the transatlantic norm of communication) barely concealed a determination on behalf of US norm leaders to wage a war against Serbia by bribing rather than attempting the difficult task to persuade European norm leaders to 'buy' US arguments. As US National Security Advisor Samuel Berger later confessed

> (w)e needed to demonstrate a real commitment to get a peaceful resolution in order to get the allies to go along with the use of significant force. (cited in: Daalder and O'Hanlon 2000, p. 89)

In reality, US norm leaders showed no intention to consult with its European members on the decision to go to war and European norm leaders seemed to be well aware of that. As Italy's Foreign Minister Lamberto Dini concluded, '(n)one of us (Europeans) likes the bombing, but in present circumstances we don't see an alternative' (Economist 1999). On 24 March 1999, NATO forces commenced air strikes against Serbia. Yet, norm disputes among norm leaders continued and threatened to undermine 'Operation Allied Force'. These disputes centered on information policy, target setting, and the introduction of ground troops contributing to the further weakening of transatlantic norms.

From the outset of the military operation, two lines of command existed within NATO, namely an American one for US sorties and a transatlantic one for all others (Joetze 2000, p. 10). This dual command structure was symbolized by the dual responsibility for the NATO operation including NATO's General Secretary Javier Solana (a European) and NATO's Supreme Allied Commander Europe (SACEUR) General Wesley Clark (an American). This division basically reflected a US determination to retain control over American forces and served to bridge a growing military and technology gap that significantly affected NATO's operation in Kosovo in a negative way. Due to this gap, for example, satellite information could not always be shared given the fact that some member states did not own common secure communication technologies. This lack of military interoperability forced some air traffic control to be executed via 'open skies' meaning that Serbian radar stations could listen in on NATO's air communication (Daalder and O'Hanlon 2000, p. 149). In some reported cases, American pilots, on return to their home bases in Italy after having conducted air strikes over Serbia, even switched off their so-called Identification Friend or Foe (IFF) systems which left NATO ground station personnel puzzled and irritated.[4] Evidently, European military inferiority entailed significant incompatibilities in communication and command structures.

What, at first glance, may seem to be only a technical issue, miscommunication in military operations is no less important than verbal exchanges among diplomats and state leaders. In fact, it can be even more important in crisis situations when the lives of pilots and ground station personnel are on the line. Thus, the persistent and in some areas even permanent lack of information sharing and air communication during the military operations against Serbia can be said to have contributed to undercutting the transatlantic norm of communication, a fact that may be less visible to the outside observer but no less significant for NATO's normative order.

The debate over deciding on what Serbian targets to hit marked another area of transatlantic norm violation. At the outset of the military operation, norm leaders had agreed on three sets of targets: Phase 1 targets (air defense systems and related military sites), Phase 2 targets (military infrastructure and Yugoslav forces in the field), and Phase 3 targets (political and civilian objects). While US norm leaders had agreed to initially hit what they referred to as 'leadership targets' (Phase 3 targets) in order to underline the 'punitive' character of the air strikes and demonstrate their resoluteness, European norm leaders including Germany, Greece, Italy, and France, citing ethical and moral arguments as well as the possibility that the civilian population might rally around Slobodan Milosevic, refused to give their consent for hitting these sites (Daalder and O'Hanlon 2000, pp. 118 and 124).

When NATO planes eventually ran out of targets by late March, its members conducted what they called 'Phase 2 Plus'. These targets were really Phase 3 targets but were not labeled as such since Germany, France, and Italy had refused to authorize Phase 3. In a further example of institutional failure, France and Britain even threatened to veto possible targets in the NATO Council, while Germany and Italy called for an urgent review of the air campaign. Instead of resolving the dispute, US General Wesley Clark simply disregarded these objections against attacking civilian targets and went ahead with the air strikes (International Herald Tribune 1999, p. 5). This lack of responsiveness at the communicative level marked another norm violation by the security community's core state. It also displayed a violation of the norm of multilateral practice as NATO members had agreed to pursue this military intervention together and to refrain from unilateral decision-making.

This is not to say that the USA did not have persuasive arguments. Indeed, US norm leaders raised the question in Washington why the core state should be responsive to the demands of smaller member states that contributed only about 25 % of all planes while American forces carried the main risks and shouldered the bulk of the military burden (Air Force Magazine 2000). As US Secretary of Defense William S. Cohen noticed

> (b)ecause we are the only nation with precision-guided ammunitions that can operate in all kinds of weather, heavy cloud cover in the early phases of the campaign at times made it an almost exclusively American operation. (International Institute for Strategic Studies 1999)

However, instead of using these arguments to persuade or confront European members with their different point of view (thereby employing communicative action), the USA simply decided that the European norm leaders were not worth the trouble. Lieutenant General Short, the US Air Force general in charge of executing the air campaign during Operation Allied Force, articulated this mindset by declaring that political interference by NATO states had been 'counterproductive' to military goals (Washington Post 1999, pp. 20–1). Thus, in the end, the USA carried out the air strikes by and large independently thereby significantly undermining the norm of communication as well as the norm of multilateral practice.

To sum up, tracing out-of-area conflict management during the Bosnian and Kosovo crises tends to support the assumption made in the beginning that the transatlantic security community entered a stage of decline during the second half of the 1990s. What can be seen in the cases of Bosnia and Kosovo is a cascade of norm violations within the transatlantic security community involving all three 'meta'-norms (values, practice, and communication). The predominant norm violator appeared to be the USA (though some European norm leaders seemed willing to follow that example).

What is striking, in both cases, is the lack of resistance on behalf of many European norm leaders most of whom objected to US norm violations in principle but were either unwilling or incapable to defend the transatlantic normative order by sanctioning these norm violations. Instead, Germany, France, Italy and other member states reluctantly backed the US position (e.g., not to seek a UN mandate in the Kosovo crisis) and thus, by and large, let the core state have its way in the diplomatic negotiations and military operations despite having strong reservations. The US strength and authority to define meanings as the security community's core state, on the one hand, and the simultaneous failure by European norm leaders to conduct successful crisis management in the Balkans, on the other hand, may account for much of this European inertia. The cascade of norm violations that occurred during the second half of the 1990s arguably injected the security community with a new dynamic. The increasing thrust and scope of norm violations, in particular by the core state, combined with institutional failures to punish these norm violations had begun to seriously undermine the normative order of the security community.

Denial

The years following the Balkan Wars introduced a phase of what seemed to be a return to transatlantic solidarity. The Kosovo crisis, in particular, had highlighted the normative disputes among norm leaders of the transatlantic security community. To bridge these disputes, norm leaders were engaged in a series of community-building symbolic interaction and organizational reforms.

Attempts to intensify the level of integration can be illustrated by the 50th anniversary of NATO in April 1999. At this summit in Washington, the members of the security community made a forceful pledge to reaffirm the transatlantic normative order. They reiterated their commitment 'to the Washington Treaty and the United Nations Charter (…) and the principles of democracy, individual liberty and the rule of law' as well as the norms of multilateral practice and communication by serving 'as provided for in Article 4 of the North Atlantic Treaty, as an essential transatlantic forum for Allied consultations on any issues that affect their vital interests (and) to consult and act together in the pursuit of peace and security' (NATO 1999c). Given the previous cascade of norm violations that had occurred during the Balkan Wars, it is interesting how much emphasis was now being placed on reaffirming the normative order of the transatlantic security community. In particular, the word 'consult' can be found 20 times in the final summit declaration.

At the same time, however, the anniversary NATO Summit remained ambivalent about the norm innovations that had been introduced in the early 1990s. While the USA interpreted the new out-of-area norm to mean that NATO would be transformed into a global war-fighting organization, most European members insisted on the regional and defensive nature of NATO eager to avoid another 'Kosovo'. In the new Strategic Concept of 1999, the norm leaders of the transatlantic security community sought to bridge this normative divide by simply combining the two conflicting meanings:

> Here in Washington, we have paid tribute to the achievements of the past and we have shaped a new Alliance to meet the challenges of the future. This new Alliance will be larger, more capable and more flexible, *committed to collective defence and able to undertake new missions* including contributing to effective conflict prevention and engaging actively in crisis management, including crisis response operations. (emphasis added, NATO 1999b)

What is also interesting is the fact that the Strategic Concept of 1999, adopted at the NATO Summit in Washington, was equally ambivalent about the transatlantic norm of common values regarding the primacy of the UN. Article 1 of the North Atlantic Treaty clearly states that NATO members agree 'to refrain in their international relations from the threat or use of force *in any manner* inconsistent with the purposes of the United Nations' (emphasis added, NATO 1949). The Strategic Concept of 1999 put this in very different terms:

> In fulfilling its purpose and fundamental security tasks, the Alliance will continue to respect the legitimate security interests of others, and *seek* the peaceful resolution of disputes as set out in the Charter of the United Nations. (emphasis added, NATO 1999b)

The word 'seek' is revealing here. It implicitly suggests a redefinition of the original transatlantic normative order by granting NATO members the authority to act collectively even without a UN mandate (albeit in exceptional cases) and thus marks a notable shift from the unequivocal wording of the NATO Treaty.

Also at the NATO Summit in 1999, the transatlantic security community extended its membership to three newcomers: Hungary, Poland, and the Czech Republic. In doing so, it made good on its promise of 'erasing the divisions imposed by the Cold War to help to build a Europe whole and free, where security and prosperity are shared and indivisible' (NATO 1999c). Moreover, NATO approved a so-called Membership Action Plan for countries wishing to join the security community promising that 'the three new members will not be the last' (NATO 1999c). The first round of NATO's Eastern enlargement was thus clearly intended to consolidate and strengthen the credibility and legitimacy of the transatlantic security community in the post-Cold War era.

Finally, the US and other non-EU NATO member states acknowledged the fact that the members of the EU had decided to build capacities for 'autonomous action' but were eager to keep these capacities within the transatlantic security community in order to avoid an open split between EU member states and non-EU member states within NATO. Despite US rhetorical praise and reassurance for ESDI, it became apparent that the construction of ESDI represented a European response to US unresponsiveness during the Bosnia and Kosovo crises. As Peter Rodman (1999, p. 4) observed,

> (t)he essence of the structural problem now is America's emergence as the 'sole superpower' in the world and Europe's response to that. (…) Europeans feel even more motivated than ever before to build the EU into a counterweight to the United States.

Indeed, the Balkan Wars had accelerated Europe's desire for greater autonomy since the wars had demonstrated that without having genuinely autonomous military forces, EU needs were more or less subordinate to US interests. Increasingly, Western European norm leaders began to question the core state's powerful position in the transatlantic security community because, as they claimed, the power asymmetry left other norm leaders hostage to US concerns and established an American veto position in joint crisis management (Rudolf 2002, p. 10).

The USA, on the other hand, feared that calls for European emancipation could lead to a marginalization of the transatlantic security community. This seemed to confirm the statement made by US Secretary of State

Madeleine Albright who, in 1998, had already warned against a possible decoupling of the EU from NATO, a duplication of NATO capabilities, and the discrimination against non-EU members within NATO (Financial Times 1998). The Western European norm leaders (most notably France and Germany), on their part, tried to reassure the USA and other members that its envisioned 'autonomous capabilities' were intended as 'separable but not separate' capabilities (NATO 1999c). To counter any impression of a European decoupling from NATO, the members of the transatlantic security community emphasized in the Strategic Concept of 1999 'the *indispensable* transatlantic link' that made 'the security of Europe and that of North America (…) *indivisible*' (emphasis added, NATO 1999b).

To sum up, even though the NATO Summit in 1999 had aimed to introduce a new era of transatlantic solidarity, its results were mixed. On the one hand, the members of the transatlantic security community made a powerful reaffirmation of the transatlantic normative order symbolized by the new Strategic Concept and the accession of new members. On the other hand, conflict over individual community norms such as the role of the UN as well as the future character (collective defense vs. collective security) and geographical scope of a future NATO remained unresolved. Most importantly, normative meanings lingered highly ambiguous and many norm leaders increasingly viewed the USA as purely self-interested and unresponsive, a view that would be reinforced by the incoming Bush Administration.

Social and Internal Change III: The 'War on Terror'

Transatlantic tensions within the security community came to the fore at the European Council Summit at Gothenburg in June 2001. Evidently, the new administration in Washington seemed to pursue a foreign policy that reflected its unrivaled military power in—as far as security and defense relations were concerned—a unipolar world. Before the new administration was three months old, French Prime Minister Lionel Jospin had already branded it a

> unilateralist administration (in that) it doesn't seem to think that some of the rules that make the international community work necessarily need to be taken into consideration on certain issues. (USA Today 2001)

Reinforcing this impression by French and other European norm leaders, President Bush eagerly and openly displayed a type of foreign policy that stressed US national interests in what he referred to as a 'distinctly American internationalism' (New York Times 2001). To an extent, this mindset mirrored the reinterpretation of transatlantic norms during the Clinton years:

> We (US) not the United Nations, decide, if it lies in our national interest to democratize Haiti or to aid the people of Somalia. We, not NATO, have to decide, if it lies in our national interest to end the killing in Bosnia. (cited in: Schneider 1997, p. 27)

Yet, US norm leaders now stated these reinterpretations more forcefully thereby in part challenging the transatlantic normative order. Specifically, it partially revoked the norm of common values; in this case, the primary authority of the UN undermined the norm of multilateral practice concerning joint military interventions and bluntly rejected the norm of communication by suggesting that there seemed to be no need to consult with the members of the transatlantic security community in future regional crisis management. Within only two years after NATO's Summit in 1999, the core state had again undermined the normative order of the transatlantic security community setting the stage for one of the worst crises in the history of the transatlantic security community.

It can be argued that the external 'shock' of 11 September 2001 established a transformative moment for US norm leaders (Rudolf 2002 p. 7). Suddenly, the terrorist attacks had left the USA with the loss of a collective feeling of invulnerability. The first attack on the American mainland since the War of 1812 abruptly turned the USA into a more ordinary nation in the sense of having experienced real vulnerabilities (Economist 2003a). As Daniel Keohane explains: 'Europeans have always felt vulnerable. But what they don't understand is that for Americans this is a new development' (Washington Post 2002).

Initially, in a sincere outcry of public solidarity, norm leaders from all levels of society in the transatlantic security community rallied to America's side. The French newspaper *Le Monde* ran a headline 'We are all Americans' (Le Monde 2001). In Belgium, complete strangers held hands, forming a human chain in front of the Brussels World Trade Center. In Norway, public trams and buses halted in tribute. Firefighters in Hungary and Poland tied black ribbons to their trucks and sounded their sirens. A total of 200,000 took the streets of Berlin to show their solidarity with the USA. In London, the US National Anthem was played during the change of guard in front of Buckingham Palace. Finally, on the day following the 11 September attacks, NATO invoked Article 5 for the first time in its history. Yet, the 'transatlantic spring' would not last.

On 7 October 2001, the Bush administration opened the military front in what it called the 'global war on terror' soon eclipsing prior non-military efforts such as diplomacy, intelligence sharing, the freezing of financial assets, and the arrests of known terrorists by law enforcement. At first, European norm leaders supported the subsequent war in Afghanistan echoing most European public opinion polls (Economist 2001a, p. 31). Great Britain, in particular, a key member of Washington's global anti-terror coalition, quickly adopted US objectives in Afghanistan.

In the early stages of 'Operation Enduring Freedom', the norm leaders of the transatlantic security community rallied around its core state in solid support for the military intervention in Afghanistan. As in the case of Bosnia and Kosovo, an external 'shock' (the 11 September attacks) was interpreted as a threat to the security community's 'way of life', in general, as well as its collective identity and norms, in particular. For example, Romano Prodi, head of the European Commission, expressed this sense of transatlantic unity and solidarity by stating that

> (t)his barbaric attack (11 September) was directed against the free world and our common values. (…) In the darkest hours of European history, the Americans stood by us. We stand by them now. (EU 2001)

Yet, beneath such sincere gestures of solidarity, many European norm leaders simultaneously sought to tame the core state and to soften the perceived unilateral tendencies of the incoming Bush administration. As Karsten D. Voigt, the then-German Coordinator for transatlantic relations, put it: 'The temptation to act unilaterally is always present (in the US) but it is up to us (Europe) whether it will become a reality' (Voigt 2008). In the aftermath of 11 September, norm leaders in Europe sought to strengthen the transatlantic partnership and to ensure European influence on whatever military reaction the USA might consider. As a result, some norm leaders began to reiterate transatlantic norms of multilateral practice and communication by strengthening symbolic interaction.

In the aftermath of 11 September, norm leaders on both sides of the Atlantic made a case for the need of enhanced transatlantic cooperation within in a multilateral framework. EU Commissioner Chris Patten declared that '(y)ou can't deal with the dark side of globalization (terrorists) (...) unless you deal with them as a result of multilateral engagement' (Washington Post 2002, p. 13). In the USA, Senator Richard Lugar argued affirmatively:

> Given the size of the problem and the resources needed, this is not a task the United States can undertake by itself. It requires a multilateral solution. In other words, we need allies. (Council on Foreign Relation 2002)

Indeed, the 11 September attacks initially seemed to trigger a major increase in symbolic interaction. NATO, for the first time in its 52-year history, had invoked Article 5 of the North Atlantic Treaty offering extensive assistance to the core state. Yet, despite this symbolic interaction of transatlantic solidarity and trust building, the US administration preferred to fight its first battle in the so-called 'War on Terror' in Afghanistan by relying largely on its own forces and equipment aided by British Special Forces. In fact, the Pentagon had initially even considered preventing the invocation of the mutual-defense clause (Nye 2002, p. xv). 'Operation Enduring Freedom' initially left the continental European norm leaders with the task to fill in for US military global commitments in Turkey, the Mediterranean Sea, and the Balkans as well as the deployment of AWACS planes to guard American skies.

The transatlantic security community now faced a peculiar paradox. On the one hand, the invocation of Article 5 had reinforced NATO's original meaning of collective defense thereby underlining the continuing relevance of its normative order. On the other hand, however, the fact that the core state of the transatlantic security community had refused to include NATO's multilateral command and control structures in Afghanistan disrupted a key symbolic ritual (invocation of Article 5) and severely undermined the norm of multilateral practice (collective defense). Moreover, NATO's institutional structures were not involved in Operation Enduring Freedom suggesting institutional failure to deal with a common security issue. Even taking into account that Article 5 does not require its members to commit troops, the unilateral decision by the core state to conduct its immediate military response largely on its own coupled with its refusal for consultation prior to the war effort violated the norms of multilateral practice and communication and thus contributed to the degeneration of the transatlantic normative order 'since NATO must be taken seriously by its strongest member if it is to be taken seriously by anyone' (Talbott 2002, p. 48).

At the same time, transatlantic symbolic interaction continued in other, less visible, areas. On one level, European norm leaders and the USA jointly conducted operations on issues of law enforcement, immigration, financial control, and domestic intelligence. On another level, NATO sought to coordinate information on nuclear, biological, and chemical weapons as well as ballistic missile programs. Yet, symbolic interaction in these less visible areas was eclipsed by the importance of the disrupted symbolic ritual on public display cited above. By rejecting the invocation of Article 5, for example, US norm leaders openly questioned the relevance of the transatlantic security community and openly challenged the meaning of the norm of multilateral practice and communication. US Secretary of Defense Donald Rumsfeld only reinforced this impression when he provocatively declared that

> NATO invoked its most sacred covenant, that no one had dared touch in the past, and it was useless! Absolutely useless! At no point has General Tommy Franks (US commander of military operations in Afghanistan) even talked to anyone at NATO. (cited in: Kitfield 2002, p. 986)

It seems difficult not to read this statement as openly challenging the transatlantic norm of multilateral practice and communication. Not only did the Secretary refuse to consult with other norm leaders but he also ridiculed the transatlantic norm of communication. Echoing Donald Rumsfeld as well as other norm leaders in the US administration, the influential columnist Charles Krauthammer now even claimed that 'NATO— once the centerpiece of the transatlantic alliance—is dead' (New York Times 2003a).

As pointed out above, institutional failure also turned into a problem for the security community. Instead of reverting to NATO, the Bush administration relied on a loose 'Global Alliance against Terror' categorizing its allies according to their respective political and military contributions instead of shared norms and identities. Washington's primary interest seemed to be now focused on the actors that could provide military and political support to the 'War on Terror'. This development had been visible before the 11 September attacks but, in the presence of a direct and vital threat against the USA, was now accelerated and advanced even more forcefully. It seemed to confirm what US Secretary of State Condoleezza Rice had argued earlier: that the purpose of US foreign policy was to 'proceed from the firm ground of the national interest and not from the interest of an illusory international community' (Rice 2000, p. 45). President Bush reiterated this uncompromising focus on US interests after 11 September when he declared that 'this country will define our times, not be defined by them' (Washington Post 2001). Apparently, this approach reflected the determination of the Bush administration to seek multilateral cooperation only 'where necessary' in contrast to its predecessor's declaration 'where possible' (Kreft 2002, p. 20). In the 'War on Terror', individual support by other norm leaders of the transatlantic security community was selectively considered useful by the core state. The institutional structure of NATO, however, was deemed insignificant as a collective entity (Gordon 2003, p. 92).

The institutional failure of NATO during Operation Enduring Freedom arguably reflected American dissatisfaction with the norm of multilateral practice, in particular the multilateral decision-making process within the transatlantic security community. As US Secretary of Defense Donald Rumsfeld explained:

> It's less important to have unanimity than it is to be making the right decisions and doing the right thing, even though at the outset it may seem lonesome. (New York Times 2002b, p. 1)

Critically, the US Secretary of Defense advocated an alternative security conception to the transatlantic security community by emphasizing more flexible institutional mechanisms like the 'Global Alliance against Terror':

> (W)ars can benefit from coalitions of the willing, to be sure. But they should not be fought by committee. The mission must determine the coalition and the coalition must not determine the mission. If it does, the mission will be dumped down to the lowest common denominator, and we (US) can't afford that. (Rumsfeld 2002)

It was not only Donald Rumsfeld who openly challenged transatlantic community norms. This 'thin' understanding of multilateralism was subsequently incorporated into official US policy (US Department of State 2002, p. 25).

Many European norm leaders (with the exception of Great Britain and most Eastern European countries) instead defended 'their' meaning of transatlantic security and the normative order it resembled. For example, Javier Solana, the former Secretary General of NATO and since October 1999 the EU High Representative for the Common Foreign and Security Policy, reacted unreceptively to American norm leaders by frankly stating that 'I don't like this principle that the "mission defines the coalition"' (cited in: Daalder and Lindsay 2003, p. 155).

In addition, by the end of 2001, Western European public opposition against the war in Afghanistan had also dramatically increased with 65 % in Germany and 69 % in Spain demanding an end to the military intervention (Mirror 2001). Anti-war protests occurred in almost every NATO member state (including the US) with 10,000 people demonstrating in Berlin, Amsterdam, New York, and San Francisco, respectively, and another 20,000 protesters marching to Trafalgar Square in London. A total of 5000 people subsequently gathered in Barcelona to protest against what they viewed as 'US world domination'. What a remarkable contrast to the public expressions of solidarity with the USA only a few months earlier!

In the end, 'Operation Enduring Freedom' signified a largely unilateral US operation under the umbrella of a 'thin' multilateral embedding. In other words, it constituted a form of multilateralism that employed multilateral mechanisms to implement the national interest of a dominant member state while in fact masking unilateral power politics (Hippler 2003, p. 20). At the very least, NATO multilateral institutions lost much of their credibility simply because its strongest member did not wish to make use of it (Heisbourg 2001, pp. 144–5). However, despite this institutional failure and apparent norm violations by the core state, many norm leaders nevertheless continued to side with the USA during the occupation of Afghanistan. In Germany, Gerhard Schröder even risked his chancellorship in a parliamentary vote of confidence in order to contribute military aid. Why did European norm leaders act in this way?

One answer to this question can be attributed to the fact that, despite a degeneration of the norms of multilateral practice and communication, transatlantic norm leaders still seemed to share common liberal–democratic values. Moreover, European norm leaders still hoped to preserve the normative order of the transatlantic security community. For example, in his speech before the German Bundestag, Chancellor Gerhard Schröder argued that contributing troops in Afghanistan was a matter of 'credibility' and 'reliability' vis-à-vis the USA and other members of the security community (Deutscher Bundestag 2001). In a similar way, French President Jacques Chirac and British Prime Minister Tony Blair declared at the Anglo-French Summit in November 2001: 'The United Kingdom and France reiterate that they stand shoulder to shoulder with the United States and the American people in the fight against terrorism. This is a cause we share with all democratic countries' (Chirac and Blair 2001).

The Polish President Aleksander Kwasniewski joined in by stating: 'As a country that has experienced tragedies many times, we know that joint action and support of allies are of great importance' (CNN 2001a). In doing so, these members arguably sought to reaffirm the level of trust within the security community at a time of severe crisis.

Thus, instead of punishing the USA for its norm violations, many norm leaders chose to persuade its core state to return to the normative order of the transatlantic security community by framing the 11 September attacks as a case of transatlantic solidarity and mutual commitment instead of a purely American affair. To US norm leaders, however, Afghanistan and the 'War against Terror' seemed to reaffirm the interpretation that the transatlantic security community resembled a declining military asset and that a normative community build on mutual trust and 'we-feeling' had little to offer in this respect.

Why did the USA choose to snub the other members of the security community in this way and why did Washington deliberately decide to violate the transatlantic normative order? One reason is that the USA appeared determined to fight and win its wars by itself (Economist 2002a, p. 27). In fact, the US administration concluded that regional institutional structures such as NATO were ill suited to conduct a modern-type military campaign unless European member states had compatible equipment and structures to offer. This precondition was only matched by Great Britain, which consequently fought alongside the USA in Afghanistan. Moreover, US norm leaders also appeared dissatisfied with the often slow and inefficient multilateral decision-making processes within integrated command structures. The war in Kosovo had already demonstrated to the USA that reaching an interallied consensus on strategic and tactical issues could slow down and eventually endanger a mission. From a US point of view, having only one European 'junior partner' involved in a US dominated military conflict such as Operation Enduring Freedom, while otherwise relying on local allies in the region, apparently seemed more desirable.

This framing of NATO as slow and inefficient became evident when President Bush compared the threat of global terrorism to earlier major threats by state actors to US national security.

> Like the Nazis and the communists before them, the terrorists seek to end lives and control all life. And like the Nazis and the communists before them, they will be opposed by free nations and the terrorists will be defeated. (White House 2002a)

It is important to point out that by 'free nations' President Bush did not mean the transatlantic norm leaders but rather any country that was willing and able to join the USA in its 'War on Terror'. The President articulated this interpretation very clearly in his statement en route to China in October 2001: 'The war against terrorism is an international war. And we're fighting with a broad, broad coalition' (CNN 2001b). In this 'war', individual NATO members were certainly invited to join the anti-terror coalition but NATO as a regional organization was not particularly welcome. As a political magazine put it eloquently: 'NATO is all dressed up with nowhere to go' (The Economist 2001b, p. 34). The ensuing process of norm degeneration culminated in the transatlantic crisis over the Iraq War that led to further disruptions in symbolic interaction and institutional failure.

The (Almost) Breakdown of the Normative Order: The Iraq Crisis

The Iraq War presented a severe crisis for the transatlantic security community. Former US Secretary of State Henry Kissinger called the transatlantic rift over Iraq 'the gravest crisis in the Atlantic Alliance since its creation five decades ago' (Washington Post 2003a, p. 1). Indeed, the crisis of how to properly deal with the threat the Saddam Hussein regime posed to the world involved a fundamental dispute over diverging views on transatlantic norms. The impact of this rift in transatlantic relations became so severe that prominent norm leaders in the USA such as former Secretaries of State Madeleine Albright and Warren Christopher as well as Senator Robert Dole and former US National Security Advisor Zbigniew Brzezinski labeled it a 'defining moment in the history of America's relations with Europe' (CSIS 2003). The transatlantic norm dispute was inherently tied to diverging meanings and interpretations of security among norm leaders. As the President of the European Commission, Romano Prodi, observed: '(W)e have witnessed *a diverging perception of reality* on the two sides of the Atlantic' (emphasis added, EU 2003). It is important to point out, however, that divisions occurred as much within Europe as across the Atlantic with some European norm leaders siding with the core state and others standing in outright opposition. If this truly was a defining moment, then it was one for transatlantic as well as European integration. While this section will focus on its implications for the transatlantic security community, it is necessary to keep this in mind.

In his speech on Iraq on 7 October 2002, President Bush laid out his political demands for Baghdad to avoid a US-led military invasion.

These demands included the declaration and destruction of any weapons of mass destruction, an end to supporting terrorism, a cessation to the persecution of Iraq's civilian population, the termination of any illicit trade outside the UN Oil for Food Program, and the release of as well as accounts for any missing US Gulf War personnel. The President ended his speech by declaring that '(b)y taking these steps, and only by taking these steps, the Iraqi regime has an opportunity to avoid conflict'. In that same speech, however, President Bush also stated that

> (r)egime change in Iraq is the only certain means of removing a great danger to our nation (…) I'm not willing to stake one American life on trusting Saddam Hussein. (White House 2002b)

These contradicting statements provided the main source for European skepticism toward the core state's position on Iraq. The sense that American norm leaders seemed determined to go to war regardless of what Saddam Hussein would do, aided by the US administration's failure to engage comprehensively and consistently with key NATO members, led some key European norm leaders, such as Germany's Chancellor Gerhard Schröder, to assume that 'they (US) are going to do it (invade Iraq), no matter what the world or their allies think' (New York Times 2002c). A number of European norm leaders, in France and Germany in particular, hence began to openly resist the core state in what they perceived as inappropriate behavior in violation of the transatlantic norm of common values, in particular a military intervention without the consent of the UN Security Council.

Conversely, the Bush administration, supported by British Prime Minister Tony Blair and other European norm leaders like Spain's Prime Minister Aznar, created an inner 'circle of trust' within the transatlantic security community while treating transatlantic norm leaders who would not agree with the core state's threat perception and policy as outsiders. This insider/outsider framing *within* the transatlantic security community became most visible when US Secretary of Defense Donald Rumsfeld discursively separated 'old' from 'new' Europe:

> Germany has been a problem and France has been a problem. But you look at vast numbers of other countries in Europe, they're not with France and Germany (…) they're with the US. (…) You're thinking of Europe as Germany and France. I don't. I think that's old Europe. (BBC 2003a)

French and German norm leaders, like German Foreign Minister Joschka Fischer, reacted to this stigmatization by openly accusing the USA of having violated transatlantic norms and referring directly to the norm of communication: 'We should try to treat each other sensibly. Our position is not a problem, it is a constructive contribution' (BBC 2003a). In France, government spokesman Jean-Francois Cope also hinted at the significance of consultation: 'An "old" continent (...) can sometimes be infused with a certain wisdom, and wisdom can sometimes make for good advice' (Radio Free Europe 2003). In the public sphere, the French newspaper *Liberation* ran the provocative headline: 'Old Europe kicks back!' and in Berlin offices, people put posters on their windows proudly reading: 'This is old Europe!' In Germany, 'old Europe' was even named word of the year in 2003.

But Donald Rumsfeld would not stop there. Instead, he went on to complain about the slowness and hardship of arguing and persuasion. This touched directly on the norms of communication and multilateralism within NATO:

> Now, we rarely find unanimity in the world. I was ambassador to NATO, and (...) when we would go in and make a proposal, there wouldn't be unanimity. There wouldn't even be understanding. And we'd have to be persuasive. We'd have to show reasons. We'd have to (...) give rationales. We'd have to show facts. (...) (I)f a country doesn't agree with us, heck, that's happened lots of times in history. (Radio Free Europe 2003)

To be fair, some American norm leaders did attempt to persuade European norm leaders of the necessity to attack Iraq. On 5 February 2003, for example, US Secretary of State Colin Powell gave a presentation to the UN Security Council in which he exhibited 'evidence' to support his allegation that Iraq possessed weapons of mass destruction. On the very next day and in response to this presentation, the foreign ministers of Albania, Bulgaria, Croatia, Estonia, Latvia, Lithuania, Macedonia, Romania, Slovakia, and Slovenia signed and published an Open Letter endorsing the US position (Foreign Ministers 2003). French and German norm leaders, however, were no longer open to persuasion since they appeared convinced that 'they (US) are going to do it (invade Iraq), no matter what the world or their allies think'. Indeed, US norm leaders came to believe that an existential threat, posed by a nexus of terrorism, rogue states, and weapons of mass destruction, made it problematic if not dangerous to rely on others—even if that included undermining the normative order of the transatlantic security community. As Charles Krauthammer noted

> we are in a war of self-defense. It is also a war for Western civilization. If the Europeans refuse to see themselves as part of this struggle, fine. If they wish to abdicate, fine. We will let them hold our coats. (Economist 2002b, p. 30)

Norm leaders in Europe and elsewhere were irritated. German Chancellor Schröder, in an interview with the *New York Times*, warned that 'I think it would be a big mistake if this feeling of needing one another should be destroyed by excessively unilateral actions'. In this interview, he also stressed his interpretation of the meaning of the norm of communication for the transatlantic security community:

> In the past it was always said: Before we do anything, we will consult with our principal allies—at least with those who take an active—very active—part in the fight against international terrorism. But consultation cannot mean that I get a phone call two hours in advance only to be told: We're going in. Consultation among grown-up nations has to mean not just consultation about the how and the when, but also about the whether. (New York Times 2002a)

In the fall of 2002, the Bush administration had, from their point of view, already 'consulted' by seeking UN approval for threatening military actions in case Iraq would not agree to account for and destroy any supposed weapons of mass destruction immediately and unconditionally. Moreover, it should not be overlooked that by unilaterally declaring that they would not support the use of force against Iraq even if the USA were to secure a UN mandate, Germany had equally violated transatlantic norms of multilateralism and communication. Yet, President Bush's decision to send troops to the Persian Gulf in order to back a UN Resolution with a credible military threat only further alienated many European norm leaders. On the one hand, US behavior supposedly pressured Saddam Hussein to agree to let the UN inspectors return to Iraq. On the other hand, the military build-up led European norm leaders such as France and Germany to believe that the Bush administration would go to war at all costs.

In this situation, the prerequisites for engaging in communicative action (mutual recognition as equals, mutual deliberation, and argumentation) were no longer given. Eventually, instrumental action led to a stand-off in the UN Security Council in March 2003 when the US administration, supported by Great Britain, Spain, and Bulgaria, sought a second UN Resolution claiming that Baghdad had effectively violated UN Resolution 1441 and thereby legitimating a military response. Predictably, Russia and China but also France threatened to veto such a resolution. This ended the diplomatic track for transatlantic norm leaders to deal with Iraq via the UN. While it is true that France's opposition made passage of a second resolution impossible, it is equally valid that the USA failed to lay the diplomatic groundwork by refusing to offer any compromise. As a result, the Bush administration was unable to achieve even a majority of the UN Security Council and was left increasingly isolated instead.

As for the transatlantic security community, the impact of the crisis over Iraq could be felt on both sides of the Atlantic but also within Europe. As explained above, the main fault line ran through the European continent, not the Atlantic Ocean, with the USA, Great Britain, Spain, Poland, Italy, Denmark, Portugal, Hungary, the Czech Republic as well as the ten members of the so-called Vilnius Group (Albania, the Baltic states, Bulgaria, Romania, Croatia, Slovakia, and Slovenia) on the one side, and France, Germany, Belgium aligning with a non-NATO member, Russia, on the other (feeding suspicion in the USA). The transatlantic security community and its institutions were left paralyzed by its internal divisions. Evidently, the dispute in the NATO Council over the US-Turkish request to prepare planning for protection of Turkey against a potential invasion from Iraq drastically demonstrated the inability to communicate with each other let alone reach a consensus. NATO's institutional failure over the US-Turkish request only reinforced the Bush administration's desire to rely on flexible coalitions (Nye 2003, p. 67).

It would be highly simplistic to label US policy on Iraq as plain unilateralism. In fact, Washington followed a more complex approach emphasizing various aspects of the spectrum between multilateralism and unilateralism as it deemed useful to serve US interests (Luck 2003). Still, by rejecting multilateral decision-making within the transatlantic security community and by failing to consult with its members, the core state openly violated if not rejected the norms of multilateralism und communication. In this sense, the core state appeared indeed "unbound" in the sense that American norm leaders seemed to be willing to cut the bonds of mutual trust and collective identity within the transatlantic security community for the sake of their own security (Daalder and Lindsay 2003). As President Bush stated in his State of the Union Address in January 2003, (t)his nation and all our friends are all that stand between a world at peace, and a world of chaos and constant alarm. Once again, we are called to defend the safety of our people, and the hopes of all mankind. And we accept this responsibility (...) we're asking them (free nations) to join us, and many are doing so. Yet the course of this nation does not depend on the decisions of others. (...) We will consult. But let there be no misunderstanding: If Saddam Hussein does not fully disarm (...) we will lead a coalition to disarm him. (Washington Post 2003b)

Winston Churchill once said that, during World War II, Britain had been 'fighting by ourselves alone, but not for ourselves alone'. In 2003, the Australian Prime Minister, Paul Keating, recycled this statement to mean that 'a lot of people in Europe think today that, in Iraq, the United States fights by itself alone, for itself alone' (International Herald Tribune 2003a, 6). This framing reveals a mindset that also circulated among many Western European norm leaders and much of European societies. Indeed, Western European public opinion stood united in opposing an American-led invasion without the consent of the UN Security Council. On 15 February 2003 alone, over ten million people worldwide took to the streets, most of them in Europe, to protest against the war in Iraq. In Berlin, 500,000 demonstrators gathered in the German capital. One million protesters joined together in London, Rome, and Barcelona, respectively. Smaller demonstrations took place in virtually every NATO member state including the USA and Canada (BBC 2003b). The *Guinness Book of Records* listed this global event as the largest anti-war rally in human history and Patrick Tyler wrote in the *New York Times*: 'There may still be two superpowers on the planet: the United States and world public opinion' (New York Times 2003b). Critically, the protests were not only anti-war protests but were also directed specifically against NATO as the institutional representation of the transatlantic security community. For example, in the Italian city of Naples, roughly 10,000 people marched in front of the local NATO base to protest.

In Washington, President Bush defended the US position by declaring that '(t)he United States of America has the sovereign authority to use force in national security' (White House 2003a). Since Iraq allegedly posed a direct threat to US national security, this framing of the issue left Washington instead of NATO with the sole decision whether the use of force would be necessary or not. Evidently, it marginalized NATO as the institutional forum for transatlantic security consultations leaving the

Europeans with the choice to either fall in line or abstain altogether reiterating President Bush's earlier statement that 'either you are with us or you are with the terrorists' (White House 2001). Regarding the role of the UN as the only legitimate organization to authorize the use of force, President Bush argued in a similar way:

> Under Resolutions 678 and 687 (from the second Gulf War in 1991)—both still in effect—the United States and our allies are authorized to use force ridding Iraq of weapons of mass destruction. This is not a question of authority, it is a question of will. (White House 2003a)

For many European norm leaders, however, an invasion of Iraq was, indeed, essentially a question of authority and respect for international law. As Javier Solana, speaking on behalf of the EU, pointed out that all nations needed to work together, 'to sustain and strengthen a world based on international rules. US dominance through force would be a return to the politics of the cave man' (Solana 2003).

In the USA, such arguments were quickly dismissed by many as an underlying European pacifist mindset (if not 'appeasement'), allegedly resulting from Europe's relative military weakness in contrast to the USA (Forsberg 2005). The astonishing unity of large majorities of Western European anti-war sentiment among the publics (including Great Britain) appeared to serve as evidence for allegations that Europeans were from Venus and Americans from Mars (Kagan 2003). For example, the *New York Post* dubbed France and Germany as members of an 'axis of weasels' for opposing the war in Iraq (International Herald Tribune 2003b). Such simplifications found their counterparts in Europe with allegations that the US war on Iraq was solely used as a pretext to obtain Iraqi oil reserves (Spiegel 2003, p. 18). Certainly, such allegations were highly overstated if not plain wrong taking into account that European norm leaders themselves were deeply divided over Iraq. However, they demonstrate to what extent the normative order (and the norm of communication in particular) had degenerated to this point.

This can be illustrated by another example of norm degeneration in the transatlantic security community. With the so-called 'doctrine of pre-emptive warfare' expressed in the US National Security Strategy of 2002, questionable treatment of prisoners at Guantanamo Bay as well as its war-like rhetoric toward Iraq, the US administration seriously undermined the norm of common values of the transatlantic security community which includes human rights and international law. For example, the Central Intelligence Agency (CIA) set up detention centers whose infamous practices were later not only confirmed but actively defended by the US president in September 2006:

> In some cases, we determine that individuals we have captured pose a significant threat, or may have intelligence that we and our allies need to have to prevent new attacks. (...) In these cases, it has been necessary to move these individuals to an environment where they can be held secretly, questioned by experts, and—when appropriate—prosecuted for terrorist acts. (White House 2006)

These inhumane practices at Guantanamo Bay and elsewhere directly challenged not only the UN anti-torture convention. They also undermined the norm of common values of the transatlantic security community which calls on its members to act in 'faith (...) (with) the purposes and principles of the Charter of the United Nations' (NATO 1949). In open defiance of these normative values, US Attorney General Alberto R. Gonzales wrote a memorandum to US President Bush on 25 January 2002, in which he declared the Geneva Convention on the interrogation of prisoners of war in relation to the circumstances underlying the 'War against Terror' as 'obsolete' (US Department of Justice 2002). Gonzales also publicly defended 'harsh questioning' in the implementation of so-called extraordinary renditions. One American official even claimed that '(i)f you don't violate someone's human rights some of the time, you probably aren't doing your job' (Economist 2003b).

Many European norm leaders strongly objected to these blatant violations of transatlantic common values. For example, German Chancellor Angela Merkel condemned the practice of rendition by stating that '(t)he use of such prisons is not compatible with my understanding of the rule of law (...) Even in the fight against terrorism, which represents an unprecedented challenge to our free societies, the end may not justify the means'. The German Minister of the Interior, Wolfgang Schäuble, also made it clear that, in the case of the ban on torture, there can be no turning a blind eye (Süddeutsche Zeitung 2006, p. 1). A senior British judge, Justice Collins, also emphasized the normative divide between transatlantic norm leaders: 'America's idea of what is torture is not the same as the United Kingdom's' (Guardian 2007). Finally, the EU Anti-Terror Coordinator, Gijs de Vries, warned that '(t)here is clearly in Europe at the moment concern in public opinion about the US balance between fighting terrorism and human rights' (Washington Times 2005).

It should be noted, however, that by voicing their opposition to US norm violations, European norm leaders were skating on thin ice. In 2006, the Council of Europe rapporteur, Dick Marty, revealed a certain degree of complicity on the part of many European governments in the practice of renditions: 'It was only through the intentional or grossly negligent collusion of the European partners that this "web" (renditions) was able to spread also over Europe' (Council of Europe 2006). As a result, European arguments opposing US torture practices were less persuasive than they could have been (Koschut 2007).

To sum up, the rift over Iraq and the subsequent US-led invasion left a degenerated transatlantic normative order. Previous norm erosion had been concealed behind friendly rhetoric and joint declarations such as during the NATO Summit in 1999. While the long-term effects of the Iraq crisis in transatlantic relations are yet to unfold, some medium-range implications can be summed up as follows. As pointed out above, there was a clear divide over the norm of common values, in particular the authority of the UN but also the meaning of the rule of law and human rights.

Another dividing line between norm leaders concerned the meaning of multilateral norms (Risse 2003, pp. 16–7). While many European norm leaders stressed the importance of transatlantic multilateral structures and procedures under the primacy of institutionalized rules and processes, the USA, in particular, emphasized a more pragmatic view as expressed by President Bush who declared that 'the success of multilateralism is not measured by adherence to forms alone, the tidiness of the process, but by the results we achieve to keep our nation secure' (White House 2003b). One significant yet often overlooked US violation of the norm of multilateralism (which, critically, includes the norm of peaceful conflict resolution) was the so-called 'Hague Invasion Clause'. In 2002, George W. Bush signed into law the American Service-Members' Protection Act, which includes the provision to take 'all means necessary and appropriate to bring about the release of any US or allied personnel being detained or imprisoned by, on behalf of, or at the request of the International Criminal Court' (ICC) placed in The Hague (US House of Representatives 2002). Put into practice, the USA may have to militarily invade the Netherlands, the seat of the ICC and a member of the transatlantic security community, to free US soldiers from the ICC. While this remains only a theoretical option for the USA and is mainly directed against the ICC and not the transatlantic security community, it does seem to contradict the meaning of the norm of multilateral practice, which prescribes that any dispute among members of the transatlantic security community must be settled without the resort to violence and war.

Finally, the prerogative to consult among norm leaders before reaching a decision on the use of force against Iraq was virtually ignored. Instead, the core state displayed an unprecedented degree of unresponsiveness that seriously undermined if not rejected the norm of communication and, ultimately, left no room for 'thick' communication. The depth of the consequences resulting from this lack of responsiveness became apparent in Prime Minister Blair's speech to the Congress directly addressing US norm leaders to 'show that this is a (transatlantic) partnership built on persuasion, not command. (…) America must listen as well as lead' (CNN 2003). The unresponsiveness of the core state seems to have been a key issue for European norm leaders even though it must be pointed out that European norm leaders certainly contributed to this.

In the end, due to the war in Iraq, the acceptance of the USA as the core of strength significantly decreased among norm leaders of the transatlantic security community. In fact, many European norm leaders started to believe that the USA now placed itself above and beyond the normative order of the transatlantic security community (Risse 2003, p. 5). This impression can also be supported by empirical evidence. For example, favorable views of the USA dropped sharply in European public opinion polls during the war in Iraq. In France, sympathy toward the USA declined from 62 % in 2002 to only 42 % in 2003. During the same period, public support for the USA fell from 50 % to a mere 38 % in Spain and in Germany from 60 % to 45 %. In 2006, a poll even revealed that 45 % of Germans viewed the USA as a greater threat to world peace than Iran (Spiegel 2006). The decline in public support was also present (although less dramatic) in Great Britain and Poland. It can thus be claimed that the USA did lose a significant amount of credibility and legitimacy as the core state of the transatlantic security community during the crisis over the Iraq War (Pew Research Center 2008).

The crisis over Iraq arguably marks a critical event in the stage of denial among transatlantic norm leaders. Why did this event not lead to the disintegration of the security community? Norm leaders can be expected to retreat into denial once the cascade of norm violations becomes intolerable and the normative order difficult to justify and defend. In this state of denial, the norm leaders of the transatlantic security community made significant tactical concessions to the US norm violator sometimes contrary to their own normative beliefs. For example, many European norm leaders such as France and Germany reluctantly agreed to the watering down of the authority of the UN in the Strategic Concept of 1999 despite their belief (developed during the Kosovo crisis) that a UN mandate was essential. This can be said to have produced a state of cognitive dissonance.

At the same time, however, norm leaders engaged in a genuine reaffirmation of their identity as part of the community. As examples, we may cite the accession of new members and the invocation of Article 5. Despite the fact that, in the latter case, the core state largely shunned offers of help from other norm leaders, it can hardly be denied that the unanimous decision (including the USA) to invoke the collective defense clause marked a sincere public recognition that security in the North Atlantic area continued to be inextricably linked. These examples demonstrate that norm leaders still felt attached to community norms and their relationship and appeared hesitant to see the normative order permanently damaged (Eznack 2012, p. 7). It should be noted, for example, that Germany, despite its opposition to the war allowed the USA to use its military bases in Germany as well as German airspace during the war in Iraq. In fact, even though the German chancellor Gerhard Schröder publicly voiced his criticism against US behavior, he also insisted that 'no matter what the difference of opinions were before, it goes without saying that healthy transatlantic relations are necessary and we'll look towards that aim in the future' (Deutsche Welle 2003). The USA reiterated this perception by emphasizing that France and Germany were still 'friends' of the USA. As US Secretary of State Colin Powell (2003) emphasized: 'The disagreement of the past is in the past, not forgotten, but nevertheless in the past. Let's move onward'.

Norm Repair

Norm degeneration initially prevailed beyond Iraq. However, as earlier as 2005, transatlantic relations were on its way toward reconciliation as the Bush administration upon entering its second term made sincere efforts to reaffirm transatlantic norms. At the Munich Security Conference in February 2005, for example, President Bush publicly reiterated the norm of communication: 'We need a place to discuss strategic issues' (Spiegel 2005). Moreover, in a meeting of the NATO Council in August 2005, US Secretary of State Condoleezza Rice reassured her Canadian and

European counterparts of America's willingness to conform with transatlantic norms in the future: 'I think it's only natural that sometimes we have these discussions. Questions and concerns arise. We should discuss them, we should discuss them in a serious way among friends' (Rice 2005).

These examples of symbolic interaction by American norm leaders resonated well in Europe. The Dutch Foreign Minister Ben Bot replied that

> given the assurances she (Rice) has given that United States will act in conformity with its own constitution and its own laws and it will also act in accordance with international agreements, I think that we have gotten guarantees and all the satisfactory answers we can hope for. (Los Angeles Times 2005)

Apparently, transatlantic norm leaders seemed determined to repair the damage done to the normative order of the transatlantic security community during the crisis over Iraq. As NATO's Secretary General Jaap De Hoop Scheffer told reporters after the meeting with the US Secretary of State: 'It is my impression that Secretary Rice (…) cleared the air' (USA Today 2005).

The election of Barack Obama as president of the USA in 2008 jumpstarted transatlantic solidarity in what the German Marshall Fund eloquently referred to as the 'Obama-bounce' (German Marshall Fund 2009, p. 1). Approval ratings among European NATO members for the handling of international policy by the incoming US president increased from 19 % in 2008 to a stunning 77 % in 2009 (German Marshall Fund 2009, p. 8). In Germany, Italy, the Netherlands, Portugal, and even France, approval ratings for Barack Obama even rose to 90 %. Desirability of US leadership in general also increased from 33 % to 49 % albeit not reaching the level of solidarity immediately following the 11 September attacks (64 %). In 2009, approval ratings of transatlantic relations rose by 23 % in Europe (EU 11) and by 21 % in the USA, respectively.

Yet, the process of transatlantic norm repair also involved temporary setbacks, the most important one being the crisis over Libya. NATO's military intervention against Libya in 2011 produced a number of serious conflicts within the transatlantic security community. Most notable among these conflicts was the push for greater military engagement in Libya by French and British norm leaders as well as the refusal by Turkish norm leaders to hand over command to NATO. The most serious conflict within the transatlantic security community, however, arouse over the abstaining vote on

Resolution 1973 by Germany in the UN Security Council. UN Resolution 1973 authorized the use of military force to enforce a no-fly zone over Libya. Since the German Foreign Minister Guido Westerwelle had previously even insisted to oppose the resolution (but was eventually persuaded by German diplomats to abstain), the vote was perceived as a 'no' by French, British, and US norm leaders. It was the first time that Germany had not sided with its fellow transatlantic community members in the UN Security Council on a major security issue. This provoked fears on both sides of the Atlantic of German 'nationalist calculations' and a 'non-aligned foreign policy' (Economist 2011). The German vote thus can be said to have undermined the normative order (in particular the norms of multilateral behavior and communication) of the transatlantic security community weakening the process of trust building and norm repair (Koschut 2014b).

Mutual trust and norm repair were further undermined when in 2013 transatlantic publics learnt about the surveillance of their electronic data by the US intelligence agency National Security Agency (NSA). While the quantity and scope of the surveillance alone gave reason to worry about the legitimacy and appropriateness of US activities, most norm leaders in Europe also criticized the lack of US responsiveness in dealing with the issue. As German Chancellor, Angela Merkel, remarked after learning that her own cell phone had been wiretapped by US intelligence services: 'Wiretapping among friends: that's a no-go' (Süddeutsche Zeitung 2013). In the USA, members of the Congress as well as the American Civil Liberties Union voiced serious doubts about the legality of the intelligence program against US citizens (though they did not question the surveillance of non-US citizens). The Obama administration defended the practice as necessary to prevent future terrorist attacks (Thimm 2014). The most remarkable fact about the NSA surveillance affair is perhaps not so much the excessive invasion of individual privacy by US intelligence agencies but the relatively weak domestic backlash against this flagrant norm violation of individual freedom in the transatlantic security community. While people in the transatlantic security community (including the USA) were certainly opposed to this gathering of private data, there was hardly any major protest on the streets. This stands in stark contrast to earlier cases such as the Iraq crisis in 2003.

That being said, transnational protests against NATO did increase in the aftermath of the Iraq War as the NATO Summits in Strasbourg in 2009 and Chicago in 2012 vividly illustrate. Many of these protesters even called for the dissolution of NATO as its member states held their summits in Strasbourg and Chicago, respectively. As one protester in Chicago, Vietnam War veteran Ron McSheffery, stated: 'I'm in total support of stopping NATO and stopping the slaughter of innocent civilians' (Reuters 2012). At the Chicago Summit, protesters raised banners with slogans like 'NATO = WW (World War) III', 'No to NATO war makers', 'NATO equals legal terrorism', and 'Abolish NATO—we need jobs not war'. In Strasbourg, protests turned violent as activists set up burning barricades and set buildings on fire resulting in over 300 police arrests. More recently, members of the World Social Forum advocated to 'strengthen our tools of solidarity among peoples such as boycott, disinvestment and sanctions against Israel and the struggle against NATO' (World Social Forum 2013). The rationale behind these transnational norm challengers can be seen as an attempt to construct an alternative meaning to the concepts of peace and security in the transatlantic area. As one pamphlet read: 'Peace and NATO are antagonistic contradictions (sic), because peace is only possible when, and without NATO and the NATO peace is superfluous' (International Coordinating Committee Anti-NATO Protests 2009). Anti-NATO protest also included political parties like the Communist Party in the USA or the Left Party in Germany as well as prominent members of mainstream political parties like Jesse Jackson of the Democratic Party in the USA.

However, the lack of internal cohesion among these transatlantic norm challengers and the lack of a clear message greatly inhibited their strength. Much of the arguments raised against NATO in Chicago and Strasbourg appeared to be related more to the global financial crisis and directed more against global financial institutions such as the International Monetary Fund or the World Bank rather than NATO proper. For example, the anti-NATO protests in Chicago were organized by a group called 'The Coalition Against NATO-G8' and supported by the Occupy Wall Street movement. As one demonstrator in Chicago put it:

> NATO is used to keep the poor poor and the rich rich. Since the end of the Cold War the alliance has become the enforcement arm of the ruling one per cent, of the capitalist one per cent. (CBC 2012)

This lack of message clarity was even seen as a problem by the activists themselves as a graduate student protester in Chicago reveals: 'It seems like there's so many messages and people aren't really sure what they want to get accomplished. People just need to figure out what their argument is going to be' (CBC 2012).

In addition, transatlantic public opinion and transnational networks of norm leaders such as the Atlantic Council, the German Marshall Fund, the NATO Parliamentary Assembly, or the Global Atlanticists pose an effective structural barrier to block the spread of alternative ideas by advocating the norms of the transatlantic security community (International Herald Tribune 2011; New Atlanticist 2012). As for transatlantic public opinion, even though the divide between Republicans and Democrats in the USA had increased on virtually any issue since the election of the Obama administration, bipartisan support for NATO remains unchanged. In 2012, 63 % of Democrats and 59 % of Republicans believed that NATO was still essential to the USA (German Marshall Fund 2012, p. 14). The corresponding number among the American public was 62 %. In European countries that were polled, including Germany, France, Spain, Italy, Poland, Romania, and the UK, popular support for the USA was now back at pre-Iraq War levels with French and Romanians respondents being the most supportive at 81 %. The same is true for the approval rating of US leadership in the transatlantic security community, which stood at 52 % in 2012 among EU members of NATO (a steep increase from 36 % in 2008) (German Marshall Fund 2012, p. 13). Even the new out-of area norm found broad acceptance if not outright approval among most publics in all NATO member states (German Marshall Fund 2010 p. 17).

In the end, it can be concluded that despite serious norm conflicts, the state of denial among norm leaders of the transatlantic security community did not induce its members to completely depart from the logic of appropriateness. While the empirical narrative displays a significant degree of cognitive dissonance among norm leaders, it apparently was not strong and widespread enough to result in overjustification or the 'crowding-out' of previous knowledge and social behavior. Instead, norm leaders continue to view each other as members of a community determined to repair a damaged normative order.

THE NORMATIVE ORDER OF THE TRANSATLANTIC SECURITY COMMUNITY REVISITED

So how does the normative order of the transatlantic security community score more than two decades after the end Cold War? What can be said with considerable certainty is that the North Atlantic area continues to be integrated in the sense that it forms a pluralistic security community. War is still unthinkable among its members and conflicts are still settled peacefully. That being said, what about the depth and scope of mutual trust, identification, and normative meanings? This differentiation is quite important. As pointed out in Chap. 2, the members of the transatlantic security community may be able to temporarily prevent violent conflict among them by maintaining a no-war community even though community norms have already eroded. If that were to be the case, the disintegration of the transatlantic security community would only be a matter of time. It is thus worth examining the scope of normative change in the North Atlantic area in greater detail.

Norm of Common Values

The transatlantic norm of common values is based on the principles laid out in the UN Charter along with the liberal principles of democracy, individual freedom, the rule of law, and free market economy. In general, we find little dispute about liberal values among norm leaders. The norm leaders of the transatlantic security community are still convinced that these values form a distinct liberal–democratic 'way of life' that is better than any alternative way of life that existed before in the North Atlantic area or outside of it. Norm leaders even appear to believe to a certain degree that their liberal–democratic way of life and norms should be promoted and extended to other areas of the globe (even though norm leaders differ about the means and methods).

That being said, it should be noted that recent allegations of the US spying on other security community members have produced some divergence on the rule of law and the meaning of individual freedom. Moreover, it can be argued that conformity with and consensus over the primary authority of the UN has been weakened to a certain degree. The USA has actively challenged this norm on several occasions and has strongly pushed for normative change in this area. This finding confirms the argument that, in a security community, it is typically the core state that acts as a norm setter with the ability to define normative meanings. It has been explicitly argued by virtually any US administration since the Somalia fiasco in 1993 that NATO should be able to militarily intervene outside its area even without a UN mandate. In fact, NATO did intervene militarily in the Kosovo case without UN approval and defended this norm violation on the grounds of promoting another transatlantic norm (human rights). As pointed out above, this partial redefinition of the transatlantic norm of common values was even enshrined in the Strategic Concept of 1999. It should also be pointed out, however, that the most recent Strategic Concept of 2010 reaffirms 'the primary responsibility of the (UN) Security Council for the maintenance of international peace and security' (NATO 2010). This suggests a return to rather than a redefinition of the norm of common values and the Libya intervention (which involved a UN mandate) seems to confirm this norm in political practice.

To sum up, the picture on normative values in the transatlantic area remains mixed. On the one hand, we generally find norm convergence over the meaning of the liberal–democratic way of life as well as over the primacy of the UN in the transatlantic security community as laid out in the North Atlantic Treaty. This is also true for the societal level. In a recent transatlantic poll, people in Europe and the USA were asked why they found NATO to be essential. A majority of respondents on both sides of the Atlantic agreed that the democratic character of its member states is key (German Marshall Fund 2013). On the other hand, norm divergence over certain transatlantic values like the rule of law or individual freedom continues to haunt the security community.

Norm of Multilateral Practice

The transatlantic norm of multilateral practice involves a normative understanding of 'thick' multilateralism, peaceful conflict resolution, and collective defense against outside threats. It has already been pointed out above that the members of the transatlantic security community continue to live in an area of stable peace with war being unthinkable between them. That being said, however, there has been an adaptation and even partial redefinition of the original norm of multilateral practice.

First of all, the norm of collective defense as laid out in Article 5 of the NATO Treaty has been extended to include not only conventional military threats by outside states (like the former Soviet Union) but also unconventional threats resulting from terrorism, migration, pandemics, and even climate change. In IR terms, NATO has transformed the meaning of collective defense from a narrow understanding of security in favor of a much broader conceptual definition. It should be noted, however, that the norm of collective defense has been undermined somewhat by the fact that the USA appeared hesitant to invoke Article 5 at a time of national insecurity.

More fundamentally, NATO has amended the norm of collective defense by emphasizing the norm of collective security. This norm amendment has produced significant implications for the members of the transatlantic security community because it adds new areas of responsibility for NATO to perform. Some of these tasks had been unthinkable prior to the end of the Cold War. Specifically, NATO has been involved in state building in Afghanistan, training security forces in Iraq, has given logistical support to the African Union's mission in Darfur, coordinated the tsunami relief effort in Indonesia, and gave humanitarian aid in the USA during Hurricane Katrina as well as in Pakistan during a massive earthquake in 2005, respectively.

Finally, a new norm has been introduced to allow for NATO members to collectively operate outside the North Atlantic area as defined by the NATO Treaty (Kitchen 2010). This new out-of-area norm emerged with the end of the Cold War and was institutionalized at NATO's Prague Summit in 2002. It essentially extends NATO's mutual-defense clause to include security threats outside the North Atlantic area turning previously unthinkable out-of-area operations into an almost day-to-day activity for NATO.[5] While it can be said that this new out-of-area norm has been firmly consolidated as part of the transatlantic normative order, its practical implementation, for example, in Afghanistan and Libya, has also produced significant domestic resistance in many member states (Koschut 2014a).

It is still too early to make any serious predictions in how far the introduction of a new out-of-area norm may undermine the level of mutual trust and identification in the North Atlantic area in the future. Based on Karl Deutsch's assumptions, it can, at best, be argued that this will probably depend on the quality and duration of military interventions on a case-by-case basis. As Karl Deutsch et al. (1957, p. 59) points out, long and enduring military commitments by one or several members against non-members place heavy burdens on the integrative capabilities of a pluralistic security community, especially if they produce only few gains and if people in the security community are unready or unwilling to bear them. Here, the current war in Afghanistan comes to mind. Emanuel Adler and Michael Barnett (1998, p. 433) equally argue that the decline of previous external threats (like the dissolution of the Soviet Union) may tempt governments and the military to become more active in 'out-of-area' operations that are meant to defend against new threats to the normative order and the distinctive 'way of life' of a particular security community.

In sum, the 'meta-norm' of multilateral practice has undergone significant innovation and reform. The norm of collective defense has been partially redefined and amended and a new out-of-area norm has been more or less consolidated. At the same time, the traditional meaning of the norms of collective defense and peaceful conflict resolution remain intact. It would thus be premature to speak of normative change in this area. Yet, the norm innovations that have been undertaken in recent years have produced serious disputes among norm leaders in the transatlantic security community. One of the reasons for this may be that the meaning of the new out-of-area norm is still only vaguely defined (e.g., under what conditions can or should NATO intervene militarily and for how long?). Moreover, transforming NATO from a regional into a globally engaged security organization has also strained the resources and capabilities of many members of the transatlantic security community (including its core state), which may, in the long run, also weaken the transatlantic norm of multilateral practice. Finally, transatlantic security issues are interrelated with economic issues. If economic conditions deteriorate or compare unfavorably with those in other areas (for example, as a result of the global financial crisis), such conditions may place an additional burden on the integrative capabilities of institutions and practices to provide for stable peace within the community as well (Deutsch et al. 1957, p. 63). The recent debate among norm leaders over cutting defense budgets due to the financial crisis may be indicative here.

Norm of Communication

The transatlantic norm of communication is characterized by the willingness among its members to be convinced by the better argument and thus follow the logic of communicative action. It rests on the norm of genuine and timely consultation and responsiveness. It is probably not exaggerated to argue that, in this area, the normative order of the transatlantic security community temporarily broke down. During the Iraq War, norm leaders displayed an unwillingness to listen to each other and to engage in the exchange of arguments and mutual persuasion. Instead, 'thin' or strategic communication became the norm—at least for a certain period of time. It took considerable time and efforts and, eventually, the election of new norm leaders, to repair this breakdown of the norm of communication.

But even after the Iraq crisis (and certainly before it), some members (especially the core state) have behaved unresponsively in their communication with each other. During the Bosnia and Kosovo crises, for example, US norm leaders hardly consulted with other norm leaders regarding strategic decisions like the lift-and-strike strategy or the decision to bomb Serbia. Likewise, European norm leaders also showed a lack of responsiveness, most recently, for example, when German norm leaders abstained in the UN Security Council vote on Libya. Hence, unresponsiveness continues to be a serious problem for North Atlantic integration. In particular, the USA seems to continue to believe that responsiveness—the willingness to listen and be persuaded by others (Deutsch et al. 1957, p. 165)—places an unnecessary burden on its freedom of action. This notion has been reinforced by the recent American focus on the Asia-Pacific region with many European norm leaders remaining reluctant to go along.

Conclusion

It is, of course, still too early to make any final conclusions on the state of the transatlantic security community. In this sense, North Atlantic integration remains an open case. What can be stated, however, is the fact that despite serious crises and a partial redefinition and adaptation of its normative order the transatlantic security community continues to exist. War among its members is still unthinkable and there is no indication of a member seriously considering the resolution of conflicts of interests by threatening the use of force. NATO as an organization (despite institutional failure during the Iraq War) also shows no signs of dissolving any time soon. There have been amendments and adaptations to the transatlantic normative order but its 'meta'-norms (common values, multilateral practice, and meaningful communication) remain largely intact or have been repaired after the Iraq crisis. Thus, dependable expectations of peaceful change among the people of the North Atlantic area still seem assured.

Furthermore, it is important to point out that the lack of responsiveness often displayed by the US core state is not a new phenomenon but continues to be a problem ever since the founding of NATO. As Karl Deutsch (et al. 1957, p. 138) concludes: 'The first capability (of a core state)—the ability to act—is present in the United States, but the second capability—to respond—is decidedly less apparent as a reliable habit.' It can be argued that this problem has intensified somewhat since the end of the Cold War and especially since the September 11 attacks. This increasing reluctance by the USA to listen to other norm leaders of the transatlantic security community follows, in part, from the predicament that 'to listen implies the possibility of being persuaded; and to be open to persuasion implies the possibility of losing part of a nation's freedom of decision, since there is an expectation that persuasion should be effective at least some of the time' (Deutsch et al. 1957, p. 139). A growing US unwillingness to be persuaded by others could thus become a significant burden for the future normative order of the transatlantic security community. For example, there have been voices in the USA that call for more freedom of action in foreign policy while seeing little need for continued North Atlantic integration. In particular, certain groups within the Republican Party are skeptical of deepening political integration within NATO. In addition, influential scholars like Justin Logan, Director of Foreign Policy at the Cato Institute, even call NATO a 'farce' and others, like Stephen Walt of Harvard University, continue to see the dissolution of NATO 'only as a matter of time' (Washington Times 2011; Walt 2010). Yet, these challenging voices are still rather isolated ones and, most importantly, run contrary to USA and transatlantic public opinion.

To sum up, despite the lack of responsiveness and serious norm contestation in the past, it is still plausible to suggest that the transatlantic security community has not (yet) entered the final stage of disintegration. As argued above, the normative order remains largely intact and norm leaders still view each other as members of the same community sharing a liberal–democratic way of life that distinguishes them from other areas of the globe. But this raises the obvious question: Why has the transatlantic security community, in contrast to the German security community presented in the previous chapter, not (yet) crossed the threshold of disintegration by moving from a stage of denial to a stage of disintegration?

It is impossible to give a definite answer to this question given the still unpredictable future of the transatlantic security community. Part of the answer has already been suggested by pointing to the apparent lack of overjustification in the aftermath of the Iraq crisis. Adding to this, two observations appear to be plausible if only preliminary explanations and, critically, both involve agency. First, in case of 'successful' security community disintegration, one would expect a general lack of norm enforcement and norm iteration that would promote social unlearning and lead to a redefinition of collective meanings. This has simply not happened in the case of the transatlantic security community. While US norm violations remained largely unpunished during the Balkan Wars and in Afghanistan, in the Iraq case, however, many European norm leaders (both state and non-state actors) openly and vehemently opposed these norm violations. These efforts show that a significant amount of norm leaders on both sides of the Atlantic continues to attach value and meaning to the security community. Thus, a 'crowding-out' effect (as present in the case of the German security community) has not occurred. Instead, by reaffirming the community's normative meanings, norm leaders' resistance perhaps saved the normative order of the transatlantic security community from further degeneration.

Second, there is no significant domestic support or transnational pressure advocating the disintegration of the current transatlantic normative order. In contrast to the previous case of the German security community, the empirical narrative in this case shows that transnational and domestic norm challengers remain marginal and divided with little support among the politically relevant strata. The presence of such norm challenging 'cross-class coalitions', however, seems to be almost a precondition for 'successful' security community disintegration as new ideas and norms tend to be introduced by 'small, scattered, and powerless movements' that take hold and turn into 'larger and more coordinated ones with significant power behind them' (Deutsch et al. 1957, p. 83). By contrast, not only is there a lack of a significant domestic or transnational social movements to challenge the norms of the transatlantic security community but, as pointed out above, there is instead a significant amount of transnational networks and institutions actively promoting transatlantic norms serving as structural barriers that successfully block the spread of alternative ideas. Adding to their weakness, norm challengers in the transatlantic area tend to have only a vague conception of what an alternative normative order might look like. Hence, despite frequent norm contestation and divergence among norm leaders, the lack of an organized group of norm challengers with a clear definition of an alternative normative order has thus far arguably saved the transatlantic security community from disintegration.

Notes

1. What is often overlooked is the fact that Deutsch remained somewhat cautious about the existence of a pluralistic security community in the North Atlantic area at the time of his writing. Deutsch's caution is understandable given that his book was written only ten years after the end of World War II. At that time, Spain and Portugal were still dictatorships, and there still was considerable mistrust among European states toward (West) Germany (Deutsch et al. 1957, p. 118).

2. The following countries make up the transatlantic security community today: Albania, Austria, Belgium, Bulgaria, Canada, Croatia, Czech Republic, Denmark, Estonia, Finland, France, Germany, Hungary, Iceland, Ireland, Italy, Latvia, Lithuania, Luxembourg, Netherlands, Norway, Poland, Portugal, Romania, Slovenia, Slovakia, Spain, Sweden, Switzerland, the UK, and the USA.
3. On the concept of the 'transatlantic West' see, for example, Miliopoulos 2007; O'Hagan 2002; Koschut 2010.
4. Interview by the author with a senior member of the German Armed Forces at the International Institute for Politics and Economics in Hamburg in 21 March 2011.
5. Article 5 of the NATO treaty limits collective defense to armed attacks 'in Europe or North America'. This territorial restriction of Article 5, increasingly blurring during the Balkan Wars, was redefined at the NATO Summit in Prague in 2002: 'Recalling the tragic events of 11 September 2001 and our subsequent decision to invoke Article 5 of the Washington Treaty, we have approved (...) to meet the challenges to the security of our forces, populations and territory, *from wherever they may come*. (...) NATO must be able to field forces that can move quickly *to wherever they are needed*' (emphasis added, NATO 2002, p. 127).

REFERENCES

Adler, E. (2001). The change of change: Peaceful transitions of power in the multilateral age. In C. A. Kupchan, E. Adler, J. M. Coicaud, & Y. F. Khong (Eds.), *Power in transition: The peaceful change of international order* (pp. 138–158). New York: United Nations University Press.

Adler, E., & Barnett, M. (1998). A framework for the study of security communities. In E. Adler & M. Barnett (Eds.), *Security communities* (pp. 29–66). Cambridge: Cambridge University Press.

Adler, E., & Greve, P. (2009). When security community meets balance of power. Overlapping regional mechanisms of security governance. *Review of International Studies, 35*(1), 59–84.

Anderson, J., Ikenberry, G. J., & Risse, T. (2008). *The end of the west? Crises and change in the Atlantic order*. Ithaca: Cornell University Press.

Asmus, R. D. (2002). *Opening NATO's door. How the alliance remade itself for a new era*. New York: Columbia University Press.

Baker, J. A. III (with T. M. DeFrank) (1995). *The politics of diplomacy*. New York: G.P. Putnam's Sons.

Bjola, C., & Kornprobst, M. (2007). Security communities and the habitus of restraint. Germany and the United States on Iraq. *Review of International Studies, 33*(2), 285–305.

Bueno de Mesquita, B., Morrow, J. D., Siverson, R., & Smith, A. (1999). An institutional explanation of the democratic peace. *American Political Science Review, 89*(4), 791–812.

Chomsky, N. (1999). *The new military humanism. Lessons from Kosovo.* Monroe: Common Courage Press.

Cox, M. (2005). Beyond the West: Terrors in Transatlantia. *European Journal of International Relations, 11*(2), 203–233.

Daalder, I. H. (2000). *Getting to Dayton. The making of America's Bosnia policy.* Washington, DC: Brookings Institution.

Daalder, I. H., & O'Hanlon, M. E. (2000). *Winning ugly. NATO's war to save Kosovo.* Washington, DC: Brookings Institution.

Daalder, I. H., Lindsay J. M. (2003). *America Unbound, The Bush Revolution in Foreign Policy.* Washington, D.C.: Brookings Institution Press.

Deutsch, K. W., Burrell, S. A., Kann, R. A., Lee, M., Jr., Lichterman, M., Lindgren, R. E., Loewenheim, F. L., & van Wagenen, R. W. (1957). *Political community and the North Atlantic area. International organization in the light of historical experience.* Princeton: Princeton University Press.

Eznack, L. (2012). *Crises in the Atlantic alliance. Affect and relations among NATO members.* New York: Palgrave Macmillan.

Fierke, K. M., & Wiener, A. (1999). Constructing institutional interests: NATO and EU enlargement. *Journal of European Public Policy, 6*(5), 721–742.

Forsberg, T. (2005). German foreign policy and the war on Iraq: Anti-Americanism, pacifism or emancipation? *Security Dialogue, 36*(2), 213–231.

Fukuyama, F. (1989). The end of history? *The National Interest, 16*, 3–18.

Gompert, D. C. (1996). The United States and Yugoslavia's wars. In R. H. Ullman (Ed.), *The world and Yugoslavia's wars.* New York: Council on Foreign Relations.

Gordon, P. H. (2003). Bridging the Atlantic divide. *Foreign Affairs, 82*(1), 70–83.

Guicherd, C. (1999). International law and the war in Kosovo. *Survival, 41*(2), 25–29.

Holbrooke, R. (1999). *To end a war.* New York: Random House.

Joetze, G. (2000). *The European security landscape after Kosovo* (ZEI discussion paper). Bonn: Center for European Integration Studies.

Kitchen, V. M. (2009). Argument and identity change in the Atlantic security community. *Security Dialogue, 40*(1), 95–114.

Kitchen, V. M. (2010). NATO's out-of-area norm from Suez to Afghanistan. *Journal of Transatlantic Studies, 8*(2), 105–117.

Kitfield, J. (2002). Pox Americana? *National Journal, 34*(14), 982–987.

Koschut, S. (2010). *Die Grenzen der Zusammenarbeit. Sicherheit und transatlantische Identität nach dem Ende des Ost-West-Konflikts.* Baden-Baden: Nomos.

Koschut, S. (2014a). Emotional (security) communities: The significance of emotion norms in inter-allied conflict management. *Review of International Studies, 40*(3), 533–558.

Koschut, S. (2014b). Transatlantic conflict management inside-out: The impact of domestic norms on regional security practices. *Cambridge Review of International Affairs, 27*(2), 339–361.
Kreft, H. (2002). Vom Kalten zum "Grauen" Krieg. Paradigmenwechsel in der amerikanischen Außenpolitik'. *Aus Politik und Zeitgeschichte, 25,* 14–22.
Loquai, H. (2000). *Der Kosovo-Konflikt. Wege in einen vermeidbaren Krieg.* Baden-Baden: Nomos.
Luck, E. C. (2003). False choices: Unilateralism, multilateralism, and U.S. foreign policy. In B. May & M. Hönicke (Eds.), *The uncertain superpower. Domestic dimensions of U.S. foreign policy after the Cold War* (pp. 161–184). Opladen: Leske and Buderich.
Lundestad, G. (2003). *The United States and Western Europe since 1945.* Oxford: Oxford University Press.
Lyman, P. N. (2000). Saving the UN Security Council. A challenge for the United States. *Max Planck Yearbook of United Nations Law, 4,* 129–130.
MccGwire, M. (2000). Why did we bomb Belgrade? *International Affairs, 76*(1), 1–23.
Miliopoulos, L. (2007). *Atlantische Zivilisation und transatlantisches Verhältnis. Politische Idee und Wirklichkeit.* Wiesbaden: Verlag für Sozialwissenschaften.
Nye, J. S. (2002). *The paradox of American power. Why the world's only superpower can't go it alone.* Oxford: Oxford University Press.
Nye, J. S., U.S. Power and Strategy after Iraq, in: Foreign Affairs 82/4 (2003), pp. 60-73.
O'Hagan, J. (2002). *Conceptualizing the West in international relations. From Spengler to said.* Basingstoke: Palgrave Macmillan.
Patrick, S., & Forman, S. (Eds.). (2002). *Multilateralism and U.S. foreign policy. Ambivalent engagement.* Boulder: Lynne Rienner.
Petras, J., & Vieux, S. (1996). Bosnia and the revival of US hegemony. *New Left Review, 218,* 3–25.
Pouliot, V. (2006). The alive and well transatlantic security community: A theoretical reply to Michael Cox. *European Journal of International Relations, 12*(1), 119–127.
Rice, C. (2000). Promoting the national interest. *Foreign Affairs, 79*(1), 45–62.
Risse, T. (2000). Let's argue! Communicative action in world politics. *International Organization, 54*(1), 1–39.
Rodman, P. W. (1999). *Drifting apart? Trends in U.S.-European relations.* Washington, DC: The Nixon Center.
Rudolf, P. (2000). Friedenserhaltung und Friedenserzwingung: Militärinterventionen in der amerikanischen Außenpolitik'. In P. Rudolf & J. Wilzewski (Eds.), *Weltmacht ohne Gegner. Amerikanische Außenpolitik zu Beginn des 21. Jahrhunderts.* Baden-Baden: Nomos.

Rudolf, P. (2002). Die USA und die transatlantischen Beziehungen nach dem 11. September 2001'. *Aus Politik und Zeitgeschichte, 25*, 7–13.
Schneider, W. (1997). The new isolationism. In R. J. Lieber (Ed.), *Eagle adrift: American foreign policy at the end of the century* (pp. 26–38). New York: Longman.
Stafford, R. W. (1996). Europe and the United States: Forging a new relationship. In H. J. Wiarda (Ed.), *U.S. foreign and strategic policy in the post-Cold War era. A geopolitical perspective* (pp. 43–66). Westport: Greenwood Press.
Starr, H. (1992). Democracy and war: Choice, learning and security communities. *Journal of Peace Research, 29*(2), 207–213.
Talbott, S. (2002). From Prague to Baghdad: NATO at risk. *Foreign Affairs, 81*(6), 46–57.
Thimm, J. (2014). *Inseparable but not equal. Assesssing US-EU relations in the wake of the NSA surveillance affair* (SWP comments 4). Berlin: German Institute for International and Security Affairs.
Voigt, K. D. (2008). Die transatlantischen Beziehungen nach der Ära Bush. *Sicherheit und Frieden, 26*(3), 132–137.
Walt, S. (2010). If NATO disappeared, Would anyone notice?, 24 September, http://walt.foreignpolicy.com/posts/2010/09/24/is_nato_irrelevant. Accessed 19 Sept 2015.
Woodward, B. (1996). *The choice.* New York: Simon and Schuster.
Wyatt-Walter, H. (1997). *The European community and the security dilemma, 1979–92.* London: St Martin's Press.
Air Force Magazine. (2000). True blue: Behind the Kosovo numbers game, 83/8. http://www.airforcemag.com/MagazineArchive/Pages/2000/August%20 2000/0800kosovo.aspx. Accessed 2 Nov 2013.
Albright, M. (1998). Press briefing at the Ministry of Foreign Affairs in Rome on 7 March. http://www.usembassy-israel.org.il/publish/peace/archives/1998/march/me0310a.html. Accessed 1 Nov 2013.
Atlantic Council. (1993). Speech by Assistant Secretary of State for European and Canadian Affairs Steve Oxman in Washington, D.C. on 12 August. http://www.c-spanvideo.org/program/EuropeanS. Accessed 1 Nov 2013.
Auswärtiges Amt. (1998). *Deutsche Außenpolitik 1995. Auf dem Weg zu einer Friedensregelung für Bosnien-Herzegowina: 52 Telegramme aus Dayton.* Bonn: RGA.
BBC. (2003a). Outrage at 'Old Europe' remarks, 23 January. http://news.bbc.co.uk/2/hi/europe/2687403.stm. Accessed 2 Nov 2013.
BBC. (2003b). Millions join global anti-war protests, 17 February. http://news.bbc.co.uk/2/hi/europe/2765215.stm. Accessed 2 Nov 2013.
CBC. (2012). Anti-NATO protesters march through Chicago to summit, 20 May. http://www.cbc.ca/news/world/story/2012/05/20/nato-summit-chicago-protest.html. Accessed 2 Nov 2013.

Chirac, J., & Blair, A. (2001). Joint declaration on Afghanistan by the French president and the British prime minister at the annual Anglo-French summit on 29 November. http://www.ambafrance-uk.org/Joint-declaration-on-Afghanistan. Accessed 2 Nov 2013.

Clinton, W. J. (1993). The president's news conference on 17 June. In Public Papers of the Presidents of the United States (Ed.), *William J. Clinton* (Book 1, pp. 867–875). Washington, DC: US Government Printing Office.

Clinton, W. J. (1994). Remarks to multinational audience of future leaders of Europe at Brussels on 9 January. http://www.usembassy.de/usa/etexts/ga-6-940109.htm. Accessed 1 Nov 2013.

Clinton, W. J. (1996). Remarks to the people of Detroit on 22 October 1996. http://www.nato.int/docu/speech/1996/s961022a.htm. Accessed 1 Nov 2013.

Clinton, W. J. (1999). Presidential address to the nation on 10 June. http://www.freeserbia.net/Documents/Kosovo/clinton10.html. Accessed 1 Nov 2013.

CNN. (2001a). Polish forces to join Afghan campaign, 22 November. http://articles.cnn.com/2001-11-22/world/ret.poland.troops_1_exercises-poland-president-aleksander-kwasniewski?_s=PM:WORLD. Accessed 2 Nov 2013.

CNN. (2001b). Bush to push anti-terror agenda in China, 17 October. http://articles.cnn.com/2001-10-17/us/ret.bush.apec_1_qaeda-populous-muslim-country-world-trade-center?_s=PM:US. Accessed 2 Nov 2013.

CNN. (2003). Address by the British prime minister to a joint session of the U.S. Congress on 17 July. http://edition.cnn.com/2003/US/07/17/blair.transcript/index.html. Accessed 18 July 2003.

Council of Europe. (2006) Alleged secret detentions and unlawful inter-state transfers involving Council of Europe member states. Committee on Legal Affairs and Human Rights, Parliamentary Assembly of the Council of Europe. http://assembly.coe.int/CommitteeDocs/2006/20060606_Ejdoc162006Partii-final.pdf. Accessed 19 Jan 2007.

Council on Foreign Relations. (2002). Remarks by Senator Richard G. Lugar on 4 March. http://www.securefrontiers.net/strategicthinkers/april02/natoafter911crisisopportunity.html. Accessed 18 Nov 2002.

CSIS. (2003). Joint declaration on renewing the transatlantic partnership on 14 May. http://www.csis.org/europe/2003_May_14_JointDeclr.pdf. Accessed 2 Nov 2013.

Daalder, I. H., Lindsay J. M. (2003). America Unbound, The Bush Revolution in Foreign Policy, Washington, D.C.: Brookings Institution Press.

Deutsche Welle. (2003). Iraq rift launches new era in German foreign policy, 17 April. http://www.dw.de/complete-archive-of-dw-worlds-iraq-coverage/a-783176. Accessed 2 Nov 2013.

Deutscher Bundestag. (2001) Speech by Federal Chancellor Gerhard Schröder on the request of the federal government on deployment of German armed forces in support of the common reaction to terrorist attacks against the United States

on 16 November. http://www.documentarchiv.de/brd/2001/rede_schroeder_1116.html. Accessed 2 Nov 2013.
Diplomatic World Bulletin. (1997). U.S. debt called 'indefensible'; Weston says it's catch-22, 28 (April-May), 1.
European Union. (1990). Transatlantic declaration on EC-US relations. http://eeas.europa.eu/us/docs/trans_declaration_90_en.pdf. Accessed 1 Nov 2013.
European Union. (2001). Statements by Romano Prodi on the attacks against the United States on 12 September. http://www.europa.eu.int/rapid/start/cgi/guesten.ksh?p_action.gettxt=gt&doc=IP/01/1265/0/RAPID&lg=EN. Accessed 2 Nov 2013.
European Union. (2003). Looking ahead in transatlantic relations. Speech by Romano Prodi in Washington, D.C on 24 June. http://www.europa.eu.int/comm/external_relations/news/prodi/sp03_322.htm. Accessed 2 Nov 2013.
Financial Times. (1995, January 6). *Each state for itself*, p. 12.
Financial Times. (1998, December 7). *The right balance will secure NATO's future*, p. 4.
Foreign ministers of Albania, Bulgaria, Croatia, Estonia, Latvia, Lithuania, Macedonia, Romania, Slovakia and Slovenia. (2003). Statement of the Vilnius Group Countries. http://www.novinite.com/view_news.php?id=19022, Accessed 21 Sept 2015.
Frankfurter Allgemeine Zeitung. (1993, July 7). Wie Gewaltfreiheit den Aggressor begünstigt. Lehren aus dem Krieg im ehemaligen Jugoslawien, p. 7.
German Marshall Fund of the United States. (2009). Transatlantic trends. http://trends.gmfus.org/archives/transatlantic-trends/transatlantic-trends-2009/. Accessed 21 Sept 2015.
German Marshall Fund of the United States. (2010). Transatlantic trends. http://trends.gmfus.org/archives/transatlantic-trends/transatlantic-trends-2010/. Accessed 21 Sept 2015.
German Marshall Fund of the United States. (2012). Transatlantic trends. http://trends.gmfus.org/category/transatlantic-trends-2012/. Accessed 21 Sept 2015.
German Marshall Fund of the United States. (2013). Transatlantic trends. http://trends.gmfus.org/transatlantic-trends/. Accessed 21 Sept 2015.
Guardian. (2007). This is a torture camp, 12 January. http://www.guardian.co.uk/commentisfree/2007/jan/12/comment.foreignpolicy. Accessed 2 Nov 2013.
Hansard Index: Canadian Parliament Historical Resources. (1948). *House of commons debates* (Vol. IV). Ottawa: Library of Parliament.
Heisbourg, F. Europe and the Transformation of the World Order, in: Survival 43/4 (2001), pp. 143-148.

Hippler, J. Unilateralismus der USA als Problem der internationalen Politik, in: Aus Politik und Zeitge-schichte 31-32 (2003), pp. 15-22.
International Coordinating Committee Anti-NATO Protests. (2009). Why we demonstrate. http://www.ag-friedensforschung.de/themen/NATO/60/programm-flyer.pdf. Accessed 2 Nove 2013.
International Herald Tribune. (1993, January 11). *For clinton a larger question looms in Somalia*, p. 8.
International Herald Tribune. (1999, September 17). *NATO lowers its tally of tanks hit in Kosovo*, p. 5.
International Herald Tribune. (2003a, July 30). *When America goes it alone, we all pay*, p. 6.
International Herald Tribune. (2003b). Meet Mr. Germany and Ms. France, 29 September. http://www.iht.com/articles/111654.html. Accessed 2 Nov 2013.
International Herald Tribune. (2011). Who needs NATO? We all do!, 18 June. http://www.nytimes.com/2011/06/18/opinion/18iht-eddaalder.html?_r=0. Accessed 2 Nov 2013.
International Institute for Strategic Studies. (1999). Speech by US Secretary of Defense William S. Cohen in San Diego, CA. on 9 September. http://www.defenselink.mil/speeches/1999/s19990909-secdef.html. Accessed 2 Nov 2013.
Kagan, R. (2003). Of Paradise and Power: America and Europe in the New World Order, New York: Alfred A. Knopf.
Koschut, S. Germany and the USA in the "War against Terror": Is Extraordinary rendition putting transatlantic cooperation under strain?, in: Internationale Politik und Gesellschaft 3 (2007), pp. 36-52.
Le Monde. (2001). Nous sommes tous américains, 13 September. http://www.lemonde.fr/idees/article/2007/05/23/nous-sommes-tous-americains_913706_3232.html. Accessed 2 Nov 2013.
Los Angeles Times. (2005). Europeans say rice allayed concerns, 9 December. http://articles.latimes.com/2005/dec/09/world/fg-rice9. Accessed 2 Nov 2013.
Lugar, R. (1993). *Remarks at the Open Forum at the US Department of State*, 2 August.
Dobbs, M. (1999). Madeleine Albright: A Twentieth Century Odyssey. New York: Henry Holt.
Mirror. (2001, November 9). *War on terror: The world questions America*, p. 1.
NATO. (1949). The North Atlantic Treaty. http://www.nato.int/cps/en/natolive/official_texts_17120.htm. Accessed 1 Nov 2013.
NATO. (1956). Report of the committee of three on non-military cooperation in NATO, approved by the North Atlantic Council on 13 December. http://www.nato.int/docu/basictxt/bt-a3.htm. Accessed 1 Nov 2013.

NATO. (1990). Declaration on a transformed North Atlantic Alliance issued by the heads of state and government participating in the meeting of the North Atlantic Council on 5/6 July 1990 (The London Declaration). http://www.nato.int/cps/en/SID-4A5A3D2C-13F8BA35/natolive/official_texts_23693.htm. Accessed 1 Nov 2013.

NATO. (1991). The new strategic concept agreed by the heads of state and government participating in the meeting of the North Atlantic Council on 7/8 November. http://www.nato.int/cps/en/natolive/official_texts_23847.htm. Accessed 1 Nov 2013.

NATO. (1992a). Final communiqué by the NATO Defence Planning Committee on 11 December. http://www.nato.int/docu/comm/49-95/c921211a.htm. Accessed 1 Nov 2013.

NATO. (1992b). *NATO ministerial final Communiqué on 17 December*. Brussels: M-NAC-2(92)106.

NATO. (1993). *Permanent representatives' lunch details athens ministerial agenda on 6 June*. Brussels: US-NATO 002532.

NATO. (1994a). Meeting of the North Atlantic Council at NATO headquarters on 1 December. http://www.nato.int/docu/speech/1994/s941201b.htm. Accessed 1 Nov 2013.

NATO. (1994b). Declaration of the heads of state and government participating in the meeting of the North Atlantic Council on 11 January 1994 (The Brussels Summit Declaration). http://www.nato.int/cps/en/SID-C129F022-F3EA069C/natolive/official_texts_24470.htm?mode=pressrelease. Accessed 1 Nov 2013.

NATO. (1995). Speech by NATO Secretary-General Willy Claes at the Munich Security Conference. http://www.nato.int/docu/speech/1995/s950203a.htm. Accessed 23 Apr 2014.

NATO. (1999a). The combined joint task forces concept. http://www.nato.int/docu/comm/1999/9904-wsh/pres-eng/16cjtf.pdf. Accessed 1 Nov 2013.

NATO. (1999b). Strategic concept, approved by the heads of state and government participating in the meeting of the North Atlantic Council in Washington D.C. http://www.nato.int/cps/en/natolive/official_texts_27433.htm. Accessed 2 Nov 2013.

NATO. (1999c). Washington Summit Communiqué. Issued by the heads of state and government participating in the meeting of the North Atlantic Council in Washington, D.C. on 24 April. http://www.nato.int/docu/pr/1999/p99-064e.htm. Accessed 2 Nov 2013.

NATO. (2002). Prague Summit Declaration on 21 November. http://www.nato.int/docu/pr/2002/p02-127e.htm. Accessed 23 Apr 2014.

NATO. (2010). Strategic concept for the defence and security of the members of the North Atlantic Treaty Organization. http://www.nato.int/strategic-concept/pdf/Strat_Concept_web_en.pdf. Accessed 2 Nov 2013.

NATO. (2013). The First Five Years 1949–1954. Part 3. Chapter 14, available at: http://www.nato.int/archives/1st5years/chapters/14.htm. Accessed 1 November 2013.

New Atlanticist. (2012). Why we need a smart NATO, 27 April. http://www.atlanticcouncil.org/blogs/natosource/why-we-need-a-smart-nato-1. Accessed 1 Nov 2013.

New York Times. (1991). Bush challenges partners in NATO over role of U.S., 8 November, http://www.nytimes.com/1991/11/08/world/bush-challenges-partners-in-nato-over-role-of-us.html. Accessed 2 Nov 2013.

New York Times. (1999a). A just and necessary war, 23 May. http://www.nytimes.com/1999/05/23/opinion/a-just-and-necessary-war.html. Accessed 1 Nov 2013.

New York Times. (1999b, January 28). *Germany's pragmatic ex-radical thinks globally*, p. A3.

New York Times. (2001, July 31). *White House says the U.S. is not a loner, just choosy*, p. A1.

New York Times. (2002a). Interview with German Chancellor Gerhard Schröder, 4 September. http://www.nytimes.com/2002/09/04/international/europe/05GERM-TEXT.html. Accessed 2 Nov 2013.

New York Times. (2002b, August 28). *Rumsfeld says allies will support U.S. on Iraq*, p. A1.

New York Times. (2002c). German leader's warning: War plan is a huge mistake, 5 September. http://www.nytimes.com/2002/09/05/international/europe/05SCHR.html. Accessed 4 Jan 2016.

New York Times. (2003a). Bridging the Atlantic divide, 6 March. http://www.nytimes.com/cfr/international/20030101faessay10223_philip_h_gordon.html. Accessed 2 Nov 2013.

New York Times. (2003b). A new power in the streets, 17 February. http://www.nytimes.com/2003/02/17/world/threats-and-responses-news-analysis-a-new-power-in-the-streets.html. Accessed 2 Nov 2013.

Newsweek. (1999, April 19). *A new generation draws the line*, p. 37.

Pew Research Center. (2008). Global public opinion in the Bush years, 2001-2008. http://www.pewglobal.org/2008/12/18/global-public-opinion-in-the-bush-years-2001-2008/. Accessed 2 Nov 2013.

Powell, C. L. (2003). Interview with German journalist Sabine Christiansen on 16 May. http://2001-2009.state.gov/secretary/former/powell/index.htm. Accessed 2 Nov 2013.

Program on International Policy Attitudes. (1999). Americans on Kosovo. A study of US public attitudes. http://www.pipa.org/OnlineReports/Kosovo/Kosovo_May99/Kosovo_May99_rpt.pdf. Accessed 1 Nov 2013.

Risse, T. Es gibt keine Alternative! USA und EU müssen ihre Beziehungen neu justieren, in: Internationale Politik 6 (2003), pp. 9-18.

Radio Free Europe. (2003). U.S.: Rumsfeld's 'old' and 'new' Europe touches on uneasy divide, 24 January. http://www.rferl.org/content/article/1102012.html. Accessed 2 Nov 2013.

Rasmussen, A. F. (2010). Renewing the transatlantic security community in the age of globalisation, speech by the NATO secretary general at the Central Military Club, Sofia, Bulgaria on 20 May. http://www.nato.int/cps/en/natolive/opinions_63773.htm. Accessed 8 Mar 2011.

Reuters. (2012). Thousands protest in Chicago as NATO summit opens, 20 May. http://www.reuters.com/article/2012/05/20/us-nato-summit-protests-idUSBRE84I09X20120520. Accessed 2 Nov 2013.

Rice, C. (2005). Press availability at the meeting of the North Atlantic Council, 8 December. http://2001-2009.state.gov/secretary/rm/2005/57805.htm. Accessed 4 Jan 2016.

Rumsfeld, D. (2002). Remarks by the US secretary of defense at the National Defense University on 31 January. http://www.defenselink.mil/speeches/2002/S20020131-secdef.html. Accessed 2 Nov 2013.

Solana, J. (2003). Mars and Venus reconciled: A new era for transatlantic relations, Lecture at the Harvard Kennedy School of Government on 7 April. http://www.useu.be/TransAtlantic/030407SolanaHarvard.htm. Accessed 2 Nov 2013.

Spiegel. (1999). Wir sollten stolz auf uns sein. http://www.spiegel.de/spiegel/print/d-12808102.html. Accessed 1 Nov 2013.

Spiegel. (2003, April 19). *Die Herren der Welt*, p. 18.

Spiegel. (2005). Bush begrüßt Schröders Reform Appell, 22 February. http://www.spiegel.de/politik/ausland/nato-gipfel-bush-begruesst-schroeders-reform-appell-a-343147.html. Accessed 2 Nov 2013.

Spiegel. (2006). US Regierung gefährlicher als Iran, 12 April,.http://www.spiegel.de/politik/deutschland/umfrage-us-regierung-gefaehrlicher-als-iran-a-411171.html. Accessed 2 Nov 2013.

Süddeutsche Zeitung. (2006, September 11). *Merkel kritisiert die USA*, p. 1.

Süddeutsche Zeitung. (2013). Abhören von Freunden, das geht gar nicht, 24 October. http://www.sueddeutsche.de/politik/nsa-abhoerskandal-abhoeren-von-freunden-das-geht-gar-nicht-1.1709525. Accessed 2 Nov 2013.

Talbott, S. (1999). The state of the alliance: An American perspective, speech by the US deputy secretary in Brussels on 15 December 1999. http://www.nato.int/usa/state/s19991215c.html. Last accessed 1 Nov 2013, Accessed 2 Nov 2013.

The Chicago Council on Foreign Relations/The German Marshall Fund of the United States, World Views 2002. European Public Opinion and Foreign Policy (European Report), Washington D.C. 2002.

The Economist. (1999, May 27). *NATO piles it on*, p. 23.

The Economist. (2001a, September 22). *Solid, but for how long?*, p. 31.

The Economist. (2001b, October 4). *NATO's super-policeman*, p. 34.

The Economist. (2002a, March 7). *Satellites and horsemen*, p. 27.
The Economist. (2002b, March 9). *Who needs whom?*, p. 30.
The Economist. (2003a, November 8). *A nation apart. A survey of America*, p. 3.
The Economist. (2003b). Ends, means, and barbarity, 9 January. http://www.economist.com/node/1522792. Accessed 3 Nov 2013.
The Economist. (2011, May 12). *The unadventurous eagle*, p. 6.
Time Magazine. (1991, February 22). *Interview with Manfred Wörner*, p. 12.
US Department of Justice. (2002). Memorandum for the president. Decision Re. Application of the Geneva Convention on prisoners of war to the conflict with al Qaeda and the Taliban on 25 January. http://news.lp.findlaw.com/hdocs/docs/torture/gnzls12502mem2gwb.html. Accessed 19 July 2007.
US Department of State. (2002). The national security strategy of the United States of America. http://www.state.gov/documents/organization/63562.pdf. Accessed 2 Nov 2013.
US House of Representatives. (2002). American Service-members' Protection Act. http://www.house.gov/legcoun/Comps/aspa02.pdf. Accessed 2 Nov 2013.
US Policy Information and Texts (USPIT). (1993). *Albright, Madeleine: Peacekeeping: A Critical U.S. Interest*, 64, 31–36.
USA Today. (2001). Spaniards protest U.S. policies on eve of Bush's trip, 6 June. http://usatoday30.usatoday.com/news/world/june01/2001-06-10-bush.htm. Accessed 21 Sept 2015.
USA Today. (2005). Rice: Abuse may occur despite U.S. torture rules, 8 December. http://usatoday30.usatoday.com/news/world/2005-12-08-rice-nato_x.htm. Accessed 2 Nov 2013.
Washington Post. (1993, June 18). *U.S. plans wider role in U.N. peace keeping*, p. A02.
Washington Post. (1999, June 20). *Allies need upgrade, general says*, p. A20/21.
Washington Post. (2001). President Bush addresses a joint session of Congress and the nation, 20 September 2001. http://www.washingtonpost.com/wp-srv/nation/specials/attacked/transcripts/bushaddress_092001.html. Accessed 2 Nov 2013.
Washington Post. (2002, March 4). *Europe U.S. diverging on key policy approaches*, p. A13.
Washington Post. (2003a, February 10). *Role reversal and alliance realities*, p. A01.
Washington Post. (2003b). State of the union address, 23 January. http://www.washingtonpost.com/wp-srv/onpolitics/transcripts/bushtext_012803.html. Accessed 2 Nov 2013.
Washington Times. (2005). CIA prisons claim discomfits Warsaw, 6 December. http://www.washingtontimes.com/news/2005/dec/06/20051206-100640-6465r/. Accessed 2 Nov 2013.

Washington Times. (2011). NATO is a Farce, 25 August. http://www.washingtontimes.com/news/2011/aug/25/nato-is-a-farce/. Accessed 2 Nov 2013.

White House. (1993). Memorandum of conversation from the presidents meeting with Italian Prime Minister Carlo Ciampi on 17 September. http://www.gpo.gov/fdsys/granule/PPP-1993-book2/PPP-1993-book2-doc-pg1526-2/content-detail.html. Accessed 2 Nov 2013.

White House. (1994). Presidential Decision Directive 25: US policy on reforming multilateral peace operations on 2 May. http://www.clintonlibrary.gov/_previous/Documents/2010%20FOIA/Presidential%20Directives/PDD-25.pdf. Accessed 1 Nov 2013.

White House. (2001). Address by the president to a joint session of Congress and the country in Washington, D.C. on 20 September. http://www.whitehouse.gov/news/releases/2001/09/20010920-8.html. Accessed 2 Nov 2013.

White House. (2002a). Alliance of freedom being tested by 'new and terrible dangers', Speech by the president in Vilnius on 23 November. http://www.whitehouse.gov/news/releases/2002/11/20021123-5.html. Accessed 2 Nov 2013.

White House. (2002b). Remarks by the president on Iraq in Cincinnati on 7 October. http://www.whitehouse.gov/news/releases/2002/10/print/20021007-8.html. Accessed 2 Nov 2013.

White House. (2003a). Remarks by the president in address to the nation in Washington, D.C. on 17 March. http://www.whitehouse.gov/news/releases/2003/03/20030317-7.html. Accessed 2 Nov 2013.

White House. (2003b). President Bush discusses Iraq policy in London on 19 November. http://www.whitehouse.gov/news/releases/2003/11/20031119-1.html. Accessed 19 Nov 2003.

White House. (2006). President discusses creation of military commissions to try suspected terrorists in Washington, D.C. on 6 September. http://www.whitehouse.gov/news/releases/2006/09/20060906-3.html. Accessed 19 Jan 2007.

World Social Forum. (2013). Declaration of the Social Movements Assembly in Tunis on 29 March. http://www.fsm2013.org/en/node/12972. Accessed 4 Feb 2014.

Yost, D. S. (1998). NATO Transformed: The Alliance's New Roles in International Security, Washington, DC: United States Institute of Peace Press.

CHAPTER 5

Conclusions

The problem of the disintegration of political communities is an all too familiar yet understudied phenomenon in IR whose importance has arguably amplified in recent years and generates increasing scholarly research on the subject (Eppler and Scheller 2013; Stetter et al. 2011; Anderson et al. 2008; Anhut 2005). One may think of the dissolution of empires like the Soviet Union, the disintegration of regional organizations like the Warsaw Pact or Southeast Asian Treaty Organization (SEATO), the breakdown of multiethnic communities like the former Yugoslavia or Czechoslovakia, the partition of postcolonial states like Sudan, the secession of newly independent entities like the Kosovo, East Timor or the Crimea, or, more recently, disintegrative dynamics in the EU such as *Grexit* (a Greek departure from the Euro) or *Brexit* (a British withdrawal from the EU).

Looking into all of these cases would be unfeasible in terms of limited space and resources available. Moreover, given the political and cultural diversity of these political communities, such an endeavor would almost inevitably lead to rather superficial results. What I have been concerned with here is both more modest and more ambitious in scope: to study the disintegration of *particular* communities. This research goal is modest in scope because its focus is limited to *security* communities in which keeping the peace among its members is the main political goal overshadowing all others. At the same time, the study pursues a highly ambitious research agenda because it essentially investigates the conditions and processes that may avert the breakdown of stable peace among nations (Deutsch et al. 1957).

This book raises a central question: What leads to the breakup of pluralistic security communities? To this end, I argued that security communities are normative communities that cease to exist when its norms are no longer followed and when collective meanings are no longer meaningful. This process involves normative change understood here as the degeneration of peaceful community norms. The scope of normative change explains why some cases of security community disintegration are 'successful' while others are not. In Chap. 2, I developed a framework to conceptualize security communities as normative communities inhabited by normative agents, and to analytically trace normative change in a security community. To this end, I provided a set of comparable analytical categories and mechanisms including the persuasiveness of new ideas, the disruption of symbolic interaction, institutional failure, and social unlearning as well as normative actors involving the interplay between norm leaders/regimes and norm challengers. This framework of security community disintegration is helpful in understanding why regional norms of peaceful change degenerate as well as to account for variations between peaceful regions undergoing normative change. It offers an original framework for norm degeneration at the regional level and advances theorizing about security community disintegration in IR.

In this final chapter, I will revisit this framework in light of the empirical findings and draw some tentative conclusions. As outlined earlier, I do not pretend to arrive at any definitive or generalized answers to the question why security communities disintegrate. These could hardly be made based on the scope of empirical cases presented in this book. Moreover, given the complexity of integration/disintegration processes along with a multitude of background conditions like history or culture, it seems even doubtful that there is a single answer to this question. Instead, by looking through the analytical lens of normative change in a security community, I present one particular but no less plausible way that contributes in significant ways to the unraveling of stable peace. Hence, instead of claiming generalized answers I wish to raise some probabilities and implications based on my theoretical argument and the historical narratives presented in this book.

This final chapter is divided into three parts. In the first part, I revisit the framework presented in Chap. 2 in order to see if and in what ways its assumptions are consistent with the empirical observations. To this end, I will not separately deal with 'external change' as a triggering factor here since its assumptions have already been extensively covered by the security community literature cited in Chap. 1. Instead, I focus on the social and internal changes leading to normative change that constitutes the main contribution of this book. In the second part, I outline a set of theoretical implications derived from this study. Finally, I offer suggestions for further research.

Analytical Implications

In this section, I revisit the analytical framework introduced in Chap. 2 in order to evaluate its empirical validity and applicability. In other words, how did the components of the framework 'score' in terms of their relative importance to each other as well as in terms of their significance and status in the overall process of security community disintegration? Again, these are not meant as definitive conclusions but rather as tentative implications based on the empirical cases above.

Persuasiveness of New Ideas

The persuasiveness of new ideas was expected to play an important role in the early stages of security community disintegration. This assumption can be tentatively confirmed based on the empirical narratives presented here. Old ideas lost traction and new ideas gained ground because, in the eyes of growing political strata, the latter appeared more capable to relate to current political and economic needs and problems. These new ideas were actively promoted by norm challengers seeking to change the normative status quo while norm leaders resisted norm innovation by erecting structural barriers and firewalls to prevent the spread of new ideas within the respective security community.

In both cases under investigation, new ideas were introduced and spread during the first stage of security community disintegration following a major external 'shock'. In the case of the German Confederation, norm challengers exploited the fact that an external 'shock' called into question the established normative order of the security community opening a window of opportunity to introduce new ideas to reform and/or replace existing norms. The external 'shock' of the July revolution in France inspired the emergence of the *Vormärz* as a transnational social movement that developed into a significant political force to challenge established community norms and grew determined to replace them with an alternative normative order. Conversely, the aristocratic norm leaders displayed a general lack of responsiveness and integrative capabilities in reaction to the norm challengers by further increasing repressive measures and by introducing firewalls (e.g., press censorship) to prevent the spread of norms in the German states. This, however, led to unintended negative consequences like the violation of member state sovereignty as well as the strengthening of the political legitimacy of norm challengers and the attractiveness of their ideas. These findings resonate with Deutsch's observation that 'the closure of the established political elite (...) tended to promote the rise of frustrated counter-elites' as an important disintegrative condition in a security community (Deutsch et al. 1957, p. 63). The findings also fit the framework presented into this book.

In the case of the transatlantic security community, normative change took a somewhat different turn. Here, norm leaders themselves introduced new ideas (in particular, the US core state) as, for example, the out-of-area norm or NATO enlargement. To be sure, the fact that norm *leaders* introduced new ideas in this case rendered the spread of these ideas no less contested (see, e.g., the British and French initial resistance). Nevertheless, the fact that these new ideas originated from within the norm regime of the transatlantic security and were actively promoted by its core state arguably made them less controversial and facilitated their eventual implementation. Moreover, the external 'shock' of the end of the Cold War did not produce the rise of norm challengers eager to take advantage of the opportunity to spread their ideas. The closest thing to a norm challenger was perhaps the USA itself but, then again, it can hardly be claimed that the USA sought to replace the normative order of the transatlantic security community.

Disruption of Symbolic Interaction

Disrupted symbolic interaction was another important factor driving security community disintegration even though it cannot be said to have agglomerated at any particular stage during the process (however, it does seem to be of little importance during the final stage of disintegration). Symbolic interaction was understood here as meaningful exchange among members of the security community. For example, symbolic rituals in a security community (summits, joint military exercises, or commemorating events) create high-order meanings necessary to maintain social norms and collective identity. Rituals involve the physical assembly of the members of a social group, their awareness and focus on a common object or action, and the sharing of similar expressions and discourse toward these objects or actions. Based on an analytical reading of the cases, it can be said that both norm challengers and norm leaders frequently employed symbols, rituals, and collective memories to reinforce or alter, respectively, the meaning of established security community norms. Moreover, it can be claimed that the disruption of such symbolic interaction facilitated misperception and incomprehension in both cases.

The disruption of symbolic interaction appears to have been an important mechanism that contributed to the alienation of the two core states of the German security community, Prussia and Austria, and initiated a vicious spiral of reciprocal retaliatory behavior. Norm challengers, on the other hand, constructed diverging interpretations of the new situation introduced by the external 'shock' via symbolic interaction, for example, during the Hambach festival. A similar process between different actors can be witnessed in the case of NATO where, in the absence of a second core state, the reinterpretation of some normative meanings was contested predominantly between the core state and varying groups of other norm leaders. For example, France and Britain openly resisted the idea of introducing an out-of-area norm leading to an undermining of ritualized symbolic interaction at NATO summits. Conversely, France and Germany defied the USA and Britain in the United Nations (UN) Security Council in the run-up to the war in Iraq. In both cases, the disruption of symbolic interaction through these ritualized encounters clearly shaped and undermined the relationship between norm leaders leading to a weakening of the norm regime thereby undermining its capability to reiterate community norms and punish norm violations.

However, the outcome of disrupted symbolic interaction differed in both cases. In the case of the German Confederation, disrupted symbolic interaction undergirded the temporary replacement of the established normative order with a new normative order during the revolution of 1848–1849. For example, norm leaders formally adopted the revolutionary colors of the *Vormärz* and the Prussian king publicly honored dead norm challengers in the streets of Berlin. By contrast, in the case of the transatlantic security community, the disruption of symbolic interaction merely resulted in a partial redefinition and reform of certain community norms such as the introduction of a new out-of-area norm. This variation in outcome indicates that, while important for producing normative change in a security community, the disruption of symbolic interaction significantly depends on the normative agents involved.

Institutional Failure

The significance of institutional failure for the disintegration of security community tends to come out even stronger than expected. In both cases and throughout all stages, we find numerous instances of institutional failures both at the regional as well as the domestic level. This undergirds the argument that the performance of domestic and regional institutions exercises an important stabilizing function for the normative order in a security community. First, it seems clear that institutions facilitate a collective response to norm violations and are involved in both the monitoring and the collective enforcement of the normative order. Second, institutions transport symbolic legitimacy as multilateral forums that are capable to promote norms of appropriate behavior in a security community and thus shape the collective identity of its members. Hence, failure to perform these roles, both at the domestic and the regional level, appears to have contributed significantly to the degeneration of community norms in both cases.

Institutional failure, for example, occurred during the German revolution of 1848–1849 when norm challengers were able to set up competing institutional structures within the framework of the security community. Subsequently, institutional failure played an important role in preventing reform of the re-established normative order in the German security community as individual member states, led by Prussia, formed alternative institutional forums such as the Erfurt Union and excluded other members from participating. In the case of the transatlantic security community, institutional failure, at times, led to the formation of an American and a (Western continental) European caucus within NATO with the EU sometimes serving as an alternative institutional vehicle excluding the USA. Institutional failure, for example, occurred during the crisis over the Iraq war when NATO was unable to serve as a multilateral forum for handling this important security issue with some norm leaders openly questioning the legitimacy of the institution.

Social Unlearning

Social unlearning seems to be a decisive factor in the process of security community disintegration because it determines the scope of normative change. To be sure, instances of social unlearning—a 'process of habit-breaking' (Deutsch et al. 1957, p. 85)—may be found in both cases studied. For example, one may interpret instances like the redefinition of the insider/outsider distinction within the transatlantic security community as articulated by Donald Rumsfeld ('old/new Europe'; 'the mission determines the coalition') or the formulation of a 'doctrine of preemptive warfare' as examples of social unlearning. Moreover, since these instances involved the core state of the transatlantic security community it seems plausible, given the importance of core states for the normative order of a security community, that these instances seriously disrupted the reiteration of community norms.

However, even though these occurrences certainly weakened the normative order of the security community it seems problematic to portray them as 'hard cases' of social unlearning since, in the end, they did not involve a replacement of previously held social identities and norms. For example, from looking at the history of US foreign policy, it seems doubtful that Rumsfeld's remarks actually represent a rejection and overwriting of previous knowledge since the USA has always shown a remarkable tendency to 'go it alone' in matters of what norm leaders perceive to be in the interest of so-called US national security. Moreover, the Obama Administration displayed an eagerness to publicly break with the policies of the Bush Administration, which it viewed as having undermined the normative order of the transatlantic security community. Hence, it appears questionable whether, in the case of the transatlantic security community, social unlearning in these few instances was strong and widespread enough to result in substantial normative change—or whether it existed at all.

Conversely, in the case of the German security community we find numerous instances of social unlearning mostly confined to the final stage of disintegration. Here, social unlearning reflects a visible pattern that involves the successful rejection and overwriting of the established normative order; first, by the norm challengers during the revolution of 1848–1849; second, by the norm regime itself leading to the replacement of the normative order of the Confederation with the normative order of the German nation-state. By the mid-nineteenth century, for example, Prussia had begun to seriously promote a reform of the established normative order of the security community allowing for the accommodation of growing German nationalism and liberalism. One group of norm leaders (following the 'Prussian way') appeared equally convinced that adapting reform could only preserve the German Confederation. However, no such process of generating new knowledge can be said to have occurred among Austrian norm leaders and its followers in the aftermath of the German revolution. As a result of social unlearning, the core states thus increasingly learnt to view each other as mutual Others thereby deconstructing the reciprocal image of a plural Self within a shared security community. Consequently, large portions of norm leaders in the member states were less and less able to identify with the meanings and symbols of the German security community.

In sum, the findings tend to confirm the assumption that (facilitated by external change) the combined impact of the introduction of new ideas, the disruption of symbolic interaction, institutional failure, and social unlearning promote a weakening of socialization processes (norm iteration) together with a lack of social control (norm enforcement). A weakening of norm iteration and a lack of norm enforcement, in turn, provide important conditions for normative change, which undermines mutual trust and collective identity and, in the end, leads to security community disintegration. As to the chronological order of things, the introduction of new ideas seems to be prominent in the early stages of norm degeneration whereas social unlearning appears to be the necessary capstone of security community disintegration. Disrupted symbolic interaction and institutional failure tend to drive norm degeneration during each stage of the process.

These findings tentatively reinforce another assumption: the centrality of agency in the process of normative change in a security community. To elaborate on this, I now turn to the conflict between norm challengers and norm leaders that arguably drives the mechanisms and process of normative change outlined above.

Norm Leaders and Norm Challengers

In this book, I have argued that agency in a security community can be framed as a conflict over collective meanings and interpretations between norm leaders and norm challengers, that is to say, between those who promote and enforce an established normative order and those who are dissatisfied with the existing normative order and actively try to change it. It was further argued that the scope of normative change in a security community depends on the ability of norm challengers to successfully replace the established normative order. To this end, norm challengers tend to be eager to contest the established normative order and to dispute the authority of norm leaders to define the meanings within a security community while norm leaders are likely to resist these efforts in order to preserve the normative status quo. Norm challengers were thus assumed to be closely associated with the mechanisms outlined above in order to contest existing norms and to mobilize a significant number of followers and resources. External 'shocks' were identified as windows of opportunities for norm challengers.

These assumptions not only resonate with Karl Deutsch's et al. (1957, p. 85) observation that the disintegration process constitutes a shift in political allegiance to new norms and identities through the emergence of new political movements that serve as alternative frameworks for mutual identification and trust-building. They also fit the empirical narrative developed in this book. In the case of the German Confederation, for example, nationalism advanced by norm challengers provided a powerful alternative to the collective identification as princes and kings in the German security community. Such shifts occurred as some norm leaders perceived their membership in the community as inhibiting their freedom of action and were hence more open for redefinition and reinterpretation of existing norms and identities (Deutsch et al. 1957, p. 89). Prussia's behavior after 1850 or US behavior after 2001, for example, can be viewed in this light when both sought to emancipate themselves from the perceived normative constraints of the security community.

Even though the empirical findings generally confirm this picture, they also reveal certain differences. One difference concerns the scope of mobilization among norm challengers. In the case of the German security community, the norm challengers of the *Vormärz* were able to gradually build a transnational and transsocietal movement that spread across member states and social milieus. Liberals and Democrats were able to align and mobilize a cross-class coalition of intellectuals, merchants, craftsmen, peasants, and workers chiefly because they were united by their dissatisfaction with the normative status quo and the unresponsive policies of aristocratic norm leaders. By contrast, in the case of the transatlantic security community such a degree of transnational mobilization was virtually absent. To be sure, there were anti-NATO protests at various summits as well as scattered domestic peace movements that called for NATO's dissolution. However, these groups certainly did not reach the scope of mobilization and societal support exemplified by the *Vormärz*. Moreover, anti-NATO protests remain a rather isolated and dispersed movement that stands in contrast to relatively stable majorities among the political strata that continues to support the normative order of the transatlantic security community.

A second and related difference between the case findings refers to the scope of normative change. In the case of the German security community, norm challengers were able to successfully replace the established normative order with a new framework. This happened in two stages. Initially, the constitutional framework of the Frankfurt Assembly temporarily replaced the normative order of the German Confederation during the German revolution of 1848–1849. Subsequently, the constitutional framework of the German nation-state replaced the re-established normative order of the German security community permanently in 1871. The norms of multilateral practice and meaningful communication were replaced by a reintroduction of war as a means of politics and strategic communication. Moreover, following the 1850s, a clear definition of the norm of common values remained void suggesting norm divergence if not norm replacement in this area as well. By contrast, the normative order of the transatlantic security community shows only marginal changes such as the extension of the norm of multilateral behavior to include a new out-of-area norm as well as a partial redefinition and extension of the concept of collective defense. Throughout the post-Cold War period, we find general convergence on the norm of common liberal-democratic values but also, reinforced by recent allegations of the USA spying on other security community members, continued norm divergence over the rule of law and the meaning of individual freedom. Even though the norm of communication can be said to have broken down during the crisis over the Iraq war, norm leaders subsequently were capable to repair it. The differences in the scope of normative change are summarized in Table 5.1. Whereas the case of the German security community displays a *complete* replacement of community norms, the case of the transatlantic security community (at least up to the present) shows only a *partial* revision and adaptation of existing community norms. Borrowing from studies of foreign policy change,[1] it is thus plausible to differentiate between genuine normative change in the former case—a fundamental break with past norms and identities—and of

Table 5.1 Scope of normative change in security communities

	Common values	*Multilateral practice*	*Communication*
German security community	Norm divergence/ replacement	Norm replacement	Norm replacement
Transatlantic security community	Norm convergence/ divergence	Norm transformation	Norm repair

norm transformation in the latter case—specific adaptations based on and in retention of established norms (Risse 2008, p. 284).

A final difference relates to the role of core states in the process of normative change. The German security community consisted of two cores, Prussia and Austria, whereas the transatlantic security community rests on a single core, the USA. From the outset, this seemed to be of minor importance since Karl W. Deutsch and his associates explicitly allow for security communities to develop around 'single', 'composite' or 'double' cores. It looks thus plausible to assume (as Deutsch did) that these quantitative variations among cores should not matter as long as the core state(s) maintain the 'power to act and the ability to respond' to the needs of other members (Deutsch et al. 1957, pp. 38 and 138). For Deutsch (as well as for Adler and Barnett 1998), the number of core states appears to be insignificant for security community development. Yet, the empirical observations in this book move well beyond this point and suggest instead that the number of core states should be considered a relevant factor in the process of security community disintegration. For example, a major reason for the failure of the norm regime of the German security community to reinstate the normative order after the unsuccessful German revolution can be attributed to the inability of the two core states to agree on the community's future institutional, geographical, and normative shape. While Prussia appeared willing to accommodate some degree of norm reform, Austria bluntly rejected any substantial changes to the established normative order. This seems to have facilitated stalemate, institutional failure and eventually even military conflict between the core states. Hypothetically speaking, had there been only a single core, the process of security community disintegration may perhaps have taken a very different turn.

The case of the transatlantic security community supports this view. Since the USA remains the single core state, it appears much easier for American norm leaders to (re)define the norms and meanings of the transatlantic security community. This is not to claim that the USA defines these norms and meanings exclusively. As Thomas Risse (Risse-Kappen 1996) shows, for example, input by smaller member states certainly matters in the transatlantic security community. Still, the absence of a composite or additional core certainly gives the USA a lot more leverage to define the security community framework in both material and ideational terms because it does not have to share this leverage or compete with other cores. For example, the introduction of an out-of-area norm as well as the redefinition of Article 5 to include a terrorist threat mainly represented the USA view of granting NATO a more active and global role in the post-Cold War world with most member states gradually falling in line. One can only speculate, of course, but had there been a viable second core (e.g., the EU) the outcome of the Iraq crisis and NATO's development might have been very different.

These differences may be indicative for theorizing and studying security community disintegration in a larger empirical context. First, the emergence of transnational social movements appears to play a significant role in the process of security community disintegration. These norm challengers, despite temporary failure, seemed to be able to promote an alternative 'way of life' through the introduction of new ideas and norms, organized mass persuasion of large parts of the populations as well as political elites, and the capability to develop alternative collective identities. For these new transnational solidarities to occur, however, there need to be high rates of legitimacy and mobilization among norm challengers that stress the injustice of the normative status and weaken the norm regime. These prerequisites can be said to have been met in the case of the German security community but were lacking in the case of the transatlantic security community. This observation introduces an important new dynamic element to recent studies of security communities, which tend to either underrate or take for granted the role of transnational movements and groups.

Second, variations in the scope of normative change observed in the cases of security community disintegration suggest that normative change is not simply an either/or case, that is to say, the absolute absence or presence of normative change in a security community. Instead, it appears to be more helpful to differentiate between various 'shades' of normative change. Based on the empirical findings presented in Table 5.1, it is perfectly possible (and indeed likely) that norm degeneration leads to very different degrees of normative change (norm adaptation, norm transformation, or norm replacement) based on the specific type of normative actors involved. Scholars of normative change in international politics may hopefully find this differentiation particular useful.

Finally, the cases indicate a strong role for core states in the process of security community disintegration. Core states were, in both cases, heavily involved in norm violations and contestation, reinterpretation of meanings, the introduction of structural barriers to the spread of alternative norms and ideas or, conversely, were themselves involved in the introduction of new ideas. One may tentatively conclude from these findings that a security community probably remains more stable with a single core whereas a plurality of cores may be conducive to instability. Of course, this assumption would need to be confirmed by further empirical research.

Theoretical Implications

This section situates these analytical implications in a broader theoretical context and outlines how the findings may be indicative for further research. In particular, based on the theoretical lens employed here it seeks to reflect on their implications for Constructivist research on norms in IR. The theoretical implications are structured around two conceptual themes (progress and agency).

Progress

One theme that carries relevance for Constructivist research on norms is that norm degeneration and processes of disintegration do not inevitably undermine progress in international politics but, on the contrary, may be conducive to progressive change (understood as regional integration). The key question with regard to normative change is thus not only how much change but also what kind of change. As pointed out in the first chapter, there is an increasing strand of Constructivist research on norm dynamics that investigates the weakening or disappearance of existing norms at the international level. These scholars have developed innovative approaches and explanations to conceptualize norm erosion, regress, degeneration, and disappearance at the international level by building on insights generated by growing research on norm dynamics and norm contestation during the last decade (Jetschke and Liese 2013; Sikkink 2013; Heller et al. 2012; Panke and Petersohn 2012; Dunne 2007). This study adds to this growing research strand by demonstrating how norm degeneration at the regional level contributes to the undermining of a particular type of regional order: a security community.

The formation of regional order and integration is still widely equated with progress in international politics (and Karl Deutsch was no exception to that). Progress tends to guide policy agendas at the international level by an implicit belief in advancing global development and the overall quality of life for human beings (Müller 2006, p. 1). The development of shared regional norms and identity is thus typically associated with reference frames like 'closer cooperation', 'economic growth', and 'social freedoms', suggesting that progressive change and integration lead the world to a higher evolutionary stage (Adler and Crawford 1991, p. 1; see also: Haas 1968). As Philippe de Lombaerde (De Lombaerde (2007) has been changed to De Lombaerde (2008) as per the reference list. Please check if okay.2008, p. 10) argues,

> From this perspective, building and developing regional institutions can be seen as a direct contribution to societal progress, inasmuch as it ensures an improvement in the availability and quality of regional public goods. Indeed, the establishment of such institutions in itself can be seen as a sign of progress, since it reveals that participating societies are starting to share a common understanding of their regional identity, which is the necessary precondition to effectively tackle their joint problems.

Integration thus describes the political and civilizational advancement of international politics through the establishment of progressive ideas, norms, institutions, and practices. In Parsonian terms, this amounts to an 'upgrading' of societies 'to a higher type of civilization than that of the native community in its original state' (Bosch 1961, p. 3; Parsons 1966). Disintegration of political communities and the degeneration of regional norms, on the contrary, are often times viewed as undermining progressive change in international politics. They tend to be most commonly associated with reference frames like 'anarchy', 'violence', and 'chaos' (Adler and Crawford 1992, p. 439; Wright 1954, p. 130).

The case of the German Confederation, however, shows that the disintegration of regional communities does not automatically inhibit progressive change but, on the contrary, eventually led to even closer integration among the German states. As this particular case suggests, the old cognitive structures, norms, and meanings of the German Confederation were deconstructed to subsequently give way (for better or worse) to a higher stage of political integration in the form of the German nation-state. The economist Joseph Schumpeter (1942) employed a similar idea in economics to describe the way in which progress in capitalism develops from the removal of a previous economic order. While such instances of 'creative destruction' may, at first, appear to most contemporary observers as an initial loss of prior progressive achievements, in the long run, they may well be part of a broader development toward reaching a higher level of integration.

From such a post-Enlightenment perspective, it would be premature to categorize disintegrative processes and norm degeneration as per se undermining progress in international politics. On the contrary, disintegration may sometimes turn out to be a step toward further integration. This has implications for theory building. Constructivist studies on norm degeneration can be helpful not just in telling us why certain norms disappear but may also add important insights to understand why new norms emerge in the first place by shedding light on the creational capacity of norm degeneration and social deconstruction.

Agency

Another theme that emerges from this book is the central role that is attributed to agency in producing normative change in a security community. A growing trend in Constructivist research on norms in particular, and global governance more generally, has emphasized the significance of agents in producing normative change at the international level and affecting policy outcomes in recent years (Müller and Wunderlich 2013; Avant et al. 2010; Wiener 2009; Rosert and Schirmbeck 2007; Slaughter 2004). It is argued that agents do not simply occupy normative structures but actively shape and transform these structures leading to either continuity or change in the international system. From this perspective, established norms are not 'locked in' the social structure of the international system but are subject to frequent contestation and conflict and thus open to potential redefinition and change. By showing that agency also takes a prominent role in processes of normative change in a security community, this study adds to this recent trend in Constructivist theory.

Karl Deutsch et al. (1957) knew the significance of purposeful agents very well. By emphasizing the role of state leaders, pressure groups, political innovators, and domestic and transnational 'cross-class coalitions' in the emergence of security community, he underlined both the diverse character and multiple dynamics of agency in the overall development of security community. Deutsch's insights on agency have been largely missing in more recent scholarly work on security communities or have been narrowly captured within a state-centric analytical framework (see, e.g., Adler and Barnett 1998; Pouliot 2008; Bjola and Kornprobst 2007). In this book, I have attempted to develop a more inclusive framework and storyline to explain the nature of normative agency in a security community in a more comprehensive way. The purpose was to show how agency—conceived through the analytical categories of norm leaders and norm challengers—plays a critical role in driving the process of security community disintegration by introducing new ideas, setting norm agendas, employing symbolic interaction as well as engaging in social (un-) learning. These interactions and interrelationships between purposeful normative agents at the micro-level can be said to play a significant role in the social construction of a meaningful normative order within a security community. What this study adds to this assumption is that those same actors may also deconstruct the normative order of a security community by creating new meanings within an altered shared social reality.

SUGGESTIONS FOR FURTHER RESEARCH

In the end, this book is far from the last word on security community disintegration but represents one step toward solving a complex puzzle. Many questions remain to be explored and more empirical research needs to be conducted to test and confirm the propositions and implications raised here and to possibly develop them further. Specifically, more work should be done into understanding how normative change affects security communities at different stages in their development. This book has only dealt with cases in which a mature pluralistic security community already existed. What about nascent or ascendant security communities?

Also, scholars could explore possible variations in the disintegration cycle resulting from different types of pluralistic security communities. The cases in this book represent what Emanuel Adler and Michael Barnett (1998, p. 30) defined as 'loosely-coupled security communities' which are 'transnational regions comprised of sovereign states whose people maintain dependable expectations of peaceful change'. It would be interesting to see if similar outcomes of normative change can be attributed to more 'tightly-coupled security communities', such as the EU, that resemble a post-sovereign system of regional governance containing a mix of supranational and intergovernmental elements. The same is true for pre-Westphalian security communities that do not conform to Karl Deutsch's notion of sovereignty such as medieval heteronomy or the ancient *polis*.

Finally, the cases in this book as well as most cases in previous works predominantly cover the Western world (Europe, North America, the North Atlantic) while only a few scholars have looked into cases of security community development in the non-Western world such as Asia, Africa, or Latin America. While the theoretical model of security community disintegration developed here can be, in principle, applied to any region of the world, its empirical findings and implications are based on Western cases and may thus well differ from region to region. A wider range of empirical studies could highlight possible regional differences and diversity in the process of norm degeneration in a security community. This should include a discussion of the strengths and weaknesses of normative orders in other possible security communities, particularly from the non-Western world, to see how these fit into the theoretical framework presented in this book. For example, ASEAN norm of non-interference in member states' domestic policies has been challenged by the refugee crisis, and the large-scale persecution of the Rohingya by Myanmar and others which is sustaining it. Moreover, the future development of regional integration in MERCOSUR, with its two core states, may encounter similar problems as the German security community whenever rivalry between Argentina and Brazil undermined its normative order, as illustrated by the suspension of Paraguay in 2012. These, and other cases, should easily fit into the framework of this book while, at the same time, emphasizing distinctive institutional forms as well as variations in spatial, cultural, sociopolitical, and historical contexts.

Until then, so far the insights from this book have already allowed to shed some more light into a dim area of IR leaving one with the impression that stable interstate peace and trust within a security community is far from 'stable' but remains a rather fragile occurrence.

Notes

1. See, for example, Holsti 1998; Medick-Krakau 1999; Risse 1999.

References

Adler, E., & Barnett, M. (1998). A framework for the study of security communities. In E. Adler & M. Barnett (Eds.), *Security communities* (pp. 29–66). Cambridge: Cambridge University Press.

Adler, E., & Crawford, B. (1991). *Progress in post-war international relations*. New York: Columbia University Press.

Anderson, J., Ikenberry, G. J., & Risse, T. (2008). *The end of the west? Crises and change in the Atlantic order*. Ithaca: Cornell University Press.

Anhut, R. (2005). Die Konflikttheorie der Desintegrationstheorie'. In T. Bonacker (Ed.), *Sozialwissenschaftliche Konflikttheorien. Eine Einführung* (pp. 381–409). Opladen: Leske and Budrich.

Avant, D. D., Finnemore, M., & Sell, S. K. (2010). *Who governs the globe?* New York: Cambridge University Press.

Bjola, C., & Kornprobst, M. (2007). Security communities and the habitus of restraint. Germany and the United States on Iraq. *Review of International Studies, 33*(2), 285–305.

Bosch, F. D. K. (1961). *Selected studies in Indonesian archaeology.* The Hague: Martinus Nijhoff.

De Lombaerde, P. (2008). International integration and societal progress: A critical review of globalisation indicators. In OECD (Ed.), *Statistics, knowledge and policy 2007: Measuring and fostering the progress of societies* (pp. 327–331). Paris: OECD.

Deutsch, K. W., Burrell, S. A., Kann, R. A., Lee, M., Jr., Lichterman, M., Lindgren, R. E., Loewenheim, F. L., & van Wagenen, R. W. (1957). *Political community and the North Atlantic area. International organization in the light of historical experience.* Princeton: Princeton University Press.

Dunne, T. (2007). "The rules of the game are changing": Fundamental human rights in crisis after 9/11. *International Politics, 44,* 269–286.

Eppler, A., & Scheller, H. (Eds.). (2013). *Zur Konzeptionalisierung europäischer Desintegration. Zug- und Gegenkräfte im europäischen Integrationsprozess.* Baden-Baden: Nomos.

Haas, E. B. (1968). *The Uniting of Europe. Political, Social, and Economic Forces, 1950-1957.* Notre Dame, IN: Notre Dame University Press.

Heller, R., Kahl, M., & Pisoiu, D. (2012). The "dark" side of normative argumentation. The case of counterterrorism policy. *Global Constitutionalism, 1*(2), 278–312.

Holsti, K. J. (1998). *The problem of change in international relations theory* (Working paper 26). Vancouver: University of British Columbia.

Jetschke, A., & Liese, A. (2013). The power of human rights a decade after: From euphoria to contestation. In T. Risse, S. C. Ropp, & K. Sikkink (Eds.), *The persistent power of human rights: From commitment to compliance* (pp. 26–42). Cambridge: Cambridge University Press.

Medick-Krakau, M. (1999). *Außenpolitischer Wandel in theoretischer und vergleichender Perspektive: Die USA und die Bundesrepublik Deutschland.* Baden-Baden: Nomos.

Müller, H. (2006). *A theory of decay of security communities with an application to the present state of the Atlantic alliance* (Working paper). Berkeley: University of California at Berkeley.

Müller, H., & Wunderlich, C. (2013). *Norm dynamics in multilateral arms control. Interests, conflicts, and justice.* Athens: Georgia University Press.

Panke, D., & Petersohn, U. (2012). Why international norms disappear sometimes. *European Journal of International Relations, 18*(4), 719–742.

Parsons, T. (1966). *Evolutionary and comparative perspectives.* Englewood Cliffs: Prentice Hall.

Pouliot, V. (2008). The logic of practicality. A theory of practice of security communities. *International Organization, 62*(2), 257–288.

Risse, T. (1999). Identitäten und Kommunikationsprozesse in der internationalen Politik. Sozialkonstruktivistische Perspektive zum Wandel in der Außenpolitik'. In M. Medick-Krakau (Ed.), *Außenpolitischer Wandel in theoretischer und vergleichender Perspektive: Die USA und die Bundesrepublik Deutschland* (pp. 33–57). Baden-Baden: Nomos.

Risse, T. (2008). The end of the west? Conclusions. In J. Anderson, G. J. Ikenberry, & T. Risse (Eds.), *The end of the west? Crises and change in the Atlantic order* (pp. 263–290). Ithaca: Cornell University Press.

Risse-Kappen, T. (1996). Collective identity in a democratic community: The case of NATO. In P. J. Katzenstein (Ed.), *The culture of national security* (pp. 357–399). New York: Columbia University Press.

Rosert, E., & Schirmbeck, S. (2007). Zur Erosion internationaler Normen: Folterverbot und nukleares Tabu in der Diskussion'. *Zeitschrift für Internationale Beziehungen, 14*(2), 253–288.

Schumpeter, J. A. (1942). *Capitalism, socialism, and democracy*. New York: Harper.

Sikkink, K. (2013). The United States and torture: Does the spiral model work? In T. Risse, S. C. Ropp, & K. Sikkink (Eds.), *The persistent power of human rights* (pp. 145–163). Cambridge: Cambridge University Press.

Slaughter, A. M. (2004). *A new world order*. Princeton: Princeton University Press.

Stetter, S., Masala, C., & Karbowski, M. (Eds.). (2011). *Was die EU im Innersten zusammenhält. Debatten zur Legitimität und Effektivität supranationalen Regierens*. Baden-Baden: Nomos.

Wiener, A. (2009). Enacting meaning-in-use: Qualitative research on norms and international relations. *Review of International Studies, 35*(1), 175–193.

Wright, Q. (1954). *Problems of stability and progress in international relations*. Berkeley: University of California Press.

References

Adler, E. (1997). Imagined (security) communities: Cognitive regions in international relations. *Millennium, 26*(2), 249–277.
Adler, E., & Barnett, M. (1998). A framework for the study of security communities. In E. Adler & M. Barnett (Eds.), *Security communities* (pp. 29–66). Cambridge: Cambridge University Press.
George, A. L., & Bennett, A. (2005). *Case studies and theory development in the social sciences.* Cambridge, MA: Massachusetts Institute of Technology Press.
Heidegger, M. (1969). *On time and being.* Chicago: University of Chicago Press.
Hurrell, A. (2001). Norms and ethics in international relations. In W. Caerlsnaes, T. Risse, & B. A. Simmons (Eds.), *Handbook of international relations* (pp. 137–154). London: Sage.
Koschut, S. (2011). Eine Gemeinschaft der Gemeinschaften. Konzeptionelle Überlegungen zur transatlantischen Sicherheitsgemeinschaft als differenziertes normatives System'. *Sicherheit und Frieden, 29*(4), 260–265.
Müller, J. (2006). *Der Deutsche Bund, 1815–1866.* München: Oldenbourg.
Taylor, A. J. P. (2001). *The course of German history: A survey of the development of German history since 1815.* New York: Routledge.
Weber, M. (1921/1968). *Economy and society. An outline of interpretative sociology.* New York: Bedminster Press.
Woods, N. (1996). The uses of theory in the study of international relations. In N. Woods (Ed.), *Explaining international relations since 1945* (pp. 9–31). Oxford: Oxford University Press.

DOCUMENTS

Bundeskriegsverfassung von 1821. In W. Rüstow (Ed.), (1859). *Die Grenzboten. Militärische Tagesfragen*. Berlin: Deutscher Verlag.

Das deutsche Volk an die sogenannte deutsche Bundesversammlung (1848/49:119/30 Nr.46; GOS-Nr. d0009991). Leipzig: Stadtgeschichtliches Museum.

Final act of the Viennese Ministerial Conferences (Vienna Final Act) of 15 May, 1820. In E. R. Huber (Ed.), (1978). *Deutsche Verfassungsdokumente 1803–1850, Vol. I, Dokumente zur deutschen Verfassungsgeschichte* (pp. 91–99). Stuttgart: W. Kohlhammer.

German Federal Act of 8 June 1815. In E. R. Huber (Ed.), (1978). *Deutsche Verfassungsdokumente 1803–1850, Vol. I, Dokumente zur deutschen Verfassungsgeschichte* (pp. 84–90). Stuttgart: W. Kohlhammer.

Karlsbader Beschlüsse (Carlsbad Decrees) von 1819. In E. H. Huber (Ed.), (1978) *Deutsche Verfassungsdokumente 1803–1850, Vol. 1, Dokumente zur deutschen Verfassungsgeschichte* (pp. 102–104). Stuttgart: W. Kohlhammer.

Reichsgesetz über die Einführung einer provisorischen Zentralgewalt für Deutschland beschlossen von der verfassungsgebenden deutschen Nationalversammlung am 28. Juni 1848 (Imperial Law on the Introduction of a Provisional Central Government of Germany Ratified by the Constituent German National Assembly on 28 June 1848). In E. R. Huber (Ed.) (1986). *Deutsche Verfassungsdokumente 1851–1900* (Vol. II, pp. 122–123). Stuttgart: W. Kohlhammer.

Six Articles, 28 June 1832. In E. R. Huber (1978). *Deutsche Verfassungsdokumente 1803–1850. Vol. I: Dokumente zur deutschen Verfassungsgeschichte* (pp. 132–133). Stuttgart: W. Kohlhammer.

The Ten Articles from 5 July 1832. In E. R. Huber (Ed.), (1978) *Deutsche Verfassungsdokumente 1803–1850. Vol. I: Dokumente zur deutschen Verfassungsgeschichte* (pp. 134–135). Stuttgart: W. Kohlhammer.

Verordnung des Königs von Sachsen Anton die Publication der, wegen des Wanderns der Handwerksgesellen unter'm 15. Januar und 12. März 1835, gefaßten Bundesbeschlüsse betreffend, erlassen am 6. Juli 1835 (Provision of the King of Saxony Anton Concerning the Publication of the Combined Federal Decrees of 15 January and 12 March 1835 Because of Hiking Journeymen, Issued on 6 July 1835. http://www.documentArchiv.de/nzjh/sachsen/1835/handeswerksgesellen-wanderung-bschl_vo.html. Accessed 30 Oct 2013.

Verordnung des Königs von Sachsen Friedrich August II. die Publication eines, auf die Abstellung der Gesellenverbindungen und Gesellen-Handwerksmißbräuche abzweckenden, unterm 3. December 1840 gefaßten Bundesbeschlusses betreffend, erlassen am 2. Januar 1841 (Provision of the

King of Saxony Friedrich August II Concerning the Publication of the Combined Federal Decree of 3 December 1840, on the Secondment of Journeymen Compounds and Journeymen Misuses, Issued on 2 January 1841. http://www.documentArchiv.de/nzjh/sachsen/1841/handwerksgesellen-verbindung-beschl_vo.html. Accessed 30 Oct 2013.

Verordnung des Kultusministeriums des Königreichs Sachsen den Bundesbeschluß vom 13. November 1834 über die Universitäten und andere Lehr- und Erziehungsanstalten betreffend, erlassen am 2. Januar 1835 (Provision of the Ministry of Education of the Kingdom of Saxony Concerning the Federal Decree of 13 November 1834 on Universities and Other Teaching and Educational Institutions, Issued on 2 January 1835. http://www.document-Archiv.de/nzjh/sachsen/1835/universitaeten-bschl_vo.html. Accessed 30 Oct 2013.

Verordnung Sr. Majestät des Königs von Sachsen Friedrich August II. zu Bekanntmachung des wegen Aufhebung der Censur in den Staaten des Deutschen Bunds unterm 3ten März 1848 gefaßten Bundesbeschlusses, erlassen am 9. März 1848 (Provision of His Majesty the King of Saxony Friedrich August II to Notice of the Application for Annulment of Censorship in the States of the German Confederation Under the Combined Federal Decree of 3 March 1848, Issued on 9 March 1848. http://www.documentArchiv.de/nzjh/sachsen/1848/zensur-aufhebung-deutscher-bund_vo.html. Accessed 30 Oct 2013.

Index

A
Afghanistan, 201–203, 205–206, 224–225, 227
Albania, 187, 209, 211
Albright, Madeleine, 181, 188, 199, 207
anarchy, 11, 104, 138, 254
arms embargo, 181–182, 184–186
Association of Southeast Asian Nations, 2, 12, 257
Austria, 28, 67, 93–97, 100, 103–108, 110–111, 113–115, 117–118, 120, 123–125, 128–129, 131, 133–136, 140–146, 148–158, 245, 247, 251. *See also* Habsburg Empire
Austro–Prussian War, 156
authority, 42, 51, 96, 123, 129, 133, 151, 182, 186, 192, 196, 212, 217, 248

B
Baden, 100, 102–106, 108, 111, 117, 120–122, 124, 131, 137, 147–148
Bavaria, 97, 100, 115, 124, 135, 141–148, 154
Belgium, 101, 200, 211
Beust, Frederic Ferdinand von, 153
Bismarck, Otto von, 147, 149, 152–153
Blair, Tony, 188, 191, 205, 208, 216
Blum, Robert, 135–136
Bohemia, 126, 133
Bosnia–Herzegovina, 180–189, 195, 198, 201, 226
Bulgaria, 209, 211
Bush, George W., 18, 199, 201, 203–204, 210, 217, 247

C
Canada, 166, 212
capitalism, 254
change
 demographic, 59
 domestic, 9
 external, 7, 16–17, 21, 55–60, 65, 70–71, 73, 75, 77, 101–108, 170–181, 242, 248
 foreign policy, 250

historical, 23
incremental, 55
in the international system, 4, 54
levels of, 28, 42
material, 4, 79
normative, 10, 14, 17, 21, 24, 27, 28, 41, 56, 60, 71-74, 81, 242-245, 248, 250-255
peaceful (*see* peaceful change)
political, 17, 102
progressive, 253-254
revolutionary, 28, 102
social and internal, 3, 7, 17, 51, 57, 60-71, 74, 79, 108-123, 181-217, 243
structural, 16, 55
China, 189, 207, 211
Chirac, Jacques, 181, 186, 191, 205
Christopher, Warren, 174, 178, 183, 207
civilization, 210, 254
civil war, 68, 136-137
Claes, Willy, 185
Clinton, Bill, 175, 178, 180-182, 184, 186, 188, 190, 200
coercion, 15, 45-46, 99, 158, 170,
cognitive dissonance, 78-79, 139, 140, 217, 221
cognitive structure, 13, 72, 254
Cold War, 18, 28, 59, 66, 166, 171-172, 179-182, 187-189, 198, 220-221, 224, 226, 244, 250, 252
collective defense, 6, 45-47, 150, 156-157, 173-174, 176, 179, 199, 202, 217, 223-225, 250
collective meaning, 6, 13, 41, 49, 51, 54, 64, 69, 80, 154, 227, 242, 248
collective security, 167, 170, 179, 181, 199, 223

communicative action, 47, 67, 150, 157, 195, 210, 225
communism, 167
communitarianism, 12, 14
communities of practice, 12
Concert of Europe, 8
conflict resolution, 6, 45-47, 98, 143, 156, 215, 223, 225
Congress of Vienna, 93
consultation, 6, 9, 46-47, 99, 113, 133, 143, 157, 169, 176, 202, 209, 225
cosmopolitanism, 14
Council of Europe, 215
Crimean War, 148-150
Croatia, 209, 211
culture, 15, 74, 95, 122, 242
Cyprus, 165
Czechoslovakia, 241
Czech Republic, 198, 211

D

Dayton Peace Agreement, 183, 186-187
decay, 3, 9, 44, 52, 68
De Hoop Scheffer, Jaap, 218
democracy, 167, 172, 177, 196, 222
Denmark, 130-131, 152-153, 156, 176, 211
Deutsch, Karl W., 2, 4-6, 13, 24-26, 41, 43, 46-52, 62-63, 70, 79, 80, 93-94, 98, 165, 224, 226, 249, 251, 253, 255-256
De Vries, Gijs, 214
diplomacy, 45, 97, 168, 184, 187, 190, 192, 201
disaggregation, 3
discourse, 5, 11, 14, 20, 23, 46, 63, 76, 179, 245
dysfunction, 8, 28, 75-77, 100, 107, 111, 170, 179, 187

E

Economic Community of West African States, 2
empire, 2, 7, 59, 131, 241
Engels, Friedrich, 136
enlightenment, 62, 254
equality, 62, 101
Erfurt Union, 142–143, 145, 148–149, 158, 246
Estonia, 209
European Defense and Security Policy, 62, 174–176, 178, 198
European Union, 2, 11, 48–49, 61–62, 64, 67, 171, 178, 181, 183–184, 192, 198–199, 204, 213, 214, 221, 241, 246, 252, 256
external threat, 25, 29, 45, 53, 78, 80, 96, 106, 120, 140, 224

F

feudalism, 114
framing, 13, 20, 28, 49, 206, 208, 212
France, 61, 96, 98, 101–102, 107–108, 110–111, 123, 135, 140, 149–150, 153, 156, 174–176, 179, 182–183, 185, 188, 192, 194–196, 199, 205, 208–211, 213, 216–218, 221, 243, 245
Franz Josef I, 151
Frederic VII, 130
Frederic VIII, 152
Frederic Wilhelm IV, 116–117, 120, 124–125, 134–136, 139, 145, 158
Free and Hanseatic City of Hamburg, 94, 96–97, 124
free market, 167, 222
friendship, 11, 172

G

Gagern, Heinrich von, 134–135, 142
German Confederation, 25, 28–29, 81, 93, 95–97, 99–101, 105–107, 111–112, 118–119, 124–125, 128, 132, 139–140, 142, 145, 148, 154–155, 157–159, 227–228, 245–247, 249–252, 257. *See also* German security community
German Customs Union, 115, 143–145, 152, 157
German security community, 28, 29, 93–159, 227, 228, 245–252, 257
Germany, 23, 71, 73, 96, 103–104, 106, 112–114, 119–120, 124–125, 127, 129, 131–138, 142–144, 148–155, 166, 174–176, 183, 188, 191, 194–196, 199, 205, 208–211, 216–221, 245
Great Britain, 98, 107, 123, 130, 135, 149, 153, 166, 174–176, 182–183, 185, 188, 192, 195, 201, 204, 206, 211–213, 216, 245
Greece, 165, 192, 194

H

habit, 5, 14, 16, 61, 70–71, 170, 226, 246
Habsburg Empire, 117, 124, 133, 134, 142, 148–150, 152, 154, 155. *See also* Austria
Hambach festival, 103–105, 112, 245
Hanseatic League, 73
Hesse
  Electorate of, 102, 143, 145, 154, 156
  Grand Duchy of, 100, 102, 143
Hessen–Darmstadt, 147

hierarchy, 18, 52, 95
Holbrooke, Richard, 175, 183, 186–187
Holstein, 130–134, 145, 152–154, 156–158
Holy Alliance, 149
Holy Roman Empire of the German Nation, 95, 97, 117, 125, 138
human rights, 12, 18, 21, 50, 167, 172, 177, 188, 192, 214–215, 222
Hungary, 103, 123, 198, 200, 211
Hussein, Saddam, 207–208, 210

I
ideas
　blocking of, 61
　changing, 58
　definition of, 5
　diffusion of, 61, 76
　established, 61, 76, 179, 243
　liberal, 113, 118, 121–122, 127, 157–158
　normative, 5, 50, 62, 69, 101
　persuasiveness of, 6, 7, 58, 60–62, 65, 77, 147, 158, 242–244
　progressive, 254
　promotion of, 4, 52, 75, 172, 174, 179, 243, 256
　spread of, 50, 105, 106, 112–113, 121, 228, 243, 244, 252
identity, 7, 9
　building of, 45
　collective, 10, 13, 15, 25, 43–45, 57–59, 64, 66, 73, 76, 81, 95, 107–108, 116, 158, 166, 168, 171–172, 201, 211, 244, 246, 248
　crisis of, 75, 171
　German, 97
　monarchical, 28, 96, 139

　national, 158
　pan-Arab, 16–17
　regional, 254
　social, 23
　and symbols, 73, 81
　transatlantic, 166
　transnational, 4, 11
　undermining of, 74
ideology, 44, 58, 95
individual freedom, 101, 167, 172, 219, 222, 250
industrialization, 117, 121
institutions
　failure of, 6–7, 21, 58, 60, 66–68, 74, 77–80, 110–111, 118–119, 121, 132, 144, 147, 158, 180, 185, 195–196, 203–205, 207, 211, 226, 242, 246, 248, 251
　of the German Confederation, 94–95, 120, 125, 127, 132, 138, 144–146, 153, 158
　and knowledge, 136
　of NATO, 166–168, 172, 179, 202, 204–205, 211–213, 224, 228
　and norms, 49, 69, 93, 95, 129, 254
　regional, 21, 47, 66, 206, 246, 254
　and security communities (*see* security community)
　societal and domestic, 3, 51, 67–68
　supranational, 113
　transnational, 7, 50, 68
integration, 1, 3, 24, 41, 47, 49, 51–53, 59, 64–65, 67, 74–75, 78–80, 94, 107, 114–115, 138–140, 144, 152, 167, 178, 180, 185, 196, 207, 226–227, 242, 253–255, 257
interdependence, 10, 47, 95
interests, 10, 46, 51, 53, 59, 66, 80, 99, 110, 143, 157, 169, 187, 200, 226

International Criminal Court, 215
international law, 66, 167, 213–214
International Monetary Fund, 220
international system, 3, 4, 12, 16, 17, 54–55, 60, 255
Iraq, 24, 28, 81, 165, 207, 212–213, 216, 217, 219, 221, 225–226, 245–246, 250
Italy, 103, 149, 176, 188, 193–196, 211, 218, 221

K
Kantian culture, 15–16
Kingdom of Hannover, 102, 107–112, 115, 135, 142–145
Kohl, Helmut, 175
Kosovo, 187–199, 201, 206, 217, 222, 225, 227, 241

L
Latvia, 209
legitimacy, 5, 8, 18, 52, 66, 77, 96, 102, 120, 123, 126, 129, 146, 172, 175, 188, 191, 198, 216, 219, 244, 246, 252
liberalism, 96, 100, 117, 157, 247
liberalization, 114, 115, 117
Lithuania, 209
Libya, 218–219, 223–224, 226
logic of appropriateness, 14, 79, 80, 140, 154, 157, 221
Lugar, Richard, 175, 202

M
Macedonia, 209
Manteuffel, Otto von, 140
Mecklenburg–Schwerin, 124
memory, 42, 49, 61, 63, 73, 245
Mercosur, 2, 257

Metternich, 95, 103, 108, 110, 112, 123, 134, 155
migration, 59, 61, 68, 102, 203, 223
Milosevic, Slobodan, 189, 194
Mitterand, François, 171
Moravia, 134
multilateralism, 45–46, 66, 133, 155, 168, 181, 190, 204, 210, 215, 223

N
Napoleonic Wars, 94
narrative, 14–15, 22–23, 28, 42, 49, 81, 159, 221, 242, 249
nationalism, 96, 101, 104, 117, 138, 157, 247, 249
national self-determination, 167
nation-state, 2, 3, 26, 81, 97, 102–103, 115, 122, 125–126, 128, 130, 133–137, 142, 147, 150, 155, 247, 250, 254
The Netherlands, 73, 176, 215, 218
neutrality, 149–150, 184
non-state-actors, 11, 50, 227
norm
  adaption, 6, 176, 252
  African, 14
  amendment, 223
  Arab, 13
  Asian, 13, 257
  collective, 2, 25, 27, 47–49, 54, 66, 70–71, 75, 81, 188
  of common values, 44–45, 58, 96–97, 108, 154–155, 167–168, 173, 182, 213, 222–223
  compliance, 5, 14, 72, 77–78, 139, 140
  contestation, 7, 8, 18, 52, 55, 58, 60, 76, 227–228, 252–253
  definition of, 5

degeneration of, 4–5, 8, 10, 14–22, 54–74, 81, 121, 140, 187, 207, 213, 218, 242, 248, 252–254, 257
diffusion, 55
disappearance, 8, 17, 20, 255
domestic, 14, 18, 67–68, 76
emergence, 4, 14–17, 20, 66
and emotions, 12
European, 13
fundamental, 6, 44
internalization, 15–16, 18, 21, 70
iteration, 6, 58, 70–71, 74, 76, 227, 248
Latin American, 13
leader and challengers, 7, 8, 20, 22, 28, 42, 48, 50–52, 54, 75–80, 95–96, 101–102, 105–107, 111, 113–114, 118, 120, 122–123, 125, 131, 137–138, 147, 158, 172–173, 175, 178–180, 190, 192, 196, 201–202, 205, 208, 215–216, 220, 225, 228, 242, 244–245, 248–253, 255
of meaningful communication, 46–47, 99–100, 113, 157, 169–170, 179, 195, 197, 210, 225–226
of multilateral practice, 12, 14, 45–46, 97–99, 108, 155–157, 168–169, 179, 195, 204, 223–225
regime, 7–8, 50, 52, 95, 118–119, 129, 131, 135, 137, 147, 188–189, 245, 247, 251–252
regional (*see* regional, norms)
repair, 52, 218–221, 250
replacement, 8, 21, 156–157, 250, 252
taken-for-grantedness of, 3, 14, 70
transatlantic, 172, 193, 218
violation, 6, 52–53, 67, 73, 76–77, 107, 110–111, 118–121, 138, 158, 179–180, 191, 194–197, 205–206, 215–217, 219, 222, 227, 245–246, 252
Western, 71
normative
agency, 7, 48–54, 73, 242, 245, 252, 255–256
behavior, 43, 48, 73, 139
beliefs, 8, 71, 78, 217
change, 10, 14, 17, 21, 24, 27, 28, 41, 56, 60, 71–74, 81, 242, 245, 248, 250, 252, 255
communities, 4, 41, 242
discourse, 5, 14, 48, 76
ideas, 5, 50, 62, 69, 101
order, 7, 9, 21, 22, 28, 42, 47–48, 50–51, 53, 56, 66, 76–77, 79–81, 95, 97, 104, 107, 110–113, 124, 141, 147–148, 154–159, 166–170, 180, 196–197, 205–207, 216, 218–219, 221–227, 243, 246–247, 256
structure, 9, 23, 27, 28, 41–48, 53, 255
North Atlantic Treaty Organization, 2, 11, 22, 24, 28–29, 48, 59, 62, 67, 81, 171–180, 184, 186, 188–189, 192, 194, 198–200, 203, 205, 207, 211–212, 215, 218, 221, 223, 225, 246, 252. *See also* transatlantic security community
Norway, 176, 200

O
Obama, Barack, 218–221, 249
Olmütz Agreement, 145
order

economic, 254
normative (*see* normative, order)
political, 3, 96, 101, 107, 124, 133
regional, 5, 13, 47, 93, 253
social, 3, 61
security, 11
Organization for Security and Cooperation in Europe, 171–172
Ottoman Empire, 149
overjustification, 78–79, 139, 221, 227

P

peaceful change, 1, 12–16, 41, 48–49, 51–52, 58, 61–62, 65, 68–69, 71, 74, 94, 97, 168, 172, 226, 242, 256
peacekeeping, 173, 182, 184–185
Peace of Malmo, 130
perception, 23, 46, 55, 65, 77, 99, 108, 139, 169, 207, 217
Persian Gulf War, 17, 208, 213
pluralism, 51, 94, 97
Poland, 53, 101, 103–104, 108, 111, 174, 198, 200, 211, 216, 221
political parties, 50, 112, 141, 220
political protest, 61, 109, 111, 122, 131, 136, 153, 170, 205, 212, 219, 220, 249
Portugal, 211, 218
power
  balance of, 11
  concept of, 53
  distribution of, 4
  executive, 128–129
  and ideas, 61
  and knowledge, 53, 57
  and language, 56
  legislative, 100, 102, 109
  material, 13, 52–53, 129, 142
  military, 137, 199
  non-material, 53
  and relationships, 52, 54, 198
  representational, 53
  separation of, 114, 128
  shifts, 59
  veto, 95, 128
practice theory, 12–13, 16, 20
progress, 15–17, 74, 110, 148, 167, 185, 253–255
protectionism, 114
Prussia, 28, 93–97, 100, 102–111, 113–123, 125, 129–159, 245–249, 251
public opinion, 27, 59, 151, 201, 212, 215–216, 221, 227

R

reconciliation, 217
region
  Africa, 176, 256
  Asia-Pacific, 176, 226, 256
  Baltic, 59
  Latin America, 256
  Middle East, 176
  North America, 256
  transnational, 256
regional
  conflict, 182, 189
  crisis, 180, 200
  governance, 256
  identity (*see* identity)
  institutions, 21, 66, 166, 206, 246, 254
  integration, 253, 257
  level of analysis, 4, 27, 45, 54, 67, 68, 242, 246, 253–254
  norms, 13, 14, 67, 242, 254
  order (*see* order)
  organizations, 6, 11, 66, 76, 189, 207, 225, 241
  security, 13, 62, 66

security complexes, 11
society, 4
spaces, 66, 166
structures, 11, 166, 206
system, 55
religion, 94, 97, 127, 166
responsiveness, 6, 9, 43, 47, 53, 61, 76, 78, 100, 111, 137, 157–158, 225–226, 244
repression, 100, 105, 107, 112, 116, 118, 120, 127, 146, 244
revolution
  American, 127
  and disintegration, 7, 59, 75–76, 96, 102, 104, 135, 139
  French, 62, 97, 101, 104, 127
  German, 104–105, 121, 123, 129, 137, 139, 141, 147, 154, 246, 250
ritual, 42, 45, 63–66, 72, 106, 179, 202, 244
Romania, 123, 209, 211, 221
rule of law, 127, 167, 172, 177, 196, 214–215, 222–223, 250
Russia, 53, 59, 101, 104, 123, 149, 171, 174–175, 183, 189–190, 193, 211, 245

S
Sardinia, 149–150, 156
Saxony, 102, 115, 124, 135, 137, 142–143, 147, 149, 153–154, 157
Saxony–Coburg, 145, 147
Saxony-Weimar, 147
Schleswig, 130, 152–154
Schröder, Gerhard, 205, 208, 210, 217
Schwarzenberg, Prince von, 134–136
security community
  and agency, 7, 20, 22, 28, 41, 48–54, 64, 75, 78, 248, 255–256
  concept of, 2, 10–12, 21, 25–26
  and core states, 52, 95, 103, 146, 155–156, 188, 196, 198, 202, 208, 222, 251, 252
  definition, 1, 42, 50
  and emotions, 12, 14
  European, 24, 27, 171, 174
  and external change, 7, 55, 59, 65, 243, 245
  German, 25, 28–29, 81, 93, 95–97, 99–101, 105–107, 111–112, 118–119, 124–125, 128, 132, 139–140, 142, 145, 148, 154–155, 157–159, 227–228, 245–247, 249–252, 257
  and ideas, 60–62, 157, 243
  and identity, 23, 45, 48, 52, 57, 59, 73, 96, 116, 188, 201, 246
  and knowledge, 53, 62
  and language, 11, 56, 69
  and meaningful communication, 46–47, 99–100, 113, 157, 169–170, 179, 195, 197, 210, 225–226
  and multilateral practice, 12, 14, 45–46, 97–99, 108, 155–157, 168–169, 179, 195, 204, 223–225
  and normative change, 10, 14, 17, 21, 24, 27–28, 41, 56, 60, 71–74, 81, 242, 245, 248, 250, 252, 255
  and normative order, 7, 9, 21–22, 28, 42, 47, 48, 50–51, 53, 56, 66, 76–77, 79–81, 95, 97, 104, 107, 110–113, 124, 141, 147–148, 154–159, 166–170, 180, 196–197, 205–207, 216, 218–219, 221–227, 243, 246–247, 256
  and norm contestation, 52, 60, 100, 197

and norm degeneration, 16–17, 19–22, 54–71, 78, 81, 123, 213, 257
North American, 68
and pluralism, 51
and power, 13, 53–54, 56
and regional institutions, 21, 66–69, 79, 158, 203, 204, 211, 246–247
and regional order, 5
and social change, 7, 60, 199
and socialization, 50, 248
and social roles, 7, 55
and social unlearning, 10, 69–71, 246–248
and sovereignty, 46
and symbolic interaction, 62, 117, 158, 244–245
transatlantic, 9–10, 24–25, 28–29, 53, 81, 165–172, 175–176, 178–180, 187–188, 192, 196–208, 210–212, 214, 216, 218–219, 221–228, 244–245, 247, 249–252
and trust, 43, 71–73, 206, 208, 257
and values, 44–45, 58, 96–97, 108, 154–155, 167–168, 173, 182, 213, 222–223
Security Council, 167, 173, 186, 189–191, 208–209, 211–212, 219, 223, 226, 245
self-restraint, 6, 45–46, 53, 66–67, 78, 99, 111, 143, 156–157, 168
sense of community, 1, 25, 43, 64, 73, 78, 171
Serbia, 183, 185, 189–194, 226
Slovakia, 123, 209, 211
Slovenia, 209, 211
social constructivism, 5, 13, 20, 54, 56, 65, 69, 253, 255
social control, 6, 7, 50, 52, 73, 248
socialization, 2, 7, 50, 73, 248
social learning, 44, 57, 62, 69–71

social movements, 8, 102, 107–108, 110, 122, 228, 252
social recognition, 3, 69
social structure, 58, 255
Solana, Javier, 188, 193, 204, 213
solidarity, 64, 96, 109, 136, 142, 150, 155, 196, 199, 200, 202, 206, 218, 220
Somalia, 181, 189, 200, 222
South East Asian Treaty Organization, 241
Southern African Development Community, 2
sovereignty, 46, 96–98, 103–104, 106–107, 109, 117, 127, 154–155, 166, 244, 256
Soviet Union, 3, 59, 170, 172, 223–224, 241
Spaak, Paul-Henri, 170
Spain, 103, 176, 205, 208, 211, 216, 221
speech act, 6, 20, 45
stable peace, 1–3, 8, 11, 49, 61, 155, 223, 225, 241, 242
status, 51, 64, 134, 142, 152–153, 243, 252
Struve, Gustav von, 131
Sweden, 165
symbolic interaction. *See* security community
symbols, 6, 14, 23, 42, 45–46, 48–49, 63–64, 71, 73, 76, 81, 105, 109, 112, 117, 138, 154, 159, 245, 248

T

terrorism, 18, 173, 176, 200, 205–210, 214–215, 220, 223
trade, 12, 107, 114–115, 119, 143, 144, 208
transactions, 50, 57, 62–63

transatlantic security community, 9, 10,
    24, 25, 28, 29, 48, 53, 59, 67,
    83n11, 165–229, 244–247, 252
trust, 1, 7, 9, 15, 25, 43–44, 57–58,
    68–69, 71–74, 76, 81, 93, 95,
    98, 107, 110–111, 140, 202,
    206, 208, 211, 219, 222, 224,
    248–249, 257
Turkey, 165, 202, 211

U
uncertainty, 1, 15, 68, 71, 81, 171
United Nations, 167–168, 177,
    180–181, 185, 190, 196–197,
    200, 214, 245
United States of America, 4, 17–18,
    22, 53, 68, 96, 135, 166, 171,
    173, 176–224, 226–227,
    244–247, 250–252
use of force, 6, 29, 46, 155, 168–169,
    189, 193, 197, 210, 212, 216, 226

V
Vietnam War, 220
violence, 68, 70, 80, 104, 138, 180,
    188–189, 216, 254

W
war, 1, 7, 9, 27, 29, 45, 48–49, 52,
    59, 68, 78, 80, 93, 97–100,
    129–132, 136–137, 143,
    145–146, 149–150, 152–157,
    166, 168, 174, 180, 182–184,
    188–189, 191–193, 197–198,
    202, 205–208, 210, 212–214,
    216–217, 220, 222, 226, 250
War of 1812, 200
War on Terror, 201–204, 206–207,
    214
Warsaw Pact, 71, 170–172, 188,
    241
Wartburg festival, 100
weapons of mass destruction, 175–
    176, 208–210, 213
Western European Union, 171, 176,
    178
Wirth, Johann Georg, 103–104
World Bank, 220
World Social Forum, 220
World War II, 71, 166, 168, 180, 212
Wörner, Manfred, 175
Württemberg, 100, 106, 115, 126,
    138–139, 142–144, 147–148,
    154

Y
Yugoslavia, 3, 66, 172, 180, 183, 188,
    241

Z
Zimmermann, Warren, 183

The manufacturer's authorised representative in the EU is Springer Nature Customer Service Centre GmbH, Europaplatz 3, 69115 Heidelberg, Germany. If you have any concerns regarding our products, please contact ProductSafety@springernature.com

Printed and bound by CPI Group (UK) Ltd, Croydon, CR0 4YY
23/03/2026
02076736-0010